Badges of the Regular Infantry 1914–1918

Badges of the Regular Infantry 1914–1918

David Bilton

Pen & Sword
MILITARY

First published in Great Britain in 2021 by
Pen & Sword Military
an imprint of
Pen & Sword Books Ltd
47 Church Street
Barnsley
South Yorkshire
S70 2AS

Copyright © David Bilton 2021

ISBN 978 1 52675 802 6

The right of David Bilton to be identified as the Author of this Work has been asserted by him in accordance with the Copyright, Designs and Patents Act 1988.

A CIP catalogue record for this book is available from the British Library

All rights reserved. No part of this book may be reproduced or transmitted in any form or by any means, electronic or mechanical including photocopying, recording or by any information storage and retrieval system, without permission from the Publisher in writing.

Typeset in Ehrhardt by
Mac Style
Printed and bound in India by Replika Press Pvt. Ltd.

Pen & Sword Books Limited incorporates the imprints of Atlas, Archaeology, Aviation, Discovery, Family History, Fiction, History, Maritime, Military, Military Classics, Politics, Select, Transport, True Crime, Air World, Frontline Publishing, Leo Cooper, Remember When, Seaforth Publishing, The Praetorian Press, Wharncliffe Local History, Wharncliffe Transport, Wharncliffe True Crime and White Owl.

For a complete list of Pen & Sword titles please contact

PEN & SWORD BOOKS LIMITED
47 Church Street, Barnsley, South Yorkshire, S70 2AS, England
E-mail: enquiries@pen-and-sword.co.uk
Website: www.pen-and-sword.co.uk

Or

PEN AND SWORD BOOKS
1950 Lawrence Rd, Havertown, PA 19083, USA
E-mail: Uspen-and-sword@casematepublishers.com
Website: www.penandswordbooks.com

Contents

Acknowledgements viii
Introduction xi

Background xxxii

Divisional Signs xxxiv

Brigade Signs xlii

Regiments
The Grenadier Guards 1
The Coldstream Guards 9
The Scots Guards 15
The Irish Guards 18
The Welsh Guards 21
The Royal Scots (Lothian Regiment) 24
The Queen's (Royal West Surrey Regiment) 30
The Buffs (East Kent Regiment) 33
The King's Own (Royal Lancaster Regiment) 36
The Northumberland Fusiliers 41
The Royal Warwickshire Regiment 44
The Royal Fusiliers (City of London Regiment) 47
The King's (Liverpool Regiment) 55
The Norfolk Regiment 59
The Lincolnshire Regiment 62
The Devonshire Regiment 66
The Suffolk Regiment 69
The Prince Albert's (Somerset Light Infantry) 73
The Prince of Wales's Own (West Yorkshire Regiment) 77
The East Yorkshire Regiment 80
The Bedfordshire Regiment 83
The Leicestershire Regiment 86

The Royal Irish Regiment	89
The Alexandra, Princess of Wales's Own (Yorkshire Regiment)	93
The Lancashire Fusiliers	96
The Royal Scots Fusiliers	101
The Cheshire Regiment	106
The Royal Welsh Fusiliers	109
The South Wales Borderers	112
The King's Own Scottish Borderers	116
The Cameronians (Scottish Rifles)	119
The Royal Inniskilling Fusiliers	122
The Gloucestershire Regiment	128
The Worcestershire Regiment	132
The East Lancashire Regiment	138
The East Surrey Regiment	141
The Duke of Cornwall's Light Infantry	144
The Duke of Wellington's (West Riding Regiment)	146
The Border Regiment	149
The Royal Sussex Regiment	153
The Hampshire Regiment	157
The South Staffordshire Regiment	162
The Dorsetshire Regiment	166
The Prince of Wales's Volunteers (South Lancashire Regiment)	173
The Welsh Regiment	178
The Black Watch (Royal Highlanders)	182
The Oxfordshire & Buckinghamshire Light Infantry	186
The Essex Regiment	190
The Sherwood Foresters (Nottinghamshire & Derbyshire Regiment)	194
The Loyal North Lancashire Regiment	198
The Northamptonshire Regiment	203
The Princess Charlotte of Wales's (Royal Berkshire Regiment)	206
The Queen's Own (Royal West Kent Regiment)	209
The King's Own (Yorkshire Light Infantry)	212
The King's Shropshire Light Infantry	216
The Duke of Cambridge's Own (Middlesex Regiment)	219
The King's Royal Rifle Corps	225
The The Duke of Edinburgh's (Wiltshire Regiment)	230
The Manchester Regiment	233

The Prince of Wales's (North Staffordshire Regiment)	236
The York & Lancaster Regiment	241
The Durham Light Infantry	244
The Highland Light Infantry	247
The Seaforth Highlanders (Ross-shire Buffs, The Duke of Albany's)	250
The Gordon Highlanders	253
The Queen's Own Cameron Highlanders	258
The Royal Irish Rifles	262
The Princess Victoria's (Royal Irish Fusiliers)	266
The Connaught Rangers	270
The Princess Louise's (Argyll & Sutherland Highlanders)	272
The Princess of Wales's Leinster Regiment (Royal Canadians)	276
The Royal Munster Fusiliers	282
The Royal Dublin Fusiliers	287
The Rifle Brigade	291
Museums	298
Regimental, Unit and Campaign Associations	298
Veterans	299
References	301

Acknowledgements

There are so many people to thank for assistance with this book. If I leave someone out it is not intentional and I sincerely apologise. This book would not have been possible without the help and early guidance of Mike Hibberd, a curator at the Imperial War Museum (IWM), now retired, who allowed me to examine the extensive collection held by the museum and to read the correspondence collected by the then National War Museum (NWM) in the latter part of the First World War. This provided the foundation on which to build this book. What is incredible about this correspondence is that in the middle of 3rd Ypres, many COs and adjutants found the time to provide information on something so inconsequential to their task.

Further information came from the many regimental museums across Britain, from the identification pamphlets produced in the 1970s by Major Waring, founder of the Military Heraldry Society, and from many enjoyable hours spent reading through folders, compiled by Haswell-Miller, among others, held by the Ogilvy Trust (now AMOT).

While most of the photographs and some of the badges have come from my own collection, many individual collectors have also provided photos and information. Unfortunately, over the intervening years since I started the project many of their names have become detached from their contributions – sincere apologies. Three names stand out for their help with the later stages of the project: Alan Jeffreys at the IWM who allowed me to photograph their badge collection; Jon Mills, a fellow member of the Military Heraldry Society who contributed many photographs to help highlight badges; and Bob Smethurst who let me photograph his badges and copy his photographs – thank you so much.

Many other collectors and libraries happily contributed: Robert Andrews, Tony Ashworth, John Bodsworth, Jerry Bond, Ted Croucher, John Gregory, Paul Hannon, Mark Holden, Martin Kerry, Norman Litchfield, Jonathan D.J. Maguire BA (Hons) War Studies (Researcher RIrF Museum), R.J. Marrion, Chris McDonald, Barrie Morris, Graham Stewart, Terry Sampson and the Taylor Library. Further assistance was provided by A. Jackson, T. Scala, T. Chadd, R. Litchfield, G. Tyson, H. Rook, L. Cable and B. Golding. As images have been sent to me by many people, far more than listed, some of whom did not want to be acknowledged, I cannot guarantee their original ownership. Keeping track was made even more difficult when my computer died; it was difficult to reconstruct even the basics, so I apologise for any inadvertent use of copyright photographs; this will be corrected in a second edition.

What made this research especially interesting, like the Kitchener book, was contact with the men who wore the badges, commoner to lord, privates, NCOs and officers from second lieutenant to lieutenant general, and even a rear-admiral who began his career in the Royal Engineers; men such as Corporal J. Armstrong of the Loyal North Lancashire Regiment: he had been captured at Ypres on 31 October 1914. *Who's Who* enabled me to track down hundreds of old soldiers, some underage on enlistment, men aged 86 to over 100, often contacted through old comrades' associations and many in old people's homes. One lieutenant colonel, aged 95, had just had a fall and asked if he could have more time to think and answer my questionnaire. Incredibly most could recall their badges, sometimes those of other units as well. One underage soldier who wanted to remain anonymous had served with the 1st Border Regiment from Gallipoli to the Armistice – he sent me a large sheet with coloured illustrations of most of the 29th Division's badges. One or two still had their badges; one had their complete uniform. But not one had a photo that showed them wearing the badge.

Many were keen to provide personal stories of their experiences. Although not relevant to their badges, many when asked provided interesting glimpses of their service life; most for the first time. Private Ashman wrote how they were pulled from the line on 9 November 1918, marched to Tournai, told they were going to Bonn, and were issued with new uniforms. As they were getting ready to go, putting up their stripes and sewing on their badges, the orders were cancelled and the uniforms taken away to be sent out to the returning PoWs. They then marched to near Brussels.

Private F. Dixon, a pre-war regular with the 1st Leicestershires, told me how his Christmas spent behind the lines in 1914, a day which should have been enjoyable, with a hot cooked meal and no shelling, resulted in a number of fatalities, none caused by the enemy.

It has been a very enjoyable experience, especially the telephone conversations. I received a snippet sent by a carer who tried to find out about badges and was told, 'sorry but Mr Hoey's memory is not too good – he had become an underage driver in 1915. He remembered very little of his uniform or flashes worn. However, he did recall driving Lawrence of Arabia.'

Or the note included with the questionnaire from Trooper Kingswell, who had landed in France with the 4th Hussars; he was attached to the Anti-Gas Services later, so could only tell me about his shoulder title with the hussars but did tell me about embarkation and the following days when he witnessed the first use of 13 pounders.

Thank you everyone who has contributed to the most complete collection of information on the badges of the regular infantry in the First World War.

A blazer badge worn by an Old Contemptible given to the writer by his younger brother during the research.

Another blazer badge, this time an Old Contemptible of the Munster Regiment. His sister felt it would be of more use to the writer than herself.

When the regular infantry arrived in France each regiment could be identified by their cap badge. This is a Sherwood Foresters cap.

All enlisted men wore metal shoulder titles that identified their regiment. Officers also wore a cap badge but generally in bronze, and instead of shoulder titles usually wore badges on their collars; often smaller versions of the cap badge.

Introduction

The purpose of this book is to answer many of the who, what, where, and when questions about the badges worn by the regular infantry during the period 1914–18. While its primary purpose is as a historical record, it will also be useful for re-enactors, collectors, family historians and those with an interest in the Great War in general. I have included a brief history of each battalion, not to detract from the main purpose of this book – a record of the badges – but to put the badges into context. I have also included other material about uniforms, such as how puttees were worn, to help identify battalions without badges.

Until 1916 many of the cap badges, like this one for the Royal Welsh Fusiliers, were in two metals.

As an economy measure in 1916, most enlisted men's cap badges were made in just one metal. For easy comparison, this is the economy version of the Royal Welsh Fusiliers badge.

A further economy measure was the introduction of Melton cloth shoulder titles in a standard rhomboid shape with white lettering.

Not all units or individuals wanted to be identical and many are found trimmed and shaped, like this Welsh Guards title.

Like my previous volume on Kitchener's Army's badges, this book is also the result of over thirty years of research using books, papers (including correspondence during the war – see below), articles, photographs, uniforms, museums, collectors and most importantly the veterans themselves – hundreds who gladly racked their brains, seventy years after the event to recall the minutiae of their uniforms; fortunately many of them could. Where there is no evidence, logic has been applied as some of the divisions used specific patterns and colours to denote brigade and then the battalion; sometimes even the man's company.

This book focuses on the badges worn at divisional, brigade, battalion and company level; the supporting arms of the army will be covered in volume four. Each regiment wore a specific cap badge and shoulder title – specified in Dress Regulations – and unless otherwise stated, all regular battalions of a regiment wore the same cap badge (later all in brass – the so-called economy version) and shoulder

When an enlisted man was moved to another battalion or regiment his badges changed accordingly. Not so with officers who kept their regimental badges regardless of the unit they were attached to. This officer was from the 1st Essex attached to the 10th Royal Fusiliers.

Introduction xiii

```
           1st  BATTN. THE NORTHAMPTONSHIRE REGT.



   1.      Western  12.8.1914 to 10.5.1919.

   2.      No distinguishing marks during the War.
           Covered with canvas.
           Officers and men identical.

   3.      Nil.

   4.      No.

   5.      -

   6.      Nil.

   7.      No.

   8.      None.

   9.      No.

  10.      No.

  11.      None.
           Neither.

  12.      None.

  13.      No.

  14.      None.

  15.      Regulation pattern.

  16.      Regulation pattern.

  17.      -

  18.      -

  19.      -
```

Regular battalions tended to regard pieces of cloth as unnecessary, as this reply from the Battalion CO shows.

xiv Badges of the Regular Infantry, 1914–1918

A copy of the original letter sent out by the National War Museum to gather information and collect the badges worn by the British Army during the war.

Reference No. 17/£.419

All communications should be addressed to—
The Secretary,
National War Museum.

Telephone Number: 9160 Victoria (15 lines).

NATIONAL WAR MUSEUM,
H.M. OFFICE OF WORKS,
Storey's Gate,
Westminster, S.W. 1.

June 13th, 1917.

Sir,

As you are doubtless aware, it has been decided to form a National War Museum, to organise which a Committee has been formed by order of the War Cabinet, with the First Commissioner of Works as Chairman and a Committee composed of representatives of the Admiralty, War Office, Ministry of Munitions,&c.

It has been decided to have a separate section for each Regiment, in which it is intended to exhibit, if possible, the following :—

(1) Rolls of the killed and died of wounds, etc., of the Regiment.
(2) Rolls of Officers and men of the Regiment who have been awarded Decorations or mentioned in Despatches.
(3) Special mention in Brigade, Divisional or Corps Orders of other Regiment, or any officer or soldier of it.
(4) Relics of special interest to the Regiment, such as guns, etc., captured by it.
(5) Badges worn by the Regiment.

It is with regard to the last item (No. 5) that I am now writing to ask your help.

The Committee wish to show not only the official Cap Badges of Regiments, but the special Battalion badges or marks of distinction worn by the Battalions on the sleeve or on the back of the Service Dress Jacket.

These badges were as you know, not made by the Army Clothing Department, and are therefore unprocurable except from the Regiments themselves. If you would send me either an actual badge, or failing that a description (with measurements or full-size colour sketch) of what was worn by your Battalion when first they went out, and any subsequent variations, with date of issue, it would be of the very greatest assistance.

It is hoped, with the co-operation of Officers commanding Battalions, to make the Regimental Sections of the Museum a complete and lasting record of the achievements of not only each Regiment, but of each Battalion composing it, as suggested in War Office Letter of 26th May, 1917, number 57/8/9532 (c.2).

It is hoped that if you have any suggestions you will let us know.

I have the honour to be, Sir,
Your obedient Servant,

Martin Conway

Director-General National War Museum.

titles – made of cloth from 1916 onwards – with officers wearing their version of the cap badge, generally the same but better quality, and usually with collar badges. As these have been covered in other specialist books (see bibliography) they are not always included here. Also included are details of special badges, created to identify particular groups of soldiers, sometimes worn for just a brief period, and wherever possible helmet signs are also included. The regiments are listed in their order of precedence.

Canadian and Australian forces had simple coloured geometric shapes for easy identification that followed a logical Army-based system unlike the British divisional systems decided by the Divisional Commander.

Unit identification was classified but understood by the population as standard for the army. This 8th Division 1917 Christmas card shows that units were easily identifiable by their badge to those in the know; all the badges displayed here are false except the cap badges.

The popular press included badges in their interpretations of the fighting on the Western Front.

Most British divisions adopted some form of cloth or painted identifying badge. However, they were not always worn, especially as many COs did not think they were essential. Looking at the myriad photographs produced, the vast majority have no badges, not even shoulder titles; they knew who they were, and as many veterans informed me they did not want the enemy to know who they were and were often ordered not to wear them. On raids they often had to leave their identity discs behind, helping explain the number of British soldiers 'Known to God' in the cemeteries across the world. Other factors were involved: lack of time or the skill to stitch them on in the correct position – very few units had the services of a battalion tailor; there was also often a shortage of cloth and/or paint.

At divisional level many of the signs were intricate and usually professionally produced. They were worn by HQ staff and many were embroidered on divisional armbands. Those worn in the trenches tended to be simple geometric shapes using both colour – sometimes regimental – and shape to identify brigade and/or battalion.

Regular battalions did not feel the need to adopt such badges until well into the war when so many of the units were Kitchener or Territorial Battalions. Like Kitchener's men, any badges, when worn, were positioned on the epaulette, back, upper arm and/ or on the steel helmet cover or painted on the surface. When correctly worn, in some units they could tell the observer the man's division, brigade, battalion, and sometimes company and function. Conversely some badges were only worn for a specific attack and then thrown away.

That these had become more or less an accepted necessity is shown by a request from the AQMG of XI Corps on 2 November 1916. He wrote: 'It is now more or less a general practice for infantry to have a distinguishing Division or Brigade patch of muslin or cloth sewn on to the jacket.'[1] He then requested details of the patches worn by the two divisions serving in the corps. It was simply a housekeeping request: he

---

1. Letter: XI Corps.O.S.18/18.

Introduction xvii

> [Letter on Imperial War Museum letterhead]
>
> THE SECRETARY,
> IMPERIAL WAR MUSEUM.
> Telegraphic Address:—"IMWARMUS, CRYSTAL, LONDON."
> Telephone Number:—SYDENHAM 2400.
>
> 5th March, 1921.
>
> Sir,
>
> The Imperial War Museum are compiling records of all the uniforms and equipment worn during the recent war. These are being made in the form of drawings by a very competent artist, Mr. A. Miller, H.L.I., who is also one of the Principals of the Art School at Glasgow. There have been so many peculiar varieties of uniform and additions to uniforms, that it is considered highly essential that records of these should be collected at the earliest possible date before their details have been forgotten by the wearers. It is especially desired to record the slight differences of uniform which may have occurred in battalions on the various Fronts, as it is considered that these will be of great interest and value in future times, both to the historian and all those connected with the regiments.
>
> As it is stated on the covering sheet, any of these details will be kept confidential if so desired.
>
> I shall be greatly obliged if you will assist my Committee by filling in the enclosed form, or by handing it to an Officer who will be able to give the necessary information.
>
> I am, Sir,
>
> Your obedient Servant,
>
> Charles ffoulkes
>
> Curator and Secretary.

In 1921 the Imperial War Museum requested information from a range of serving officers: this is the letter sent out.

wanted the information so that they could be 'officially sanctioned in order to enable the materials to be provided from the base'. Why this was being asked is unclear when two months previously the corps had been informed by the divisional commander that they were not worn except on helmets by some battalions. This led to a considerable

xviii   Badges of the Regular Infantry, 1914–1918

One of the more informative replies received by the museum. This is from the CO of the 2nd Royal Berkshire Regiment.

1st Bn. The Argyll & Sutherland Highlanders.

1. Left India. October 1914.
   To France. December 1914.
   To Salonika. " 1915.
   To Constantinople after the Armistice.

2. No markings.
   Khaki covering, with back flap for protection against the sun was worn in Salonika. No variation in the case of Officers.

3. Tartan Patch on the left side. Number of folds in puggaree eight. No variation in the case of officers.

4. In 1915 a soft felt hat was issued in Salonika. Left side was pinned up. Khaki puggaree 4 folds. No distinguishing patch. The hat was originally a grey-green but faded in the sun to Pink.

5. The Battalion landed in France with glengarries. A few balmorals were issued to battalion shortly after landing in France, and in July 1915 this was changed to a fawn colour, and issued to all. With both these bonnets the Regimental Cap Badge was worn on the left side and no rosette.
   Early in 1916 a Tam-o'-Shanter, known by the Ordnance as "Caps Balmoral, large crown khaki cloth" was issued and is still in use. Officers wore the same patterns in all three occasions but a special tam-o'-shanter was eventually made by Banard & Sons, London. This make all Officers wore in the last year of the war. It had ribbons at the back, 12 inches in length.

6. Tartan patch was worn on helmet only.

7. No in both cases.

8. The only marking on tunic was started in Salonika in 1915. This was a 27th Divisional Mark, a khaki drill band of about ½ inch wide, worn on the outside of the shoulder strap of jacket.

9. No.

10. Regimental Collar badges were worn by Officers.

11. Nil.

12. Equipment as at present worn i.e. Pattern 1908 Web Infantry Equipment. The equipment was worn as shown in the manual on this equipment dated 1913. In winter great coats when not worn were either carried in the pack, or if transport was available were carried in limbers or on pack mules. Blankets 3 (sometimes 4) per man always carried in transport.
    In Summer Great coats were withdrawn also all blankets except one which was carried in the pack or by transport. Mess tins, bivouac sheets and poles, waterproof sheets, and later waterproof capes instead, carried in the pack.

13. In action officers wore the Government pattern equipment without pouches, and out of the line Sam Browne Belts.

14. Nil.

15.

A lengthy reply from the 1st Battalion Argyll & Sutherland Highlanders.

15. Are trousers worn folded in any special way over puttees? State if shorts worn, and when if turned up, or of Salonika pattern.

    Shorts worn on fatigue and at nights when on the plain during summer (Salonika pattern), otherwise the kilt was always worn.

16. Describe any regimental or battalion method of wearing puttees. If shorts worn, any special feature, such as a coloured hose top.

    Short khaki puttees (3' turns) were worn over the top of boots. Khaki hosetops worn with kilt and shorts.

17. (Scottish Regiments.) When puttees were adopted, whether long or short puttees worn, and nature of hose tops in various battalions.

    Boots and puttees were taken into use when the battalion left England for France. A shortputtie, 3½ folds-4 foinger breadths, finishing on the centre of the outside of the ankle. The ordnance pattern of khaki hosetops worn throughout the war.

18. (Scottish Regiments.) Any special pattern of kilt, apron, or sporran, apart from regulations?

    The half khaki apron was worn throughout the war.

19. (Scottish Regiments.) Describe special features of pipers' uniform in various battalions (e.g., special badges, rosettes, belts, sporran, hose tops, garters).

    Pipes dress. Web equipment without packs. Revolvers on right side, no rifles.

20. Any regimental pattern of breeches and leggings worn by officers?

    Tartan breeches worn out of the line with black field boots or leggings.

21. Are buglers' lines worn, and in what manner?

    Only when the bugle was carried.

22. State any peculiarity of band uniform, if any (badges on pouch, belts, etc.).

    The band were all used as stretcher bearers.

23. Was any provisional uniform (blue, grey, etc.), or equipment worn at early stages of war while training? (Photo and description if available.)

    No.

Part two of the reply from the CO of the 1st Argyll & Sutherland Highlanders.

From,

    The Office Commanding,
        1st Battalion THE GORDON HIGHLANDERS.

To,

    The Secretary,
        National War Museum,
            L O N D O N.

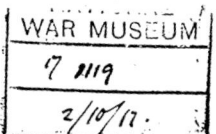

        In answer to your letter I received some little time ago asking for any relic of this Battalion's actions during the present War. I am sending you the colours worn by the Battalion subsequent to the Battle of the Bluff.

        These colours are being forwarded for inclusion in the collection of war material etc., for exhibition in the National Museum if you think them of sufficient interest for this purpose.

        A short explanatory account is given hereunder to add a little informationas to the colours, and which I hope will prove of some small interest to the future generations who may be concerned in upholding the tradations of THE GORDON HIGHLANDERS.

PATCH. - KHAKI CLOTH WITH BLACK ST ANDREW'S CROSS ON BLACK GROUND.

        During the Battle of the Bluff which was fought on the morning of 2/3rd March 1916. This patch was worn by the Battalion on the back of the Service Dress Jacket, between the shoulders.

        This was the first occasion the Battalion went into action with any special distinguishing mark, and it proved the soundness of its adoption by the easiness with which the men knew each other when they occupied the captured German trench in the uncertain light of early morning.

SHOULDER COLOURS. - WORN BY THE DIFFERENT COMPANIES AS FOLLOWS.

        "A" COY............ BLUE.
        "B" " .... GREEN.
        "C" " .... RED.
        "D" " .... YELLOW.
        "Headquarters COY..... MAUVE.

        The above colours were worn on the two shoulder straps during the Battles of DELVILLE WOOD fought on 18/7/16 and GUILLEMONT fought on 18/8/16 on the SOMME, and on one shoulder strap (Right.) during the Battle of ARRAS fought on 9/4/17. AND Battle of SERRE fought on 13/11/16

        The usefulness of these shoulder colours became apparent in helping to distinguish the men of the different companies when they became casualties during the fighting and were adopted permanently as part of the "Fighting Kit" of the 1st Battalion THE GORDON HIGHLANDERS.

In the Field.
23/9/17.
        F. T Pine Capt /fr   Major,
        Commanding 1st Battalion THE GORDON HIGHLANDERS.

The 1917 reply from the CO of the Gordon Highlanders.

amount of very negative correspondence from the 5th Division, evidenced by the reply below from Brigadier Turner. However it did result in some of the battalions receiving cloth for their badges: 14th Royal Warwicks received ten square feet of Royal Blue and five of yellow; 15th Royal Warwicks received 69 yards of regimental ribbon and the 2nd KOSB received 50 square feet of Leslie tartan.

Many regular battalions saw no need for them and consequently did not adopt them. A number also saw no need to assist the NWM (National War Museum). The attitude displayed by many regulars to the subject was not that shown by those commanding Service Battalions, like Lieutenant Colonel W. Peacock, CO of the 9th Royal Inniskilling Fusiliers, who wrote on 29 July 1917 that he would be 'very pleased to give you any further information you require, or to do anything in co-operation with you, to make the Regimental Sections of your Museum a complete and lasting record of the achievements of the Regiment to which I have the honour to belong.'[2] Unlike the COs of many regular battalions, Lieutenant Colonel Welsh, commanding 1st KOSB, was also happy to help: he provided details about badges worn on Gallipoli and on the Western Front on helmet and tunic.

By December 1916, in a letter to the three divisions in XI Corps, Major General Hobbs, DA & QMG, First Army, told the divisions that 'the principle of wearing distinguishing patches has been concurred in and the cloth required will in future be supplied by the Army Ordnance Department.' Even so the 5th Division refused to cooperate.

More standard of the attitude by regulars to such badges was that of Lieutenant Colonel Crofts' reply of 25 July 1917. Commanding 1st Battalion Queen's, serving in a Kitchener Division that did not wear badges, he recorded proudly that 'no fancy badges are worn by this Battalion.' In a similar vein, the CO of 1st Buffs told the NWM that his battalion had 'not at any time during the campaign worn any Distinctive Badges other than those authorised by Dress Regulations.' This was echoed by the CO of the 1st Royal Welch Fusiliers who wrote that no badge had been worn by the battalion since its arrival on the Western Front in 1914. However, officers, warrant officers and staff sergeants wore the 'flash' at the back of the collar. Similarly, the 2nd Battalion Black Watch were only identified by a red hackle, which unfortunately they were unable to send to the museum because they could not get the materials needed to make them in France or Belgium. In the case of the 2nd Division they were just not worn, probably because they were worn by New Army Battalions; simply a case of being superior and snobbish.

---

2. Letter F2119 30/7/17th (Service) Battalion Royal Inniskilling Fusiliers to Secretary NWM.

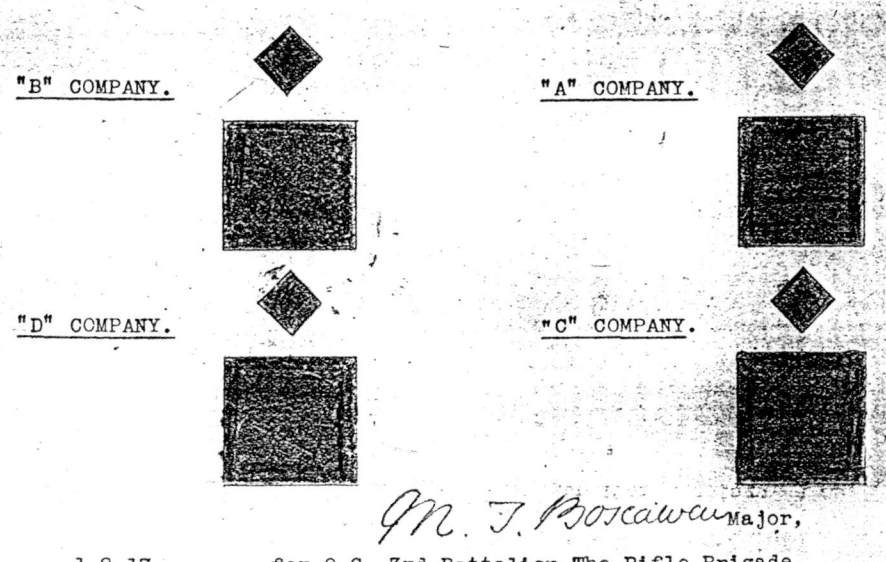

Subject:- Distinguishing Marks.

Director General,
National War Museum.

Reference attached.

Herewith attached distinguishing marks worn by all ranks of this Battalion on both arms, just below the shoulder.

The large RED square is a Battalion distinguishing mark and the small coloured diamond pieces are Company marks, which are worn just above the Battalion marks.

No distinguishing marks are worn on the back of the jacket and the attached were first worn before going into action at GUILLEMONT (on the Somme) on 18th August, 1916.

Previous to this, no distinguishing mark of any description was worn by this Battalion.

"B" COMPANY. "A" COMPANY.

"D" COMPANY. "C" COMPANY.

M. J. Boscawen Major,
1.8.17.   for O.C. 3rd Battalion The Rifle Brigade.

In August 1917 the 3rd Battalion second in command sent the NWM details of the badges worn by his men.

xxiv   Badges of the Regular Infantry, 1914–1918

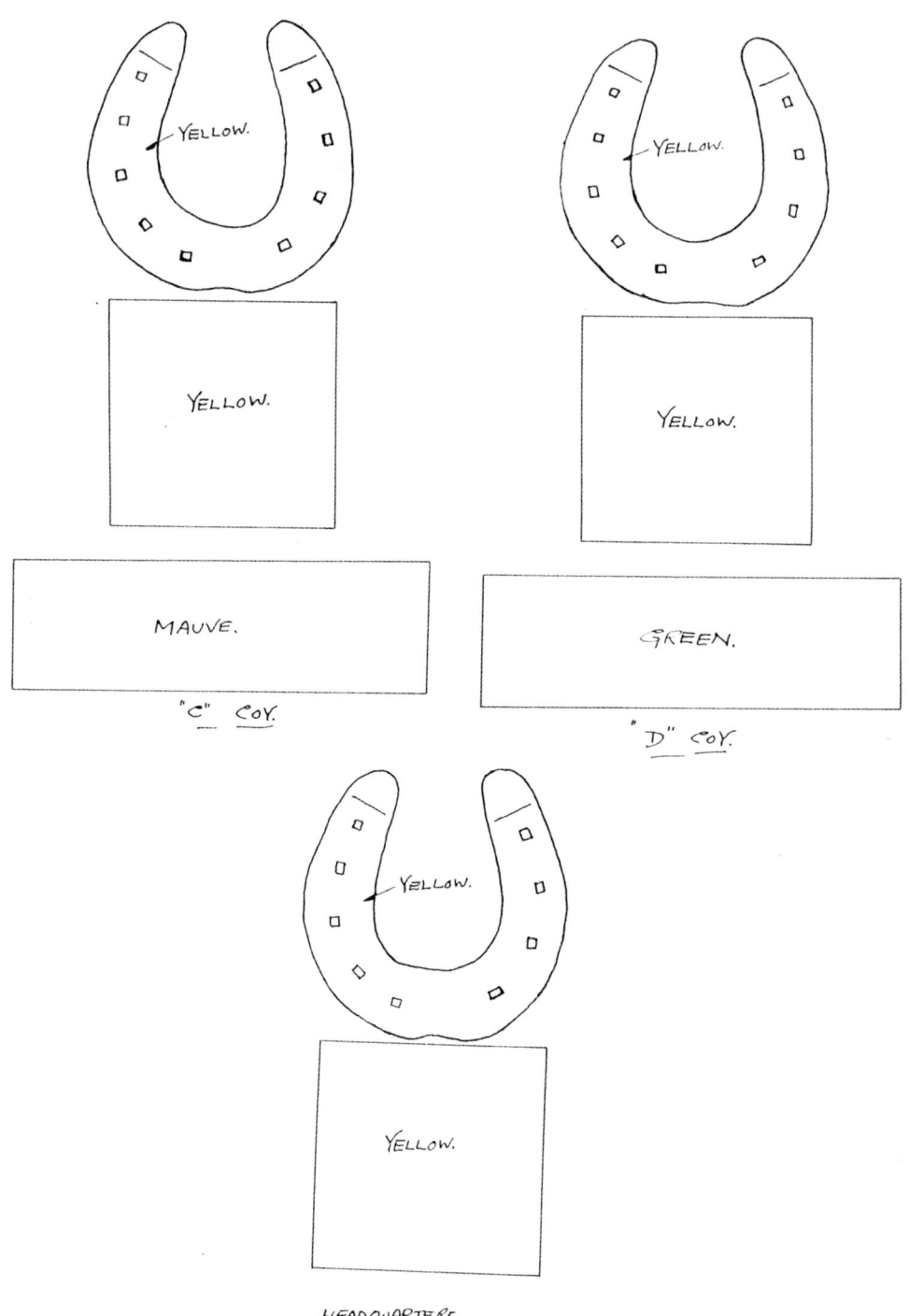

In the early 1920s Haswell-Miller started to draw the badges worn by the British Forces in the war. This is one of his early drawings; in this case 8th Somerset Light Infantry in 37th Division – a Kitchener battalion.

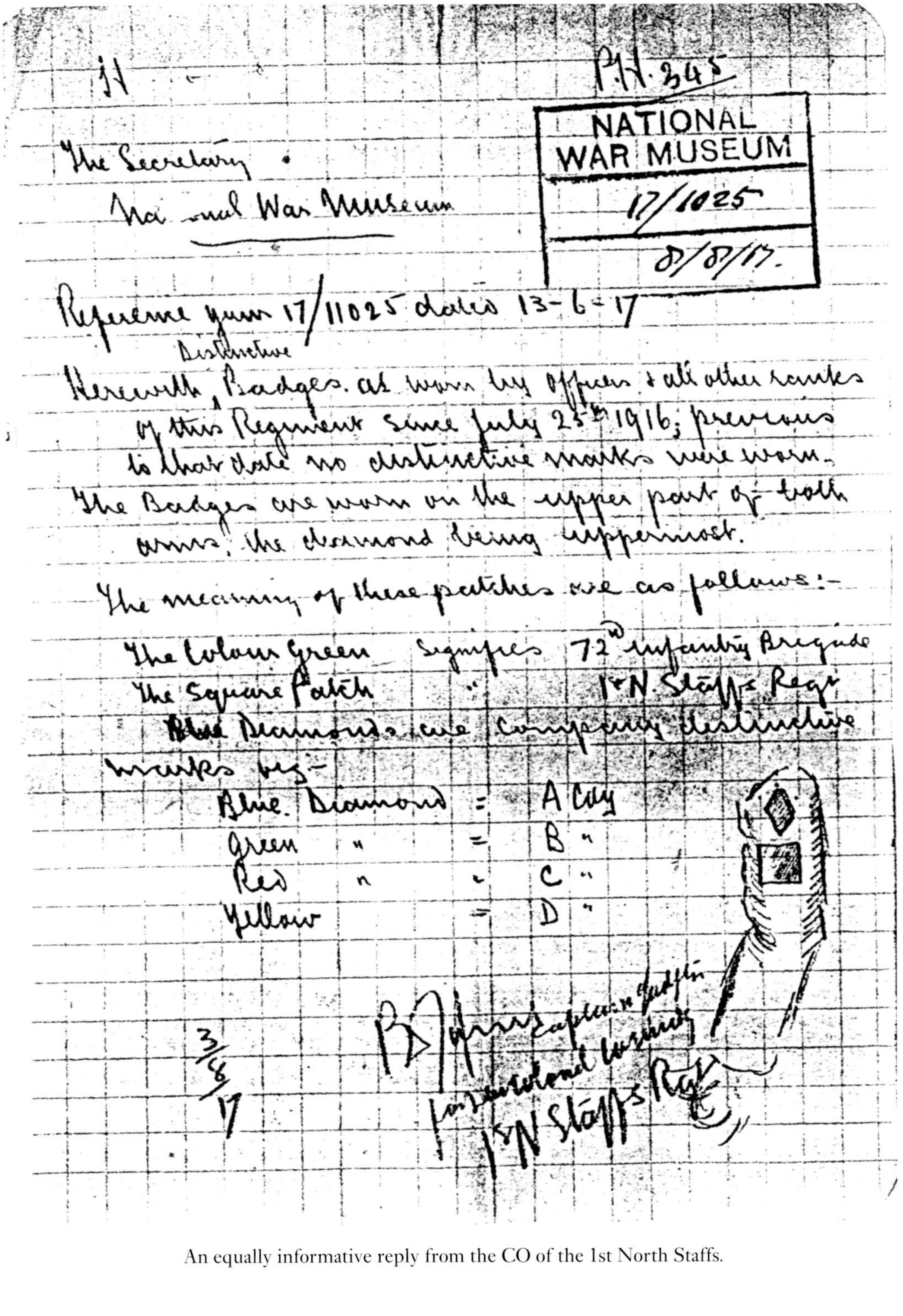

> P.H. 345
> NATIONAL WAR MUSEUM
> 17/1025
> 8/8/17.
>
> The Secretary,
> National War Museum.
>
> Reference your 17/11025 dated 13-6-17
>
> Herewith, Distinctive Badges as worn by Officers & all other ranks of this Regiment since July 25th 1916; previous to that date no distinctive marks were worn. The Badges are worn on the upper part of both arms; the diamond being uppermost.
>
> The meaning of these patches are as follows:—
>
> The Colour Green   Signifies 72nd Infantry Brigade
> The Square Patch   "   1st N. Staffs Regt.
> Blue Diamonds are company distinctive marks viz:—
>
> Blue Diamond = A Coy
> Green   "   = B "
> Red   "   = C "
> Yellow   "   = D "
>
> 3/8/17
>
> B. Johns Captain & Adjutant
> 1st N. Staffs Regt.

An equally informative reply from the CO of the 1st North Staffs.

xxvi   Badges of the Regular Infantry, 1914–1918

Members of the BEF marching through Le Mans in August 1914. Even though they had just arrived in France some have no cap badge and some have no shoulder titles – one of the reasons that many men could not be identified when they were killed.

Brigadier General Jones, commanding 13th Brigade, felt they were unnecessary and he would not advocate wearing them; and Brigadier General Lord Gordon-Lennox, 95th Brigade CO, serving with the 5th Division, could not 'understand exactly what purpose' they served. Brigadier Turner, commanding the 15th Infantry Brigade, felt very strongly about them, expressing his feelings in a reply dated 5 November 1916 to a letter AM/7387 dated 3 November 1916: 'No unit in the Brigade wears a distinguishing mark on their uniform. All units in this Brigade strongly oppose the idea of these patches on the jackets. The Division has now been in the field for over 2 years and up to the present time no idea has ever been entertained of having these patches except by New Army units. The Brigade had very recently fought three big battles and all Commanding Officers are agreed that distinctive patches would have been of no value as, firstly, it would be necessary for individuals to know all the marks of the Division and, secondly, it is necessary to be very near the person before the badge is visible. The 16th Battalion Royal Warwickshire Regiment wore badges when they joined the Brigade but found them of no value and so removed them.' He also appended the views of his battalion COs, adding that he entirely concurred with their comments. Major Patterson, commanding the 1st Norfolks, considered them

IMPERIAL WAR MUSEUM.

Questionnaire that was circulated — with very unsatisfactory results

1. Theatres of war in which unit has served. Approximate dates of proceeding to and leaving.

(a) *Brigades and Divisions in which unit has been, date of transfer if any.*

2. What have been the markings on steel helmets, approximate when adopted, and if altered, when? Nature of covering and any peculiarity. Any variation in case of officers.

3. State what have been the patches on topees, lines in puggaree, or if badge worn (state on which side). Any variation in case of officers.

4. Has any experimental or special headdress been worn at any time? State nature and attach sketch, photo, or example, if possible.

5. (Scottish Regiments.) State any peculiarity in tam o' shanter, balmoral, etc., e.g. nature of rosette, tails, special badge, hackle, etc. Any variation in case of officer

6. Describe any patch worn on service cap.

7. Is the cap badge different in any battalion? (If so, please send specimen). Any variations in case of officers.

8. What are the recognition marks on tunic? State correct positions and measurements. State any changes in these, and dates approximately. If available, please forward specimens. Any variations in the case of officers. *Explaining origin if any and what portion denotes battalion, brigade and division.*

9. Are collar badges worn by other ranks; if so, what?

10. Are any special or different collar badges worn by officers in any battalion?

11. What regimental badges, if any, are worn by N.C.O.s over (or upon) chevrons? State if gold or silver chevrons are worn

12. State any peculiarity in equipment or regimental or battalion methods of assembling or wearing (e.g. fastening buckles, arranging loose ends in different orders of dress, positions of w.p. sheet, mess tin, blanket, in marching order)

13. Any special pattern of equipment or Sam Browne belt worn by officers.

A copy of the original letter sent out by Haswell-Miller in 1921 to gather information about the badges worn; note his comments and additions.

unnecessary, determining that 'it would be very deeply resented by all ranks of the Battalion especially as it would be of no military value.' The 1st Bedfordshires felt it was a distinction not to wear them while Lieutenant Colonel Barker, CO of the 1st Cheshires, as well as seeing no use for them, felt they also broke with tradition and would be looked on with 'intense disgust'.

To other regulars they were expected and so were grudgingly worn, which probably explains the replies from some battalions. The 1st Somerset Light Infantry and 1st Worcesters did not start wearing them until February 1917 and the 1st King's Own until 10 March 1917. Some regular battalions on joining Kitchener Divisions wore badges to conform to the divisional pattern. However, 1st Dorsets, while serving in the 5th Division, had introduced a special identifying title in April 1915 and on joining 32 Division they continued to wear it and adopted the divisional system of badges that showed division, brigade, battalion and company.

Some regular divisions accepted and wore them throughout the war. The 4th Division even included the badges in its orders. The National Archive (TNA) has a sheet marked secret, with the distribution of troops with reference to 4th Divisional order No. 61 with illustrations of the badges worn by the attacking troops (date

Apart from regulation badges there are no battalion flashes visible in this 1919 victory parade.

A draft leaving from London in October 1914 clearly showing that on departure men wore their regulation badges.

unknown – provided by a correspondent many years back). On 20 June 1916, Major Stenhouse, 31st Division GS, issued a staff order that supplied information on the badges to be worn by the 4th Division for the offensive – cloth badges that were to be worn on sacking covering the steel helmet. 'The colours will be:- 10th Brigade – Green; 11th Brigade – Yellow; 12th Brigade – Red.' He then provided the size and direction of wear of the five allotted shapes.

Along with the cloth badges worn to indicate a soldier's unit there were other cloth adornments wrapped round or stitched to his tunic. Stripes, crowns and pips indicated rank; letters in laurel leaves indicated his trade/speciality, as did coloured bands and brassards. Inverted stripes were the sign of a well-behaved soldier – or one who had not been caught wrong-doing – and short vertical yellow cloth or metal bars indicated that

Although no regimental or battalion badges are visible, this photograph clearly shows the issue helmet cover.

Many of the replies from the battalions detail bugle lines. This is a typical example – battalion unknown.

In many of the battalion returns the use of armbands is detailed. This shows the ways in which signallers were identified: crossed flags and/or an armband - in this case above the elbow: more usually below. Again non of the three are wearing shoulder titles.

they had been wounded. This book will not look at the multitude of trade badges worn or good service stripes and wound badges unless they feature in a photograph. Like shoulder titles and cap and collar badges, trade badges have their own specialist books. However, to help readers, each section includes the standard cap badge; I have included officers' cap badges where these differ from other ranks, apart from colour/material. Also included are many of the cloth replacements for brass shoulder titles. Some useful extra books are suggested in the bibliography to aid identification.

I have tried throughout to provide photographs of the badge or of it being worn. Given the rarity of many of the badges I have been unable to trace examples of them all so I have included drawings or made mention of them in the main text. If any reader has examples of the missing badges or photos showing their wear or any additional information I would be extremely grateful if they could contact me through the publisher. Any new information or examples will be included in the next volume or in a second edition. Any errors are solely my responsibility.

Introduction   xxxi

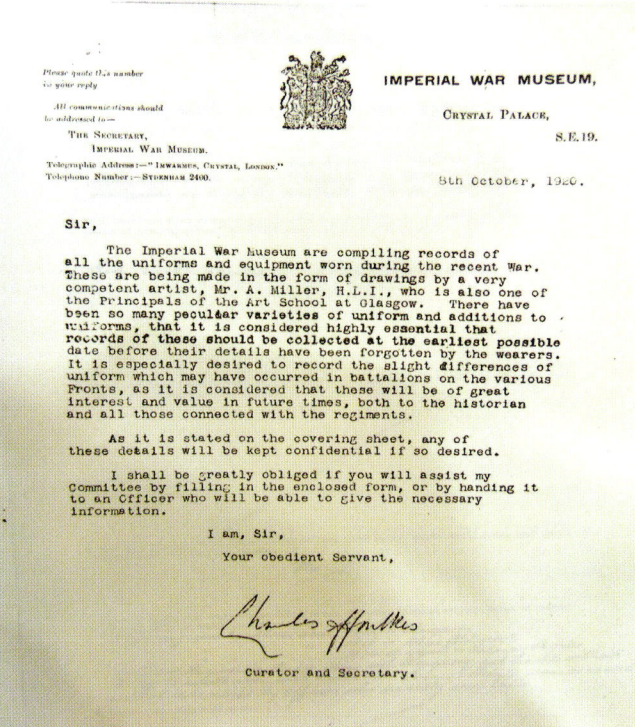

The letter from the IWM curator detailing their work and asking for assistance with the development of the museum for future generations.

A copy of a secret document distributed by the 4th Division detailing the badges to be worn for an attack.

Background

Instant recognition of friend and foe has always been essential in warfare. Differing clans or groups distinguished their commonality with some form of easily recognisable marking: face paints, body scars, motifs on shields, flags, helmet style.

Probably the first recognisable 'flash' was the ivy leaf shoulder patch worn by the Herculi Legion circa AD 286–305; the army of King Cadwallader in 640 wore a leek in their caps. The advent of mass armies led to the introduction of a uniform that distinguished between enemy and ally. Variations in the uniform highlighted 'leader and led, expert and novice.'[3] The Romans wore a uniform and armour, the crusaders wore crosses, and in the Middle Ages men wore garments that showed their loyalty. During the reign of Richard II, English soldiers wore a red cross on a white doublet. By the mid-1500s soldiers were beginning to wear clothing that not only showed their allegiance, their district, but often their function. Archers sent to Ireland from Liverpool in 1566 were dressed in blue cassocks with two small blue laces; Staffordshire men wore red. In 1574 soldiers wore blue coats, artificers red, and artificers from Lancashire wore white coats with red and green laces. By the seventeenth century, dress, field marks, and the equipment of the soldiers, were used to differentiate both rank and function. During the Siege of Bristol in 1643, Royalist troops were identified by their lack of neckwear. Over a hundred years later in the War of Independence, each side chose to wear their allegiance in their hats: loyalists wore pine-twigs and Americans slips of paper during an action in South Carolina in 1780. Mass conscript armies led to uniforms that clearly identified allegiance, status and often function. Individual regiments could be identified by numerals, coloured facings, head gear, epaulettes and sashes.

The introduction of mass-produced clothing, and more practical designs, led to the introduction of easily recognised badges for rank, function and unit. As uniform clothing grew more practical and visually less obtrusive, badges became more discreet. During the First World War the rapid increase in size of the British army led to the need to be able to identify a man's unit at close range, especially in the confusion of battle, to stop men becoming mixed up and moving away from the objective.

---

3. Rosignoli, 1987.

While the French and German armies kept unit identification to a minimum, usually detailing only arm of service and regiment, British and Empire troops were often festooned with cloth badges: Corps, Divisional, Brigade, Regiment, Battalion, order of seniority in a brigade, rank, function, long service and whether wounded or not. One veteran recalled that the reason for the replacement of metal badges 'was that a figure in the field of battle would be less easily discerned.'

Although the badges were worn, many were ignorant of those used by units not in their immediate proximity – they didn't want or need to know: units were family; they were secret and could not be disclosed. 'Distinguishing signs which have been adopted by units and formations, and the signs authorised for certain transport vehicles, are secret, and must not be disclosed in correspondence.'[4] This was issued around the time when the NWM was asking for examples. A further order as well as insisting on secrecy went further: they could 'not be reproduced for unofficial purposes, nor [could] their meaning be disclosed to unauthorised persons.'[5] Secrecy meant anonymity: 'we were not allowed to wear any badges or anything that would identify us,' noted one veteran. Some signs however, while not providing unit recognition, were worn to identify the participant to others.

By 1917, to those on the home front the wearing of such badges was synonymous with serving in the army abroad. This is clear from adverts and postcards where the soldiers usually had some form of distinguishing badge on their upper arm.

The NWM request for information in 1917 provided a large but incomplete collection of the badges worn during the war. After the war, between 1919 and the early 1920s, the artist Haswell-Miller circulated a detailed questionnaire to ex-COs about the distinctions their unit wore. Most replies were from regular officers who were still serving and had seen service abroad with the regular battalions. While providing extra information it was sometimes contradictory and was still not complete. Some badges can be deduced, others guessed at, some are mentioned in passing in books, journals and letters, others seen in photographs. Correspondence with veterans in the 1980s also provided much new material. This book, using the above sources and more, is the summation of close to a lifetime's work, ably assisted by other enthusiasts and by the dedication of those Great War veterans who responded to my requests and often re-requests for further clarification.

---

4. GRO 2463.
5. GRO 3043.

Divisional Signs

The original expeditionary force consisted of six infantry divisions with supporting units and cavalry. A further five divisions were formed during 1914 and early 1915 from regular battalions returning from overseas postings with the Guards Division being formed from the battalions serving on the Western Front during 1915. Not all the regular battalions returned home, some were left to garrison the Empire, assisted by battalions of territorials; these are also described.

'Since the beginning of organized military formations, both the participants and in many cases the implements of war have been formally identified by the use of field signage or differencing marks.'[6] Before the war British and Dominion forces 'were using an alphanumeric system of Unit identification markings on their military horse transport and equipment that appears to have been accepted as quite adequate for its time.'[7] With transport, staff brassards and directional signs and noticeboards all bearing a unit's number, the enemy could quickly deduce who they were opposing. To remove this threat a letter was sent 'to the three Army Corps and Indian Corps, pointing out that our methods for facilitating the identification of units and individuals by our own troops are probably of considerable assistance to the enemy. Suggestions are made and opinions requested.'[8] The divisional and brigade sign was born; others followed later.

This is confirmed by Captain V. Wheeler-Holohan, ex-12th London Regiment, in the preface to his book *Divisional and Other Signs* in 1920. 'The origin of the Army, Corps and Divisional sign was the necessity of having some means of immediately recognising the transport and personnel of any unit or formation. It was also intended to mystify the enemy and to prevent his discovering the identity of the Corps or Division which was opposing him.'[9]

---

6. Dux & Hibberd, *British & Dominion Formation and Unit Vehicle Signage*, preface p. 1.
7. Ibid.
8. Ibid, preface p. 1.
9. Wheeler-Holohan, p. xiii.

Notes on divisional signs

The images in this book show the designs used by regular divisions, illustrated with artwork taken from Player's cigarette cards published after the war and original signs. The best known sign was the 'eye' of the Guards, designed by Major Sir Eric Avery, Bart., MC, who commanded the Divisional MT Company. It was painted on vehicles and worn by staff; attached units wore a different sign in various colours and differing letters. A marine signals flag that represented the number one was used by the 1st Division. The three stars of 2nd Division showed its seniority in the original BEF – 2nd Division in the 1st Corps. Lieutenant General Sir Aylmer Haldane used 'one of the charges in his Armorial Bearings'[10] for the 3rd Division. A ram's head was used by the 4th Division; it represented the family crest of the commanding officer, Major General the Hon. Sir William Lambton. The original 5th Division sign was a yellow diagonal bar which was placed across existing signs. Over the course of the war it evolved into a blue square with a yellow diagonal bar. The sign adopted by the 6th Division was simply a straightforward design with no history; similarly those of the 7th and 8th Divisions. Distinctive marks in Salonika were simple coloured bars worn on the shoulder straps, adopted by both the 27th (described by units as yellow, khaki or buff) and 28th Divisions. The 29th was a half diamond designed by Lieutenant General Sir Beauvoir de Lisle,[11] to remind all ranks of the importance of the diamond as a military formation in open fighting.

Not all the signs are represented by an original badge. This is for a number of reasons: some signs were only used on a staff officer brassard; a few were purely for use on vehicles and other equipment, and others were simple coloured loops which have survived on just a few tunics. As well as vehicle use, many were painted on steel helmets and did not exist as a cloth badge, and some were produced in such small numbers - because they were only worn by headquarters staff – that there are probably none left in existence; they may exist but I have been unable to trace them. On the other hand, a few divisional signs are relatively common because they were worn by all ranks in the division.

---

10. Ibid. p.36.
11. 'He found that junior officers had much difficulty in understanding minor tactics, especially advanced guards, and as he strongly advocated the efficacy of the diamond formation, he adopted the diamond as the 29th Divisional sign, half being worn on each shoulder.' Wheeler-Holohan p.62.

xxxvi Badges of the Regular Infantry, 1914–1918

The Guards Division eye designed by Major Sir Eric Avery.

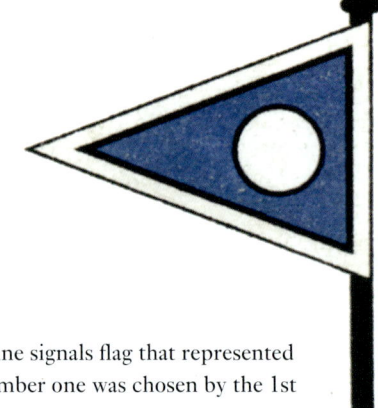

A marine signals flag that represented the number one was chosen by the 1st Division.

The three stars of the 2nd Division showed its seniority in the BEF: second division, I Corps.

Lieutenant General Sir Aylmer Haldane chose one of the charges in his Armorial Bearings to represent the 3rd Division.

A ram's head was part of the family crest of the CO of the 4th Division.

The original sign of the 5th Division was a yellow bar placed across existing signs. During the war it evolved into a yellow diagonal bar over a light blue square.

Divisional Signs   xxxvii

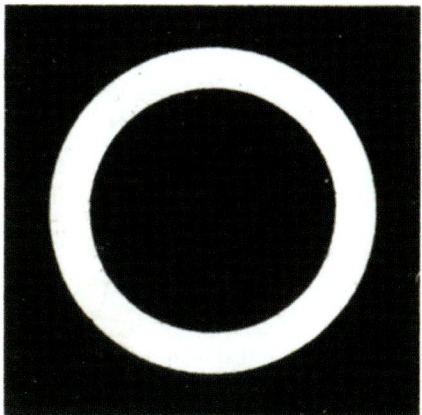

The sign of the 6th Division was a simple geometric design with no history.

Ease of application was probably paramount in the design of the 7th Division sign.

There was no history attached to the design of the 8th Division.

In Salonika badges were kept to a minimum with each division adopting a coloured bar on the shoulder strap; yellow for the 27th Division.

As part of the Salonika Army, the 28th adopted a red bar on the shoulder strap.

On the Western Front, the 29th Division adopted a red triangle designed to remind all ranks of the importance of the diamond as a military formation in open fighting.

xxxviii   Badges of the Regular Infantry, 1914–1918

Two senior NCOs clearly displaying the 29th Division red triangle.

Most officers working in divisional headquarters wore a red armband, usually with the division's sign. This was worn by HQ staff in the Guards Division.

Divisional Signs xxxix

A 1918 Christmas card from a member of the 2nd Division. The divisional sign is cleverly disguised in the tree.

An officer of the Lovat Scouts who was attached to 4th Division HQ at the end of the war. The Lovat Scouts in 1918 were Corps Troops on Lines of Communication (LoC) duties but many were attached to units as scouts and snipers.

The sign of the 3rd Division was simple and easy to manufacture and came in a range of materials, sizes and shades of yellow.

Major General the Hon. Sir William Lambton, 4th Division CO, chose his family crest as the sign for his division.

xl Badges of the Regular Infantry, 1914–1918

In the 5th Division non-regulation uniform badges were not allowed but markings on helmets were. This divisional sign was worn on the sandbag cover of an unknown unit.

Colloquially known as Honnicker's balls, staff in the 8th Division wore two red circles side by side.

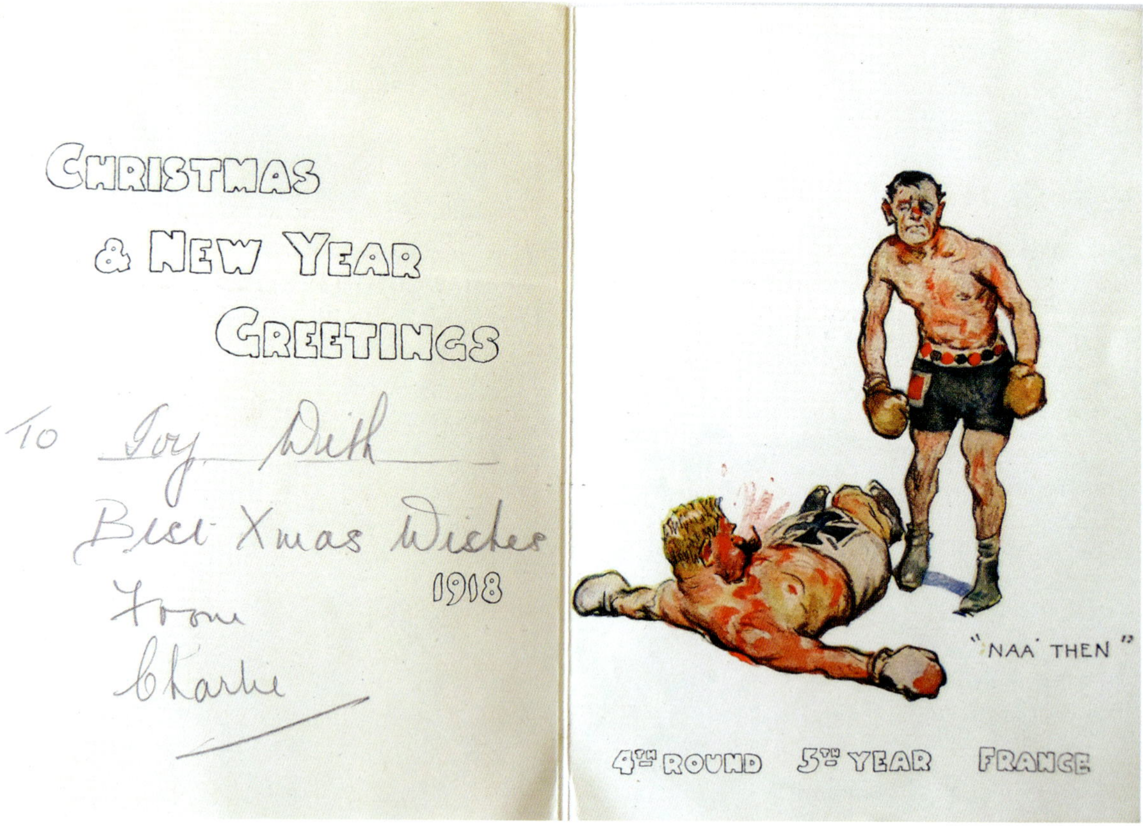

The sign for the 8th Division was cleverly positioned on the standing boxer's shorts in this 1918 Christmas card.

Bravery and good work was rewarded in the 29th Division by an entry in the Divisional Record, an individual certificate signed by the G.O.C. and by the award of an Honour Badge which was worn above the divisional sign on the right sleeve; amended by Special Order No. 11 of 14 January 1918 which stated that it was to be worn in the centre of the divisional sign.

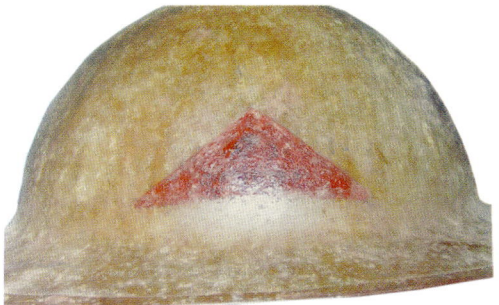

The red triangle was worn on the front of the steel helmet.

After the war many of those awarded the divisional Honour Badge wore it as a lapel badge.

Brigade Signs

Very few brigades saw the need to adopt an independent sign, as in many cases the colour or shape of the patch already identified both the brigade and the battalion. As these were only worn by a few men at any one time, existing badges are very rare and are more likely to exist as part of a combination badge showing brigade, battalion and regimental seniority. Brigade badges were generally used to denote brigade troops, such as RE Field Companies, sometimes to identify members of brigade headquarters. The decision to use a special brigade sign was taken at divisional level, with all three brigades, for the most part, adopting such a badge.

Brigade badges were not generally used by the regular battalions. However, all three brigades of the 4th Division wore a badge that identified the division and brigade at the same time. In the 7th Division only the 91st Brigade has a confirmed colour, initially pink and then blue. The most badged divisions were the 8th and 29th but only the former identified brigades. In Salonika, of the six regular brigades, only the 81st Brigade wore an identifying badge. In 1915 a number of regular battalions were transferred to the newly arrived Kitchener divisions to bolster them; they wore their adopted division's badges.

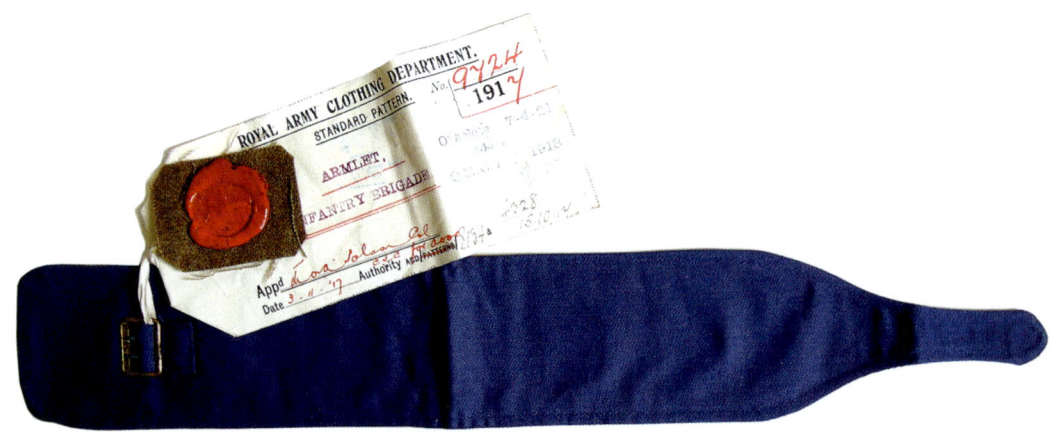

A standard-pattern Infantry Brigade armlet from 1917 with official authority tag and seal.

Brigade Signs   xliii

When a brigade had no separate badge the divisional sign, in this case the 2nd, was sometimes worn on the armlet.

The headquarters badge for the 10th Infantry Brigade dated 23 September 1917.

All three Infantry Brigade HQs of the 4th Division wore a sign. This is the 11th Brigade; it was worn vertically.

A red square with black vertical central stripe was worn by HQ personnel in the 12th Infantry Brigade.

Although the 5th Division did not wear uniform badges the 14th Infantry Brigade HQ sent the NWM a red diamond but did not specify its position of wear. The brigade was serving with the 32nd Division and had adopted the divisional scheme.

xliv   Badges of the Regular Infantry, 1914–1918

Before the adoption of cloth signs the 14th Brigade wore an embroidered armlet.

All three Infantry Brigade HQs in the 8th Division wore a cloth sign. That of the 23rd was a green arc; the arc signified the brigade, the colour the unit: Brigade HQ.

The 24th Infantry Brigade wore different colour circles to show the unit: white for the Brigade HQ, the shape for the brigade.

A square indicated the 25th Infantry Brigade; the colour – yellow – was used by the headquarters.

A number of regular battalions were transferred to Kitchener divisions and wore their badges. On joining the 74th Infantry Brigade, the 2nd Royal Irish Rifles wore the 25th Division's red horseshoe and the brigade bar on their back.

The Grenadier Guards

The most senior British infantry regiment raised six battalions during the war of which three were in existence at the outbreak; four served on the Western Front. Four of them served on the Western Front. The 5th was a reserve battalion, supplying drafts to the active battalions and the sixth, formed for a specific purpose was short lived. All wore a standard cap badge in different styles and qualities.

All battalions wore curved cloth shoulder titles GRENADIER GUARDS in white embroidered on red, adopted in May 1916[12] but not approved until 19/6/16. Before the adoption of a cloth title a metal GG with a separate grenade above was worn on the epaulette. Cloth titles were not worn by officers. Unknown battalion: officers steel helmet, 1918, vertical rectangle divided vertically in equal sections blue/maroon/blue with gold grenade on black backing on both sides of cover; at Brooklands in January 1916 an officer was recorded as wearing a square diamond vertically divided equally into blue/red/blue.

1st Battalion

Stationed at Warley on 4/8/14 as part of London District troops it joined the 20th Brigade, 7th Division in September 1914 at Lyndhurst, landing at Zeebrugge on 7/10/14. After serving with the division, on 4/8/15 it transferred to the 3rd Guards Brigade, Guards Division.

---

12. NWM correspondence with adjutant 3rd Battalion.

Badges: a single vertical red bar was worn below the shoulder title on both sleeves, 1¼ × 5⁄16″.[13]

2nd Battalion

Stationed in Chelsea on 4/8/14 it was part of the 4th (Guards) Brigade, 2nd Division, landing at Le Havre on 15/8/14. It transferred on 20/8/15 to 1st Guards Brigade, Guards Division.

Badges: white embroidered 2 on red rectangle 1″ × 1³⁄16″ worn below shoulder titles.[14] Guardsman Calvert recalled that all the battalions wore a battalion number under the shoulder title.

3rd Battalion

Stationed at Wellington Barracks, London District, on 4/8/14 it joined the 2nd Guards Brigade, Guards Division in France on 19/8/15.

Badges: on 28/7/17 the battalion adjutant wrote that 'on arrival in France, this Battalion wore the brass numerals supplied by Ordnance; in May 1916 they were done away with and "Grenadier Guards" sewn on the sleeve directly under the shoulder straps… In January 1917 the 3 numerals were added to denote Battalion.' The three numerals were three vertical red bars 1¼″ × ¼″ worn below shoulder titles.[15] Guardsman G. Knights, as well as recalling his brass and red and white titles being worn on active service, also recalled having the Guards cap badge soldered on the front. He was a Lewis gunner and wore a yellow square on the right arm.

4th Battalion

Formed at Marlow on 14/7/15 it joined the 3rd Guards Brigade, Guards Division in France on 19/8/15. On 8/2/18 the newly formed 4th Guards Brigade replaced a brigade in the 31st Division. On 20/5/18 4th Guards Brigade was transferred to GHQ Reserve.

---

13. IWM ART 3045; Q2678 photo Pilkem 5/8/17.
14. IWM photograph Q9182 Bavincourt 3/6/18 and ART 4116.
15. IWM photograph Q6966 and Q6979 August 1918.

Badges: red Roman numeral **IV** below shoulder titles, 1⁵⁄₁₆″ high, bars ⁵⁄₁₆″ wide.[16] Guardsman W. Spencer, who served with the battalion from 1915 to 1919, clearly recalled always wearing the red and white shoulder title.

5th (Reserve) Battalion

Formed at Kensington as 4th (Reserve) Battalion in August 1914 it remained at Chelsea during the war as a draft finding unit and was disbanded after the war.

Badges: Guardsmen Calvert and Knight trained with the battalion and confirmed that the battalion only wore regulation metal badges.

1st Provisional Battalion

Formed at Aldershot on 7/8/18 for duty at the Senior Officers School, it was disbanded after the war.

Badges: only regulation cloth and metal were worn.

Officers wore a gold wire cap badge on cloth backing on the service cap.

Warrant Officers, Orderly Room Sergeants and the Band Sergeant wore a cap badge with the Royal Monogram on the grenade.

---

16. IWM photograph Q17619 shows transport sign, Divisional sign with IV below grenade badge). The battalion sign is illustrated in the Haswell-Millar drawing – ART 4116.

An early war officer's cap showing the badge and gold on the visor.

Each battalion adopted an extra badge that showed its seniority. The 1st Battalion wore a red vertical bar.

Cloth shoulder titles were adopted in 1916 to economise on metal. Line infantry wore khaki Melton, the Guards wore coloured embroidered arcs.

The 2nd Battalion wore a white 2 on a red square just below the title.

Guards' officers wore rank on their shoulder straps. This lieutenant clearly shows how an officer dressed in the early part of the war.

This transport guardsman – note the reinforced trousers and stirrups – has the cap badge on the front of his cap and the cloth arc at the top of his shoulder.

The Grenadier Guards 5

With mounting officer casualties many officers wore an enlisted man's jacket in action with the same tunic badges but with rank on the straps.

In this photo taken near the front a guardsman of the 2nd Battalion is wearing the title and 2 on his right shoulder.

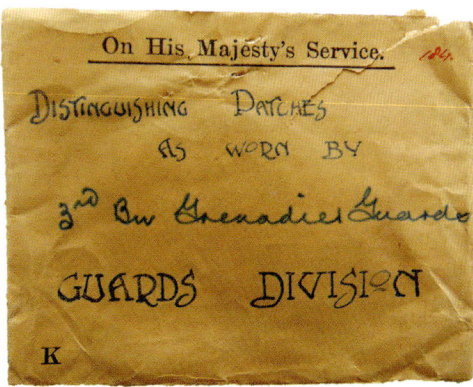

The envelope used by the 3rd Battalion to send examples of its badges to the NWM.

A guardsman with two years' service at the front – two inverted chevrons on the lower right arm – and the badges for the 3rd Battalion.

The envelope contained a piece of tunic with the battalion badges stitched to it: three vertical bars under the title.

This photograph was sent in May 1914 and shows regulars stationed in London. They are at the Soldiers' Christian Association room in Olympia. The corporal on the left side of the left table – no hat – is wearing a curved Grenadier Guards title with 3 underneath proving that cloth titles were in use before the war.

Formed in July 1915, it went to the front wearing metal titles. Along with the other battalions it adopted a cloth title but with a roman IV underneath.

In mid-1916 a Melton shoulder title was authorised but does not seem to have been worn at the front.

A close-up of a guardsman clearly showing the cap badge and shoulder title. He is also wearing regimental buttons.

The Grenadier Guards 7

Like other regiments at the beginning of the war there was not always enough to go around for the new recruits. Here, at the Guards Depot in Caterham some of the recruits are in civilian clothes.

This photograph clearly shows that even when cloth titles were available many preferred to continue wearing the metal ones.

Corporal Gilbert's Squad in March 1915. Even though they are posing for their photo at the end of the course not all are wearing shoulder titles.

Two 1st Battalion Guardsmen acting as stretcher bearers. One is wearing metal titles, the other cloth.

The Coldstream Guards

Like the Grenadier Guards, the Coldstreams consisted of six battalions by the end of the war, three of which were in existence in August 1914. Unlike the other Guards Regiments it formed a pioneer battalion. The 5th was a reserve battalion supplying drafts for the front and the sixth was formed for duty at the Senior Officers' School. All wore a standard cap badge in different styles and qualities. Other ranks wore a shoulder numeral in metal, CG below a white metal rose.

All battalions wore embroidered shoulder titles COLDSTREAM GUARDS in white on red – approved for wear on 19/6/16. From late 1917 the red cloth title was changed for a standard khaki shoulder strap title, however both the metal and red cloth title continued to be worn. Metal and cloth titles were not always worn with the numerals. Officers in all the battalions wore the regimental star on the front of the helmet cover.

1st Battalion

Stationed in Aldershot on 4/8/14 as part of the 1st (Guards) Brigade, 1st Division landing at Le Havre on 14/8/14. On 25/8/15 it moved to the newly formed 2nd Guards Brigade, Guards Division.

Badges: red Roman numeral **I** worn below shoulder titles on both sleeves: numerals 1³⁄₁₆″ high, ⁵⁄₁₆″ wide with serifs. Examples also exist in embroidered form, 1½″ high with bar ¼″ wide.[17]

---

17. IWM photograph Q 7056 Noreuil 6/9/18.

2nd Battalion

The battalion was in Windsor on 4/8/14 as part of 4th (Guards) Brigade 2nd Division landing in France on 13/8/14. On 25/8/15 it joined the newly formed 1st Guards Brigade, Guards Division.

Badges: red Roman numeral **II** worn below shoulder titles, bars 1¼″ high, ⅜″ wide.

3rd Battalion

At Chelsea Barracks on 8/14 with the 4th (Guards) Brigade, 2nd Division. It landed at Le Havre on 13/8/14. On 20/8/15 it moved to the 1st Guards Brigade, Guards Division, transferring on 8/2/18 to the 4th Guards Brigade, 31st Division. On 20/5/18 4th Guards Brigade became part of GHQ Reserve.

Badges: red Roman numeral **III** worn below shoulder titles, bars 1¼″ high, ⅜″ wide, with serifs.[18] Officers wore metal titles. Lieutenant Colonel J. Codrington, who served with the battalion from May 1917, informed the writer in June 1989 that he also wore a cap badge on the front of his helmet and his men wore the red and white shoulder title. Guardsman A. Barlow was a Lewis gunner with the battalion. In correspondence with the writer in 1988, he recalled wearing a yellow square on his forearm instead of LG in a wreath.

4th Battalion (Pioneers)

Formed at Windsor on 17/5/15 as the Guards Pioneer Battalion but soon became the 4th Battalion. On landing in France on 15/8/15 it joined the Guards Division and it became Pioneer Battalion, Guards Division. It served with the division for the duration.

Badges: red embroidered Roman numeral **IV** on 2″ square of khaki serge, numerals 1½″ high, serifs ⅜″, bars 3⁄16″ & ⅛″ worn on both sleeves below shoulder titles.[19]

5th (Reserve) Battalion

Formed as the 4th Reserve Battalion in August 1915 at Windsor it became 5th (Reserve) Battalion in July 1915. The battalion was stationed in Windsor for the duration providing 'drafts of 16,860 all ranks'. It was disbanded after the war.

Badges: regulation cloth and metal.

---

18. IWM photograph Q 3011 Langemarck 12/10/17.
19. IWM photograph Q6047 Houlthurst Forest 10/10/117.

1st Provisional Battalion

Formed at Aldershot on 7/8/18 for duty at the Senior Officers' School, it was disbanded after the war.

Badges: regulation cloth and metal.

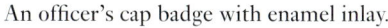

Like the Grenadier Guards, a red and white cloth title was adopted in 1916.

An officer's cap badge with enamel inlay.

The 1st Battalion wore a red Roman I under the red and white shoulder title.

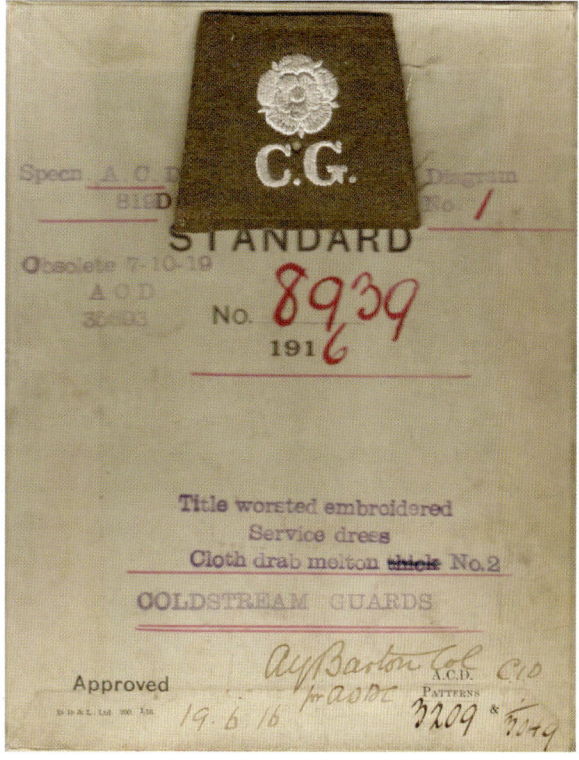

In June 1916 a Melton embroidered title was authorised but does not seem to have been worn by many.

Two vertical red bars under the title indicated the 2nd Battalion.

The 3rd Battalion wore a red Roman III under the title.

A Guardsman of the 2nd Battalion wearing metal titles and red cloth bars.

Taken near the front, a group of Coldstream men pose for the camera. The guardsman on the left is wearing metal titles and three red bars. Those in the centre are wearing cloth titles.

The Coldstream Guards 13

A late-war Coldstream Guard wearing only metal badges.

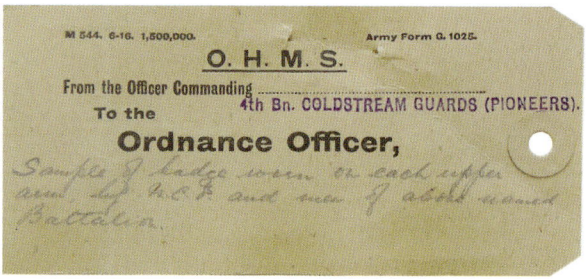

Army Form G. 1025 accompanied the badges sent by the 4th Battalion; they were worn by NCOs and men only.

Under the shoulder title the battalion was indicated by the Roman numerals IV.

The 4th were the only Pioneer Battalion in the Guards Regiments and consequently wore crossed rifles and picks on their collars – clearly shown here along with the metal titles and cloth badge.

The 4th Battalion wore crossed rifle and pick to show they were a pioneer unit.

14   Badges of the Regular Infantry, 1914–1918

Cpl. G. McVITTIE'S Squad, Coldstream Guards. May, 1918.

Corporal McVittie's Squad in May 1918 clearly shows that all regulation badges worn are of metal and that even that late in the war men were being trained with obsolete firearms; in this case the Lee-Metford which went out of production in 1896.

The Scots Guards

The Scots Guards consisted of two active service battalions and a reserve battalion. All wore a standard cap badge in different styles and qualities. Other ranks wore a shoulder numeral in white metal, SG below a white metal thistle.

All battalions wore cloth shoulder titles: **SCOTS GUARDS** embroidered in white on red above a white thistle.

1st Battalion

Stationed in Aldershot on 4/8/14 as part of the 1st (Guards) Brigade, 1st Division it landed at Le Havre on 14/8/14. On 25/8/15 it moved to the 2nd Guards Brigade in the newly formed Guards Division with which it served for the rest of the war.

Badges: dark blue Roman numeral **I** worn both sleeves below shoulder titles. Numerals were 1⅜" high ½" wide, serifs ¾". The numerals were also found without serifs, 1¼" × ⅜" (IWM). A Royal Stewart tartan rectangle of silk ribbon, 1⅛" × 1⅞", was worn on the headband on both sides of forage cap. The ribbon was cut to display single white stripe vertically in centre with single white stripe horizontally across centre. Both examples were provided by the battalion QM on 27/9/17.[20]

---

20. IWM ART 4115.

16 Badges of the Regular Infantry, 1914–1918

2nd Battalion

Serving at the Tower of London on 4/8/14 as part of London District Garrison, in September it joined the 20th Brigade, 7th Division at Lyndhurst, landing at Zeebrugge on 7/10/14. On 9/8/15 it moved to the newly formed 3rd Guards Brigade, Guards Division, with which it served for the duration.

Badges: a dark blue Roman numeral **II** was worn both sleeves below shoulder titles, sizes as 1st Battalion. Rectangle of diced cap band 2½″ × 1½″ worn horizontally on both sides of khaki service dress cap and later painted on the steel helmet; in use in France 12/1917.[21] Officers wore dicing round their cap until 1917 when it was altered to dicing of nine squares. Other ranks' shoulder titles exist with the number 2 instead of the thistle. During the Somme battles a tin square was worn on the helmet cover to aid identification by the RFC. The cap badge was painted on the front of the steel helmet.

3rd (Reserve) Battalion

Formed on 18/8/14 at Chelsea Barracks it moved on 31/8/14 to Esher and on 2/10/14 to Wellington Barracks. By the end of the war it had provided drafts of 11,201 all ranks.

Badges: Private (later Captain) T. Clark trained with the battalion in 1914/15 and recalled the regulation metal badges but late war cloth titles exist with the number 3 in place of the thistle.

An officer's cap badge was essentially the same but better quality and sometimes made in silver.

Cloth shoulder titles were introduced in mid-1916.

---

21. IWM photograph Q17607 Cartigny 12.1917, Q17505 Battalion and Divisional signs on transport, 1916 and ART 4115.

The Scots Guards 17

Around the same time as the red title was introduced a Melton title was introduced.

VC winner Sergeant McAulay DCM served with the 1st Battalion. His shoulder title is above the dark blue vertical bar – just visible – worn by the battalion.

The 1st Battalion sent a title and bar with information as to its position of wear.

An officer's version of the forage cap badge with a silver wire cap badge.

A piece of Royal Stewart tartan was worn on each side of the forage cap.

Dice worn horizontally on each side of the forage cap; the same design was painted on the steel helmet.

Numerals and title worn by 2nd Battalion men.

The Irish Guards

In August 1914 the regiment consisted of a single battalion. During the war it raised a second active service battalion and a reserve battalion. All wore a standard cap badge. Other ranks wore a metal shoulder numeral, **IG** below the star of the Order of St. Patrick.

All Battalions wore embroidered shoulder titles **IRISH GUARDS** white on dark green – approved 19/6/16. On the introduction of pipers, a 4″ square vertical saffron diamond badge was worn behind the piper's large white cap star.

1st Battalion

Stationed at Wellington Barracks at the start of the war in the 4th (Guards) Brigade, 2nd Division, it landed at Le Havre on 13/8/14. On 20/8/15 it joined the newly formed 1st Guards Brigade, Guards Division with which it served for the remainder of the war.

Badges: dark green bar 1½″ × ¼″ was worn vertically below centre of shoulder titles – IWM example has bar sewn touching the bottom edge of the title.[22]

---

22. IWM photograph Q3011 Langemarck 12/10/17, Q3352, Q3364 & Q3365 Maubege 12/11/18; ART 4112.

2nd Battalion

The battalion was formed on 18/7/15 at Warley Barracks. On 17/8/15 after landing at Le Havre it became part of the 2nd Guards Brigade, Guards Division. After the 1918 divisional reorganisation it moved on 8/2/18 as part of 4th Guards Brigade to the 31st Division. On 20/5/18 the 4th Guards Brigade went into GHQ Reserve.

Badges: two dark green bars worn vertically below shoulder titles, sizes as 1st Battalion.[23] Pipers wore a special title: Irish Guards in yellow on green.

3rd (Reserve) Battalion

Formed as the 2nd (Reserve) Battalion in 1914 at Warley it became the 3rd (Reserve) Battalion in July 1915. It was a draft finding unit.

Badges: regulation cloth and metal.

An officer's cap badge was of similar design to that of the men but much more detailed and stylish with central enamel inlays.

An unknown Irish Guardsman wearing the economy uniform, identified only by his cap badge.

---

23. IWM Photograph Q2636 Pilkem 31/7/17.

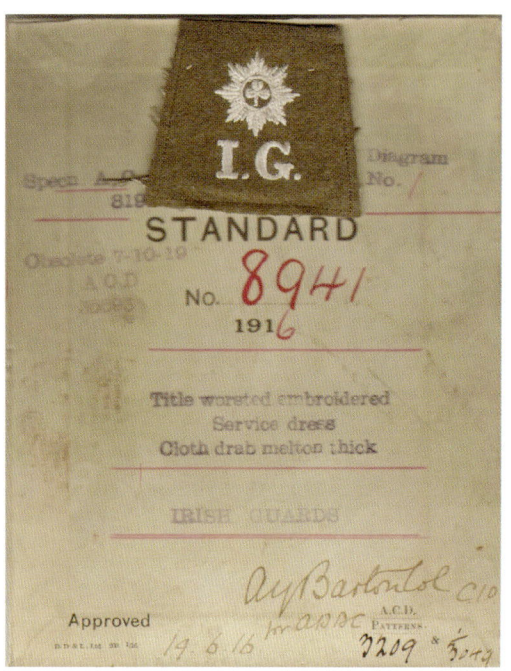

In June 1916 a drab Melton shoulder title was authorised.

More commonly worn was the green and white title with vertical green bar underneath.

The 2nd Battalion wore two vertical green bars under the title.

A miniature version of the cap badge above the letters IG was worn on the shoulder strap of enlisted men.

The Welsh Guards

The newest and smallest of the Guards regiments it consisted of two battalions: one active, the other a draft-finding unit. All wore a standard cap badge. Other ranks wore a metal shoulder numeral, WG below a leek.

Both battalions wore embroidered shoulder titles **WELSH GUARDS** white on black – approved on 22/6/16.

1st Battalion

Raised by Royal Warrant on 26/2/15 and formed at White City. On 28/4/15 it was at Sandown Park and on 4/6/15 Wellington Barracks. After nearly six months training on 18/8/15 it joined the 3rd Guards Brigade, Guards Division on the Western Front.

Badges: black Roman numeral **I** 1½″ high ¼″ wide, serifs ⅝″. According to Lieutenant Colonel Douglas Gordon writing to the NWM on 20/8/17, this was worn ½″ below the centre of the title on both arms by WOs, NCOs and men but only by officers prior to an attack.[24]

---

24. Haswell-Miller drawing ART 4153; Q17618 Divisional sign and Leek.

2nd (Reserve) Battalion

The battalion performed Home Service as a draft-finding unit from its formation in 8/1915 at Wellington Barracks. Moved to Marlow, the Tower of London, Tadworth, Orpington, Tadworth again and finally to the Ranelagh Club, Barnes, until the end of the war.

Badges: regulation cloth and metal.

In 1916 the regiment adopted cloth titles in white on black.

The 1st Battalion wore the title and a black Roman numeral I.

The officers badge was similar but in gold wire on a cloth backing.

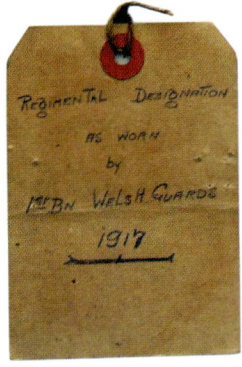

Although the 1st Battalion were wearing the black and white title the battalion sent the NWM a Melton title with this tag.

The Army Clothing Department (ACD) authorised a drab Melton cloth shoulder title at the same time as the curved coloured title was adopted.

The future King Edward, pictured during the war, was the colonel of the regiment.

A member of the 1st Battalion clearly showing the shoulder title and numeral. The bandolier shows he is a member of the transport section: they were only worn by mounted personnel.

A proud son copying his father.

The Royal Scots (Lothian Regiment)

The most senior line infantry regiment consisted of two regular battalions and a reserve battalion based at Glencorse Barracks, Penicuik, to train new recruits and to deal with time-served soldiers recalled for service. Officers wore a different cap badge to other ranks and also wore collar badges; enlisted men wore metal shoulder titles – **ROYAL SCOTS**.

1st Battalion

Stationed in Allahabad at the start of the war it returned to England to form part of the 81st Brigade, 27th Division. It landed in France on 20/12/14 and left for Salonika on 29/11/15. The battalion served in France, Salonika and Bulgaria.

Badges: topee – left side only, Hunting Stewart tartan patch – 2″ square – with red and yellow stripes running diagonally from corners. On right side, ½″ × 2½″ vertical yellow stripe with ends turned in over top and bottom of pagri, indicating seniority of battalion within brigade. The pagri had four turns and consisted of ten folds. Slouch hats were worn until August 1916 with a pagri of four turns and five folds; the regimental cap badge was worn on the turned-up left side. A khaki strip across the base of the shoulder straps indicated the 27th Division.

    Puttees were worn on all occasions with two turns round the ankle and leg and the third and fourth turned over 'V' shaped; the puttees then passed around the leg to just below the knee-cap with the top of the puttee turned over to hide the puttee tapes. Pipers had short puttees with khaki hose-tops and bright red flashes. Pipers wore a 'black glengarry with special silver badge same as the men's, only solid. Leather sporrans white with two black tails (pipe major three black tails). Hose tops Hunting Stewart with green garters to match.'

Steel helmets were adopted in August 1916 and were worn with a drill khaki cover and sun curtain at the back. No badges were worn on the steel helmet, which was covered with drill khaki. The tam-o'-shanter and Balmoral bonnet 'were worn as issued with the cap badge but without any rosette'.

2nd Battalion

In Plymouth on 4/8/14 forming part of the 8th Brigade, 3rd Division, with which it landed on 14/8/14 at Boulogne. It served on the Western Front for the entire war with the 3rd Division.

Badges: in October 1915 the battalion adopted a rosette of Hunting Stewart tartan worn on the left front of the Balmoral bonnet. In March 1917 it was painted on the left side of the steel helmet – Lieutenant Colonel Lumsden, Battalion CO in July 1917.

During the Battle of the Somme in July 1916 and on the Ancre in November 1916 shoulder straps were covered with coloured cloth: A Company – blue; B Company – green; C Company – red; D Company – yellow. The shoulder straps of signallers were blue and red, snipers green and red, Pipes and Drums blue and green, orderlies wore a small yellow patch on the left forearm – 2″ square – with white streamers from the shoulder.

For the Arras offensive in April 1917 the battalion was allotted a distinguishing colour – blue and companies and HQ a specific shape: A Company – 1½″ square; B Company – 1½″ equilateral triangle; C Company 1½″ sided vertical diamond; D Company – 1½″ circle; HQ 1½″ four point star. Orderlies wore a red band on the forearm and signallers a blue band with a 2″ blue band on the shoulder strap.

From October 1915 a rosette of Hunting Stewart was worn on the left of the Balmoral and was painted on the left of the steel helmet from March 1917.

3rd (Reserve) Battalion

Shortly after the start of the war the battalion moved from Glencorse to Weymouth, returning to Edinburgh in May 1915. At the end of 1917 it moved to Ireland being stationed at Mullingar until the cessation of hostilities.

Badges: regulation cloth and metal with a silver thistle on the shoulder straps.

The officer's cap badge was similar in shape and design but different.

A regimental officer in his British Warm coat and glengarry with cap badge on rosette.

Enlisted men's collar badges.

Enlisted men's shoulder title.

Officers' collar badges.

A pre-war postcard for the Lothian Regiment showing badges, headwear and regimental tartan.

The Royal Scots (Lothian Regiment)

Three young soldiers of the 1st Battalion showing their collar badges and pagri patch – a 2″ square of Royal Stewart tartan.

For the Arras offensive in 1917 the 2nd Battalion was allotted the colour blue with companies using different shapes. A square was worn by A Company.

B Company wore a triangle in April 1917.

C Company wore a blue diamond during the 1917 Arras offensive.

During the Battle of Arras, D Company wore a blue circle.

A four-point star was worn by HQ personnel during the Battle of Arras.

28 Badges of the Regular Infantry, 1914–1918

The Royal Stewart tartan patch worn on the left side of the pagri in Salonika.

A helmet worn by the 1st Battalion in Salonika.

During the Somme and Ancre battles, companies and a man's function were identified by coloured shoulder straps: from left to right, signallers, A Company, B Company, C Company, and D Company.

Orderlies were identified during the Somme and Ancre battles by a yellow square on the left forearm.

As well as the yellow square, orderlies wore a white streamer from the shoulder.

The Royal Scots (Lothian Regiment)

All ranks in the 1st Battalion wore a yellow/khaki band on the shoulder straps.

Private Scott Campbell, 2nd Battalion, was killed in action on 2/8/1918 according to his Company Commander, dated as 2/9/18 on his death certificate and 3/9/18 by the CWGC. He is wearing a Glengarry with a rosette backing to his cap badge.

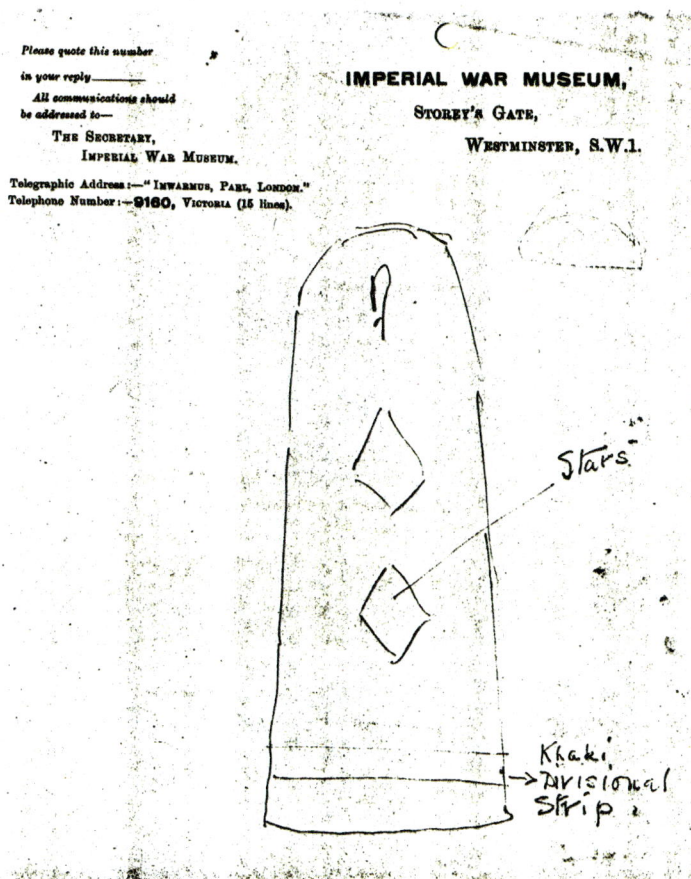

A copy of a sketch describing the badge worn by the 1st Battalion.

The Queen's (Royal West Surrey Regiment)

The regiment consisted, in August 1914, of two regular and a reserve battalion. The regimental headquarters was at Stoughton Barracks, Guildford. All wore a common cap badge, with officers having collar badges and enlisted men wearing metal shoulder titles – **QUEEN'S**.

1st Battalion

On 13/8/14 the battalion left Bordon, as part of the 3rd Brigade, 1st Division, for Le Havre transferring to I Corps troops on 8/11/14. On 21/7/15 it transferred to the 5th Brigade, 2nd Division and on 15/12/15 it moved to the 100th Brigade, 33rd Division. Remaining with the 33rd Division until the end of the war it transferred to the 19th Brigade in the same division.

Badges: throughout the war the battalion only wore regulation badges. This was confirmed in July 1917 by the CO, Lieutenant Colonel Crofts, who told the NWM that the battalion was wearing the same badges they had landed with in August 1914 and that there were 'no fancy badges worn by this battalion'. Signallers wore a blue band on the lower left arm and a blue band under both epaulette titles. Sergeant E. Turner and Private H. Fosdyke, writing in 1987, both noted that they wore no signs on uniform or helmet while serving with the battalion from March 1917 until the end of the war. Serving in the signal section Private Fosdyke confirmed Colonel Crofts' comments adding that he wore brass crossed flags on the armband.

2nd Battalion

Moving from Pretoria to Cape Town it landed at Southampton where it formed part of the 22nd Brigade, 7th Division. It landed at Zeebrugge on 6/10/14. On 20/12/15 it transferred to the 91st Brigade, 7th Division, and fought with the brigade for the duration.

Badges: NWM correspondence records that a pink badge was worn which probably refers to X which signified the senior battalion in the brigade. Responding to the NWM request for information, Captain Driver, responding for the CO on 8/9/17, recorded that the battalion was wearing a horizon blue serge cross with bars ⅝″ wide by 3¼″ long on the right shoulder; it was adopted on 12/8/17 and was only worn by other ranks.

3rd (Reserve) Battalion

The battalion moved to its war station from Guildford to Chattenden as part of the Medway Defences for the war where it remained.

Badges: Sergeant E. Turner who served with the battalion from February 1915 to March 1917 recalled only wearing regulation cloth and metal badges during that time; similarly the other battalions in the Medway Defences only wore regulation badges.

An enlisted man's shoulder title.

The brass badge was replaced by the Melton cloth title from 22/6/16.

32 Badges of the Regular Infantry, 1914–1918

An officer's collar badge.

In August 1917 the 2nd Battalion adopted a blue cross as an identifier but it was only worn by other ranks.

The blue armband worn by signallers like Private Fosdyke in the 1st Battalion.

Taken some time in 1918, George is wearing the 2nd Battalion badge on his shoulder and two years overseas service chevrons on his cuff.

The first badge worn by the 2nd Battalion was a pink cross.

The Buffs (East Kent Regiment)

In line with most infantry regiments the Buffs consisted of two regular battalions with a reserve battalion at Howe Barracks, Canterbury, the home depot. All wore a common cap badge, with officers having collar badges and enlisted men wearing metal shoulder titles – **BUFFS**.

1st Battalion

Based in Fermoy, it formed part of the 16th Brigade, 6th Division, landing in France on 10/9/14. It spent the entire war on the Western Front with the division.

Badges: on 25/7/17 the Battalion CO told the NWM 'that the Battalion has not at any time during the Campaign worn any distinctive Badges other than those authorized by Dress Regulations.' There is no evidence that any were adopted after that date.

2nd Battalion

Left Bombay on 16/11/14 and joined the newly formed 85th Brigade, 28th Division on 23/12/14. It went to France on 23/12/14 and after fighting on the Western Front moved to Salonika in November 1915 for the remainder of the war.

Badges: the only non-regulation badge was the red ½″ strip on the base of the shoulder strap – the 28th Division sign.

3rd (Reserve) Battalion

On 8/8/14 the battalion moved from Canterbury to Dover where it formed part of the Dover Garrison for the duration.

Badges: regulation cloth and metal.

The cap badge faced to the left but officers' collar badges were in facing pairs.

All other ranks wore a metal shoulder title – BUFFS. This was a reference to the buff coats issued to it when it first served abroad in the Low Countries. It was later given buff-coloured uniform facings (collar, lapels and cuffs) and waistcoats to distinguish them from other regiments.

All ranks of the 2nd Battalion wore a red band on their shoulder straps. Other ranks also wore a shoulder title.

The Buffs (East Kent Regiment)

The typical dress and badges of both regular and reserve battalions during the war.

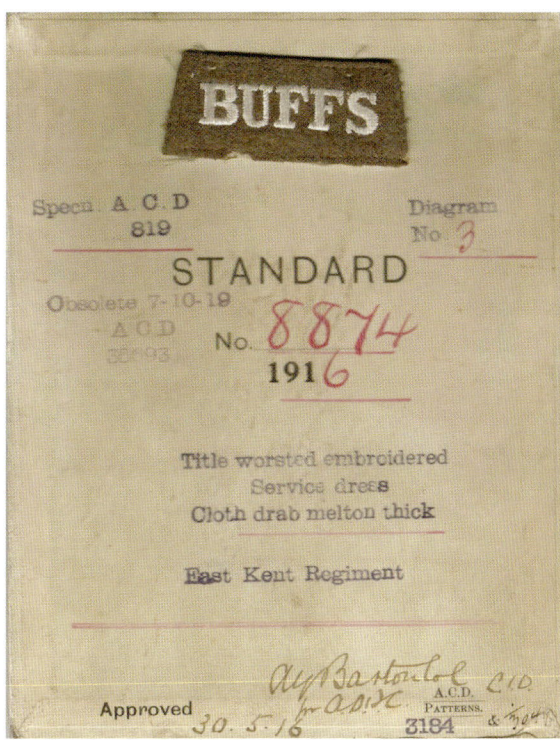

The ACD authorised a Melton title for the regiment on 30/5/16.

The King's Own (Royal Lancaster Regiment)

The King's Own was a standard regiment of two regular and one reserve battalion with the regimental headquarters being at Bowerham Barracks, Lancaster. All wore a common cap badge, with officers having collar badges and enlisted men wearing metal shoulder titles – **KING'S OWN**.

1st Battalion

Based in Dover as part of the 12th Brigade, 4th Division on 4/8/14 moving to France on 23/8/14. From 4/11/15 it served in the 12th Brigade, 36th (Ulster) Division, for three months before returning to the 4th Division.

Badges: the first badge, adopted on 10/3/17 was a red cotton bar worn on the top of both sleeves by all ranks. It was also worn on either side of the green painted helmet. On 25/7/17 the CO wrote that it was 3″ × 1″ but the NWM questionnaire states 2″ × 1″. This is contradictory to a Staff Order from the 31st Division before the Somme offensive that stated the battalion would wear a horizontal red rectangle on the helmet cover.

The red rectangle was discontinued in March 1918 and replaced with a patch of horizontal silk regimental ribbon, 2″ × 1″, split centrally – dark blue left and orange – worn 2″ below the shoulder seams surrounded by a khaki serge edge – ⅛″ wide. Above was the divisional sign, a ram's head, in maroon, indicating the 12th Brigade.

Until December 1917 a red bar, 2″ × ½″, was painted on both sides of the steel helmet. In March 1918 it was replaced by a vertically bisected orange and blue rectangle ½" × 1" painted on both sides. RSM G. Hudson recalled all of these signs in 1988. From December 1917 the regimental lion was stencilled on the front. A white lanyard was worn plaited round the left shoulder and in the left breast pocket. Band members wore the regimental lion on a red cloth patch on the pouch.

2nd Battalion

The battalion sailed from India on 19/11/14 and in England joined the 83rd Brigade, 28th Division. The battalion landed in France on 16/1/15 and after nine months service on the Western Front moved to Egypt in October 1915 and Salonika in the December. It remained in the Balkans until the end of the war.

Badges: on the Western Front from January to May 1915, officers wore a 3" blue square on the back of the tunic under the collar. From October 1915 until the end of the war all ranks wore a ½" red strip across the base of the shoulder straps. In Salonika a royal blue diamond with regimental badge superimposed was worn on the left side of the pagri by all ranks during the summers of 1917 and 1918.

No badges were worn on the steel helmet and covers which were made from sandbags until khaki covers were issued in early 1916. Transport men wore a lanyard which was white and worn plaited round the left shoulder, end in the left breast pocket. Puttees were worn without crossings and finished off on the outside of the leg. No hose tops worn. Salonika pattern shorts worn.

3rd (Reserve) Battalion

Stationed in Lancaster at the start of the war, it also served in Saltash, Sunderland, Plymouth and Harwich. It was a draft finding unit.

Badges: regulation cloth and metal with a lion (colour unknown) stencilled on the front of steel helmets; date of introduction unknown but in use during September 1917.

38 Badges of the Regular Infantry, 1914–1918

Although the Melton title was sanctioned for wear from mid-1916, many preferred to keep their metal titles.

The standard metal title worn by other ranks.

The red ram's head worn by members of the 12th Brigade: the colour the brigade, the shape for the division.

Three staff officers, centre and right, and the CO of the 1st Battalion on the left. He is wearing on his left shoulder the divisional sign above the battalion badge.

From March 1918 until the end of the war all ranks of the 1st Battalion wore a piece of regimental ribbon on a khaki backing on both arms.

The King's Own (Royal Lancaster Regiment)

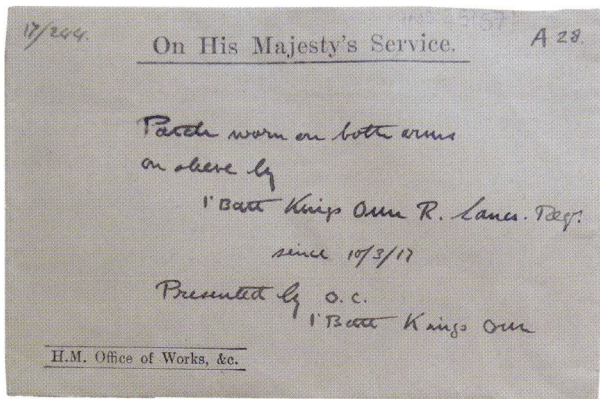

The 1st Battalion identifier was a red cotton bar, adopted 10/3/17. It was worn on both upper sleeves and on the helmet. No further details were provided, but it was probably worn horizontally.

The only non-regulation badge worn by the 2nd Battalion was the red strip on the epaulettes identifying the 28th Division.

Taken just before the war, the pagri badge of a blue diamond with cap badge can be clearly seen.

40 Badges of the Regular Infantry, 1914–1918

A 2nd Battalion private at the end of the war. The divisional band can just be seen on his left shoulder strap.

All ranks wore a blue diamond with cap badge on the pagri in Salonika.

All ranks of the 2nd Battalion wore a red band in Salonika; other ranks wore a shoulder title as well.

The 1916 cloth title did not copy the metal title but instead called the regiment the King's Own Royal Regiment – K.O.R.R.

Other ranks wore a cap badge shoulder title on their shoulder straps in France.

The Northumberland Fusiliers

Considering the size of the recruiting area, and the number of Service Battalions raised during the war, it is surprising that the regiment only consisted of two regular battalions; the 1st at Plymouth, the 2nd at Sabathu, and a reserve. The regimental HQ was at Fenham Barracks in Newcastle. All wore a common cap badge, with officers having collar badges and enlisted men wearing metal shoulder titles – **NgrenadeF**, although the obsolete grenade above NF pattern was seen throughout the war.

1st Battalion

In Portsmouth at the start of the war, as part of the 9th Brigade, 3rd Division, it went to France on 14/8/14. It served on the Western Front throughout the war with the division.

Badges: coloured 1½″ worsted herringbone tape with triple diagonal pattern worn on the right shoulder strap identified a wearer's company: Blue – W Company; green – X Company; red – Y Company; yellow – Z Company; gold – HQ Company. However the IWM index gives the HQ colour as brown braid and the companies as W, X, Y and Z, not the standard A, B, C and D Companies.

2nd Battalion

The battalion sailed from Karachi on 20/11/14. On arrival at Portsmouth it went to Winchester and became part of the 84th Brigade, 28th Division, landing in France on

18/1/15. After nine months on the Western Front it went to Salonika via Egypt. It was transferred back to France in late June 1918 joining the 150th Brigade, 50th Division.

Badges: red ½″ red strip was worn across the base of the shoulder straps – the 28th Division badge. A vertically bisected circle, red left and black right, was worn on the pagri. In France it wore a yellow square on both arms.

3rd (Reserve) Battalion

In Newcastle-on-Tyne at the beginning of the war the battalion moved to East Boldon, near Sunderland, where it remained, forming part of the Tyne Garrison throughout the war.

Badges: regulation cloth and metal.

As a fusilier regiment the shoulder title included the regimental initials and a grenade.

In mid-1916 cloth titles were authorised in Melton but were actually manufactured in a range of materials. This is a woven version.

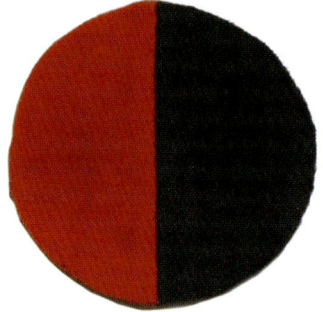

Most of the battalions in the 28th Division only wore the divisional red band on their straps. However, some wore a pagri patch. A vertically divided red and black circle was worn by all ranks of the 2nd Battalion.

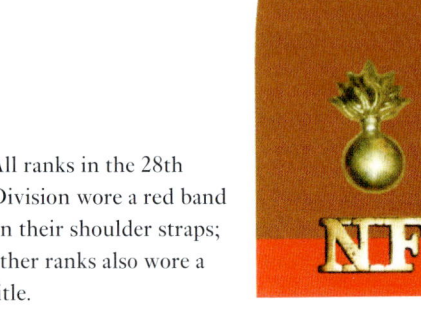

All ranks in the 28th Division wore a red band on their shoulder straps; other ranks also wore a title.

The Northumberland Fusiliers

Although it had been discontinued before the war, some men still wore a two-part shoulder title with a simple grenade above NF.

The 1st Battalion used a woven tape on the right shoulder strap to identify the wearer's company. The shoulder title is worn above the tape.

The only non-regulation badges worn by the battalion were different colour herringbone tapes worn on the right shoulder; gold – HQ Company; blue – W Company; green – X Company; red – Y Company; yellow – Z Company.

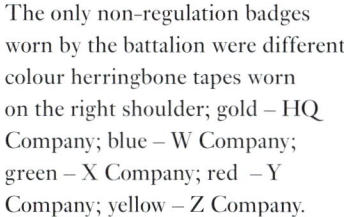

The Royal Warwickshire Regiment

As the recruiting area for the regiment was Birmingham, the regiment had two regular battalions, a reserve battalion and an extra reserve battalion which could be used as an active service battalion, to garrison alongside the reserve battalion or act as an independent garrison battalion. Most extra reserve battalions stayed in the country and were used as draft finding units. The regimental headquarters were at Budbrooke Barracks, Budbrooke. All wore a common cap badge, with officers having collar badges and enlisted men wearing curved metal shoulder titles – **RWARWICKSHIRE**.

1st Battalion

The battalion left Shorncliffe as part of the 10th Brigade, 4th Division, and landed in France on 22/8/14. It remained with the division on the Western Front for the duration.

Badges: a green horizontal $3'' \times 1''$ cotton rectangle was worn on the helmet for the Somme offensive and issued in December 1916 for wear on both sleeves; it continued to be worn on the steel helmet cover parallel to the brim. The badges were worn by all ranks. In June 1917 the rectangle was replaced by the regimental colours worn in two styles: officers wore a $1'' \times 1\frac{1}{4}''$ rectangle of silk regimental ribbon, dark blue with central $\frac{3}{16}''$ orange stripe; other ranks had the same badge painted between the lettering on the cloth shoulder title worn on the top of the sleeves or a painted version of the officer's badge when a metal title was worn. The 10th Brigade green ram's head was worn above or below the battalion badge but not always worn.

2nd Battalion

On arrival from Malta the battalion joined the 22nd Brigade, 7th Division. It landed at Zeebrugge on 6/10/14. After three years in France and Belgium it moved to Italy in November 1917 where it remained.

Badges: during the Somme battles most of the infantry battalions of the division wore some form of recognition mark; in the case of the Warwicks it was almost certainly a purple cross, 1" wide, 4" high, worn on both arms.

3rd (Reserve) Battalion

A home service battalion; it served in Warwick, Portsmouth, Isle of Wight and finally Dover as part of the Dover Garrison.

Badges: regulation cloth and metal.

4th (Extra Reserve) Battalion

The 4th served with the 3rd Battalion throughout the war.

Badges: regulation cloth and metal.

The first badge worn by the 1st Battalion was a horizontal green bar on the tunic and helmet.

1918 soldiers wearing only metal titles and a cap badge.

46   Badges of the Regular Infantry, 1914–1918

The 10th brigade sign that was worn by the 1st Battalion above the regimental colours.

From June 1917 three variations of the same badge were worn. The first was a painted blue/orange/blue painted rectangle on the shoulder title.

When metal shoulder titles were worn a painted version was worn on the sleeve.

The third type was worn by officers on both upper sleeves: the regimental colours in silk.

The Royal Fusiliers (City of London Regiment)

As the biggest city in the Empire, it also had the biggest regiment in the British army, fielding four regular battalions, two reserve and an extra reserve battalion. The latter became an active service battalion in 1916. Hounslow Barracks was the regimental HQ. All wore a common cap badge, with officers having collar badges and enlisted men wearing metal shoulder titles – **RF** worn with a separate grenade above, a plain **RF** or towards the end of the war a one-piece title **RgrenadeF**.

1st Battalion

In Kinsale at the beginning of the war, the battalion landed in St. Nazaire in September 1914 as part of the 17th Brigade, 6th Division. In October 1915 the 17th Brigade transferred to the 24th Division where it remained for the rest of the war.

Badges: red cloth cross, 3¾" square, bars ⅝", worn diagonally on both upper sleeves. This indicated that it was the second senior battalion in the brigade. This was worn below four-pointed stars/diamond – to show the wearer's company: blue – A Company; green – B Company; red – C Company; yellow – D Company. The lack of a star indicated HQ Company. These were adopted at the end of July 1916.

2nd Battalion

The battalion, stationed in Calcutta, landed in England in January 1915 and joined the 86th Brigade, 29th Division. It served continuously with the brigade in Gallipoli, Egypt and on the Western Front.

Badges: on landing in Gallipoli a blue and red/maroon diagonally-bisected 3″ cloth square was worn on the back of the right shoulder seam with the top right corner at the junction of the shoulder strap. In March 1916 it was moved to the centre of the back directly below the collar. The 29th Division red triangle was also worn on both sleeves after landing in France.

3rd Battalion

Stationed at Lucknow, India, it arrived in England in December 1914 and formed part of the 85th Brigade, 28th Division. The battalion landed in France in January 1915 and fought on the Western Front until October 1915 when it moved to Egypt. It fought at Salonika between December 1915 and July 1918 when it joined the 149th Brigade, 50th Division, in France.

Badges: the divisional sign, a red strip on the shoulder straps, was worn by everyone in the battalion with a horizontal yellow rectangle on the left side of the pagri. In the 50th Division the yellow rectangle was worn horizontally on both shoulders.

4th Battalion

After leaving Parkhurst as part of the 9th Brigade, 3rd Division, it landed in France on 13/8/14. It served with the division on the Western Front for the entirety of the war.

Badges: apart from regulation badges there were no badges to identify the battalion from others in the division. However, company identification marks in woven tape were worn on the right shoulder strap under the brass shoulder title: HQ – red over blue (4″ wide); W Company – mid blue; X Company – mid-green; Y Company – red; Z Company – yellow cotton folded 1½″ strips. They were introduced around 22/2/16.

5th (Reserve) Battalion

The battalion moved to its war station days after the start of the war and remained there as part of the Dover Garrison.

Badges: regulation cloth and metal.

6th (Reserve) Battalion

At the end of 1917 the battalion parted ways with the 5th and moved to Carrickfergus.

Badges: regulation cloth and metal. In his reply to the NWM Major Westwood-Henderson, the Battalion CO, did not mention his battalion wearing any special badges (suggesting regulation badges only) but indicated the function of his battalion by August 1917 – a recuperation unit. 'Many returned Expeditionary Force men come here, wearing different badges, but, as I do not know if these are authentic, I think it would be better if you were to obtain badges direct from the Battalions abroad.'

7th (Extra Reserve) Battalion

One of the few extra reserve battalions to serve overseas, it spent nearly two years in Falmouth before leaving for France on 24/7/16. It joined the 190th Brigade, 63rd Division, in July 1916 and served with the division until the armistice.

Badges: regulation cloth and metal until it arrived in France. On joining the 63rd Division, in July 1916, 2″ squares of cotton cloth were adopted. Initially red over blue with a central horizontal ⅛″ yellow line, replaced with a 2″ square of regimental ribbon: red over blue with three central horizontal lines, blue (1/16″), yellow (⅛″), and red (1/16″). The badges were worn on both sleeves just below the shoulder. Under the battalion sign was a square company colour: red – A Company; blue – B Company; yellow – C Company; green – D Company; no badge – HQ Company. Private A. Chatfield who joined the battalion in May 1918 had clear memories of these badges when corresponding with the writer; he was in A Company. There is also evidence that only the company colours were worn in action and by 1918 they were only being worn on the left arm, and that many also wore the divisional sign with the company colour.

50 Badges of the Regular Infantry, 1914–1918

A group of 1st Battalion officers sometime in summer 1918. The battalion X can be seen on both arms below a coloured diamond denoting the company.

The 1st Battalion badge was one-piece red cloth saltire.

The badge of the 2nd Battalion was a simple geometric shape in the regimental colours.

The 4th Battalion HQ wore a large two-coloured badge on their right strap.

The Royal Fusiliers (City of London Regiment) 51

On landing on Gallipoli, all ranks wore a blue/red diagonally bisected cloth square on the back of the right shoulder. This is a contemporary piece of artwork sent to the NWM during the war.

On arrival in France the badge was transferred to the centre of the back; again illustrated by an original piece of artwork.

A private in the 4th Battalion clearly displaying his company indicator – worn only on the right shoulder strap.

A corporal in the 7th Battalion showing his battalion badge. He is wearing regimental buttons and a brass Lewis gunner's badge in his chevrons rather on the lower left sleeve.

52 Badges of the Regular Infantry, 1914–1918

Woven tape in different colours was used to identify wearer's company: mid-blue – W Company; green – X Company; red – Y Company and yellow – Z Company.

The first badge used by the 7th Battalion was adopted on joining the 63rd Division in July 1916.

There is no known reason why the 7th Battalion changed its badge to a piece of regimental ribbon other than it was readily available and cheap to purchase.

In mid-1916 the metal title was replaced by one in Melton cloth.

In the 29th Division all ranks wore the divisional sign on both arms.

The Royal Fusiliers (City of London Regiment)

A second lieutenant somewhere in France. Rank is worn on the shoulders and he is wearing cap and collar badges and no battalion badges.

A head-and-shoulders studio portrait of a private in the 4th Battalion. His company identifier is under the shoulder title; they were only worn on the right shoulder.

A rather portly 3rd Battalion policeman somewhere in Salonika. He is wearing a hackle in his pagri and police armband with the regimental designation.

The badges worn by an anonymous 2nd Battalion veteran who after being wounded was sent to the King's Regiment, serving in the 18th and 20th Battalions.

54 Badges of the Regular Infantry, 1914–1918

Shoulder title worn by all other ranks in the regiment.

A post-1916 tunic showing the position of the badge worn by the 2nd Battalion in the 29th Division.

In the 1st Battalion, companies were identified by stars or diamonds above the battalion badge: A Company – blue; B Company – green; C Company – red; D Company – yellow.

All ranks of the 3rd Battalion wore a red band on the shoulder strap; other ranks also had a shoulder title.

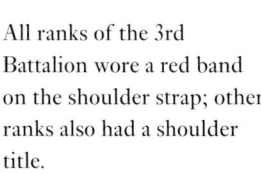

In Egypt and Salonika the 3rd Battalion wore a horizontal yellow rectangle on the left side of the pagri.

The King's (Liverpool) Regiment

As a regiment recruited in a large city, it had two regular, a reserve battalion and an extra reserve battalion which, unusually, served on the Western Front: both reserve battalions were at Seaforth. Although the Liverpool Regiment, their barracks were in Warrington. All wore a common cap badge, with officers having collar badges and enlisted men wearing metal shoulder titles – **KING'S**.

1st Battalion

As part of the 6th Brigade, 2nd Division, the battalion left Aldershot and landed in France on 13/8/14. They spent the entire war on the Western Front as part of the 2nd Division.

Badges: apart from regulation cloth and metal badges no other distinguishing marks were worn.

2nd Battalion

The battalion remained in Peshawar, India, throughout the war.

Badges: the battalion wore the pre-war pagri flash: a red rectangle 2⅝″ × 2″ embroidered **KINGS** in white cotton on the left side by all ranks. This was worn in action and on field service on the north-west frontier in 1915–16 according to correspondence from Lieutenant Colonel Hislop dated 29/8/17. Officers attached to the battalion wore the red flash with a horizontal white tape bar in the centre 1¾″ × ¼″. He also reported the use of an unusual cap badge which differed from the regulation cap badge and was similar to an obsolete badge worn many years before; it was worn in the blue 'Austrian pattern' field service cap and was used in action during 1915–16.

3rd (Reserve) Battalion

Stationed at Seaforth, Liverpool, the battalion left for Hightown, moving in July 1915 to Pembroke Dock and in late 1917 to Cork.

Badges: regulation cloth and metal.

4th (Extra Reserve) Battalion

Also stationed at Seaforth, it was one of the few extra reserves to go abroad; the battalion landed in France in March 1915 and joined the Sirhind Brigade, Lahore Division, and in November it moved to the 137th Brigade, 46th Division. During December 1915 it was attached to the 56th and 57th Brigades before moving permanently, in February 1916, to the 98th Brigade, 33rd Division.

Badges: regulation cloth and metal. Serving in divisions before such signs became normal and then in units that did not use them, they only wore regulation badges. The wearing of only regulation badges was confirmed in July 1987 by Sergeant E. Turner who was certain that such things were only worn by brigade and divisional staff.

The official shoulder title from mid-1916 was made from cloth.

The pagri flash of the 2nd Battalion worn in India throughout the war.

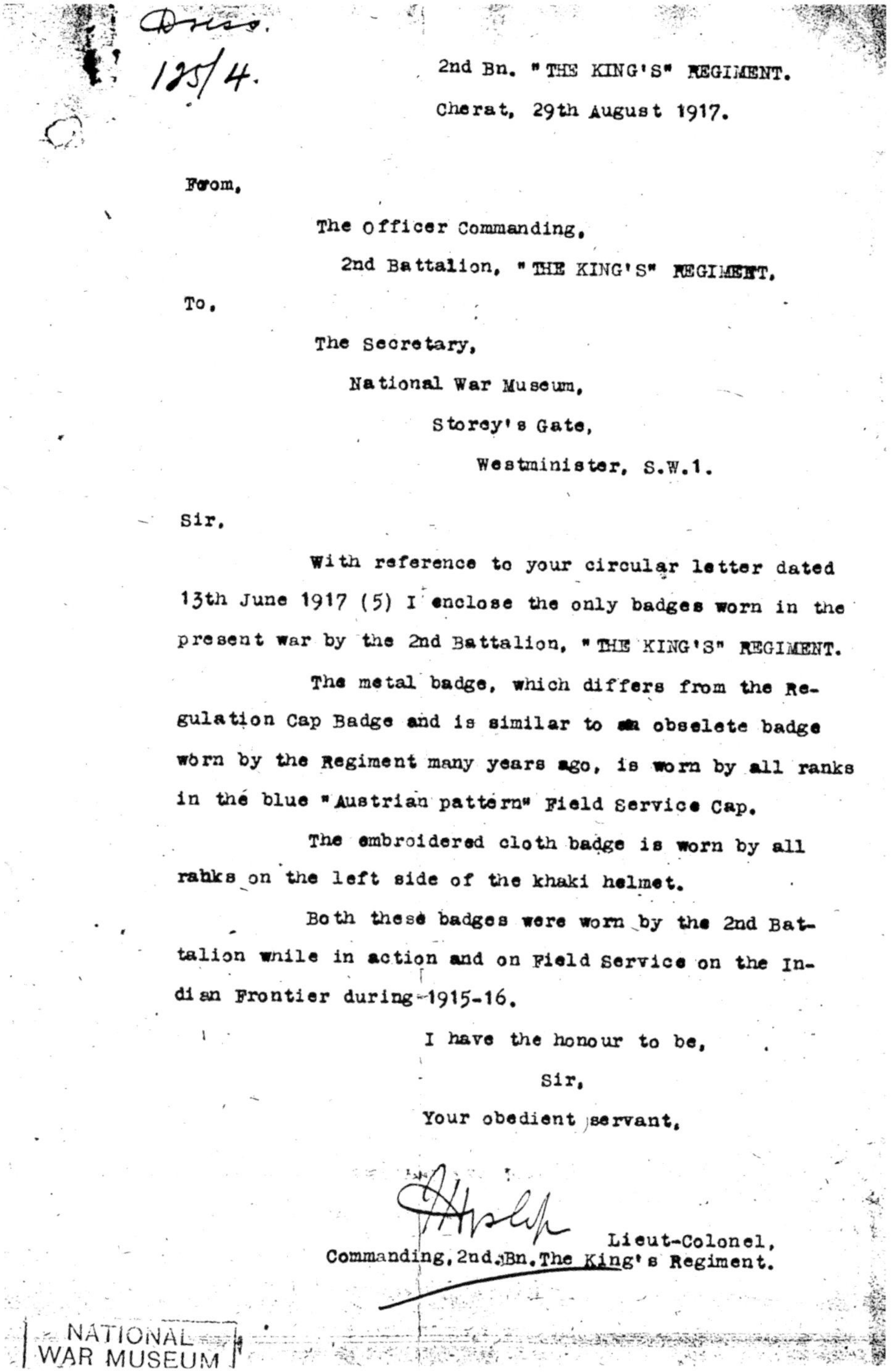

2nd Bn. "THE KING'S" REGIMENT.
Cherat, 29th August 1917.

From,

    The Officer Commanding,
        2nd Battalion, "THE KING'S" REGIMENT.

To,

    The Secretary,
        National War Museum,
            Storey's Gate,
                Westminister, S.W.1.

Sir,

    With reference to your circular letter dated 13th June 1917 (5) I enclose the only badges worn in the present war by the 2nd Battalion, "THE KING'S" REGIMENT.

    The metal badge, which differs from the Regulation Cap Badge and is similar to an obsolete badge worn by the Regiment many years ago, is worn by all ranks in the blue "Austrian pattern" Field Service Cap.

    The embroidered cloth badge is worn by all ranks on the left side of the khaki helmet.

    Both these badges were worn by the 2nd Battalion while in action and on Field Service on the Indian Frontier during 1915-16.

        I have the honour to be,
            Sir,
        Your obedient servant,

                Lieut-Colonel,
    Commanding, 2nd.Bn. The King's Regiment.

In August 1917 the 2nd Battalion CO informed the NWM about the badges worn by his men.

58 Badges of the Regular Infantry, 1914–1918

An unknown officer wearing the standard uniform and badges.

Two 2nd Battalion soldiers pose for a photograph to send home. The pagri flash is clearly visible.

A typical group photo from India before and during the war. These are men from the 2nd Battalion as evidenced by the badge on the tropical helmet.

The Norfolk Regiment

At the beginning of the war the regiment consisted of two regular battalions with a reserve battalion at Britannia Barracks, Norwich. Officers wore a different cap badge to the other ranks and also wore collar badges, and enlisted men wore metal shoulder titles – **NORFOLK**.

1st Battalion

As part of 15th Brigade, 5th Division, stationed in Hollywood, it landed in France during August. In December 1917 it moved to Italy, returning to France in April 1918.

Badges: only pre-war regulation badges were worn on the uniform but by the end of the war a painted sign was applied to the steel helmet: 1¾″ square with black diagonal from top left to bottom right dividing red (top) and yellow.

2nd Battalion

The battalion left India for Mesopotamia in November 1914 as part of the 6th (Poona) Division. It was captured at Kut al Amara and the drafts and recovered wounded of the battalion and 2nd Dorsets joined temporarily to form the Norsets. Reformed in July 1916 it joined 37th Brigade, 14th Indian Division.

Badges: on 29/8/12 a sign was sanctioned for wear on the pagri. It was to be provided at regimental expense and permission for its wear was given by Major General

Birdwood, CO of the 6th (Poona) Division. The sanction was not to be quoted as an authority for wearing the patch outside India. However, it was worn throughout the battalion's campaigns in the Middle East on the left side, maximum size to be 3″ × 2″: a vertical cloth patch of yellow with a narrow black stripe down the centre. In correspondence with the writer in May 1987, Lord Ailwyn recalled wearing the flash on the left hand side of the topee.

3rd (Reserve) Battalion

Moving from Norwich to Felixstowe it formed part of the Harwich Garrison for the war.

Badges: regulation cloth and metal.

The officer's badge only contained the central design of the other men's cap badge.

A group of three 1st Battalion officers, probably company commanders, showing the officer's cap badge and collar badges. The captain on the right has two wound stripes and two years overseas service chevrons visible; he is also wearing his rank on his shoulders. Two have the 1914–15 Star ribbon, suggesting the photo was taken in early 1919.

The Norfolk Regiment 61

The metal shoulder title was replaced in mid-1916 by a Melton title.

The only non-regulation badge worn by the 2nd Battalion was a vertical yellow cloth patch with narrow vertical central black stripe.

In the 5th Division uniform badges were frowned upon but most units wore a marking on their helmet. The 1st Battalion wore a 1¾" square with black diagonal from top left to bottom right dividing red (top) and yellow.

A young recruit training with the 3rd Battalion. He is wearing standard pre-war uniform with a soft cap dating the photograph after late 1916.

The Lincolnshire Regiment

The regiment consisted of the standard two regular and a reserve battalion at Sobraon Barracks, Lincoln. Officers wore a different cap badge to other ranks and also wore collar badges; enlisted men wore metal shoulder titles – **LINCOLN**.

1st Battalion

Stationed in Portsmouth, it formed part of the 9th Brigade, 3rd Division, landing in France on 14/8/14. It was transferred to the 62nd Brigade, 21st Division, and fought with the division until the end of the war. From June 1915 a contingent of the Bermuda Rifle Volunteers Corps served with the battalion.

Badges: according to Captain Neilson, writing on 29/7/17 all ranks wore a red cloth diagonal cross, 2″ × 1½″ worn on the centre of the back of the tunic from June 1916; **X** represented the regiment's seniority. On the steel helmet a blue Lincolnshire Imp, 1½″ × ¾″ with red eyes and red **X**, superimposed, gilt for officers, was painted on the dull-grey steel helmet. The IWM questionnaire indicates a further badge was worn later: a blue imp with red **X** worn 2″ below the shoulder seams on both sleeves. The Bermuda Volunteers Corps wore their own cap badge but Lincolnshire cloth badges.

2nd Battalion

The battalion left Bermuda for England in September 1914, arriving in October after passing through Halifax, Nova Scotia. At Hursley Park it joined the 25th Brigade, 8th Divsion, landing at Le Havre on 6/11/14. In February 1918 it joined the 1st Battalion in the 62nd Brigade.

Badges: writing from Grimsby, the CO of the 3rd Battalion indicated that the battalion wore, on both sides of the helmet, a 1½″ blue square with a red **X** in the centre. The IWM questionnaire also indicates that a red **X** on blue background, 2″ square, in worsted, was worn on both arms 2″ below each shoulder. A red over green horizontal rectangle was worn during offensives.

3rd (Reserve) Battalion

As a home service battalion it left the depot in Lincoln just days after the war began and served in Grimsby and from early 1918, Cork.

Badges: regulation cloth and metal. Although the correspondence from the Battalion CO gives details of a number of badges worn by the Lincolnshire Regiment, no special badges are mentioned for the 3rd Battalion. This was confirmed in 1991 by Private F. Perry who trained with the battalion in the second half of 1915.

The only similarity between the officer's and other rank's cap badge was the central Sphinx over Egypt.

Like other regiments the metal title was replaced in mid-1916 by a cloth title.

A red **X** was worn on backs by all ranks in the 1st Battalion.

Lance-Corporal Stuttard sent this photo to family friends in December 1916 from Woodcote Park Convalescent Hospital in Epsom; he was serving with the 2nd Battalion when he was wounded.

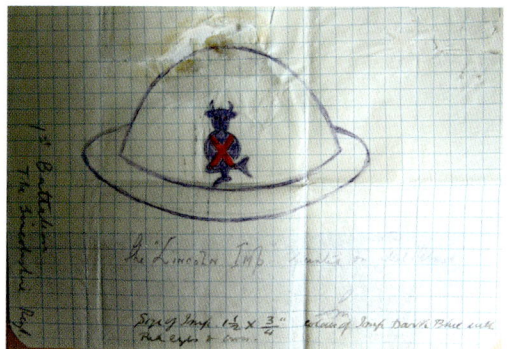

The battalion also sent a drawing of the helmet sign with details of its size.

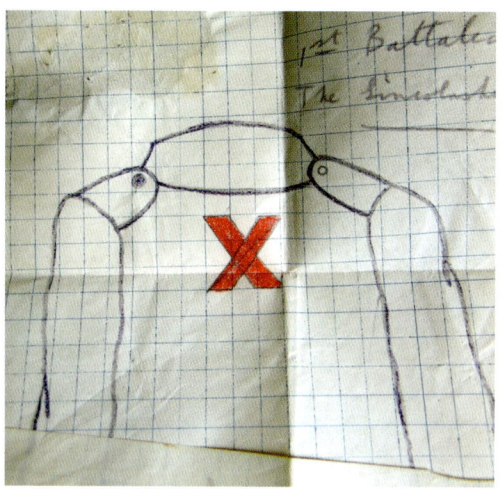

A drawing sent by the battalion to the NWM detailing position of wear.

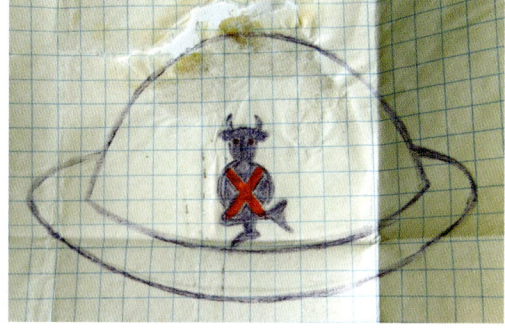

A close-up of the original drawing clearly showing the red eyes of the Lincoln Imp.

This photograph clearly shows that the 2nd Battalion did wear the red X at the end of the war.

The cap badge of the Bermuda Rifle Volunteers who served with the 1st Battalion from June 1915 until the end of the war.

The front and reverse of the 2nd Battalion sign showing how well it was made.

The Devonshire Regiment

The regiment had three regular battalions: two active, the 1st in the Channel Islands, the 2nd in Egypt and a reserve at Topsham Barracks, Exeter. All wore a common cap badge, with officers having collar badges and enlisted men wearing metal shoulder titles – **DEVON**.

1st Battalion

After leaving Jersey it moved to France on 21/8/14, where it initially joined the 8th Brigade, 3rd Division before moving to the 14th Brigade, 5th Division. In January 1916 it joined the 95th Brigade which had transferred from a Kitchener division. From December 1917 to April 1918 it served in Italy returning to France where it ended the war.

Badges: only regulation badges were worn on the uniform in the 5th Division. However, helmet markings were permitted. The battalion wore a horizontal painted rectangle 1¼″ × 1¾″ horizontally divided equally, green over dark red over green, on the steel helmet.

2nd Battalion

In September the battalion left Cairo and in England joined the 23rd Brigade, 8th Division. From landing at Le Havre on 6/11/14 it remained with the division on the Western Front throughout the war.

Badges: when signs were introduced by the 8th Division, the battalion wore a curved bar, split into three equal sections – green/dark red/green. In February 1918 the curved bar, 3″ × 1″, the colours were inverted to red/green/red, Private S. Walker remembered wearing this badge when he was taken PoW at Bois-des-Buttes on 26/5/18. Both signs were worn at the top of both sleeves.

3rd (Reserve) Battalion

A home service battalion that travelled from Exeter to Plymouth and back before becoming part of the Plymouth Garrison, stationed at Devonport.

Badges: Second Lieutenant G. Stone served with the battalion in 1917 and was definite that he and other ranks only wore regulation cloth and metal badges.

The ACD pattern card showing the replacement cloth shoulder title.

The 2nd Battalion wore a curved badge to show the brigade with the colours showing the battalion. In February 1918 the colours were inverted.

This is a platoon of the 3rd Battalion late in the war. Interestingly, only one soldier is wearing the cloth title.

A mounted corporal serving with the 1st Battalion clearly showing the lack of non-regulation badges.

Battalion badges on uniforms were deemed to be unnecessary but helmet markings were allowed: the 1st Battalion wore a green/red/green rectangle.

The Suffolk Regiment

The regiment comprised two regular battalions in Egypt and Ireland, with the reserve battalion at Gibraltar Barracks, Bury St Edmunds. All wore a common cap badge, with officers having collar badges and enlisted men wearing metal shoulder titles – **SUFFOLK**.

1st Battalion

The battalion landed at Liverpool in late October 1914 from Khartoum. At Hursley Park it joined the 84th Brigade, 28th Division. The Battalion landed in France on 18/1/15 and fought on the Western Front until 30/10/15 when the battalion left for Egypt and then to Salonika where it remained.

Badges: only regulation badges were worn in France. In Salonika, following the divisional pattern, all ranks wore a red ½″ tape across the base of both shoulder straps. Due to a shortage of yellow cloth, the pagri badge adopted in May 1916 was a red castle

The 1st Battalion wore a yellow castle in Egypt before returning to England. It was re-introduced in 1917 when stocks of yellow cloth were available. It was worn on a piece of pagri cloth that was tucked into the pagri.

– part of the regimental cap badge. Before this, before the war, the battalion had worn a yellow castle on the pagri while serving in Egypt. The red castle was short-lived and was worn on the left side of the slouch hat when they were worn. With the availability of the correct coloured material in the summer of 1917, all ranks wore a yellow castle on the right side of the pagri. There were no markings on the steel helmet which was khaki covered and had a neck flap.

2nd Battalion

After leaving The Curragh, the battalion landed in France on 17/8/14 as part of the 14th Brigade, 5th Division. As a result of heavy casualties at Le Cateau the battalion became GHQ troops, joining the 8th Brigade, 3rd Division in October 1914 before transferring in October 1915 to the 76th Brigade, 3rd Division. It fought with the division on the Western Front for the duration.

Badges: a black silk 2½″ square in the centre of a 6½″ yellow square was worn on the centre of the back between the shoulders during the battle of the Bluff; this was the only occasion on which distinguishing patches were worn by the battalion. However, the battalion wore a yellow rectangle on the small pack during the Somme battles and according to Lieutenant Colonel Peebles the Battalion CO in November 1919, a three turret castle was painted on the front of the steel helmet in yellow. Coloured shoulder straps were worn to denote the different companies: blue – W Company; green – X Company; red – Y Company; yellow – Z Company; on the Somme on both straps but afterwards only on the right strap. Specialists were identified by bands on the right forearm: orderlies – red; snipers/scouts – green; signallers – blue. All battalion vehicles were painted with a yellow three turret castle.

3rd (Reserve) Battalion

As part of the Harwich Garrison it remained in Felixstowe for the war.

Badges: regulation cloth and metal.

The Suffolk Regiment 71

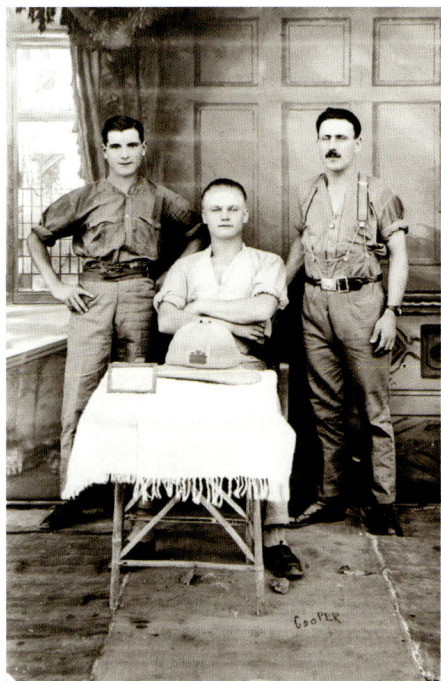

At the Battle of the Bluff all ranks wore a black square on a yellow rectangle on their backs.

Three 1st Battalion soldiers; the one on the right is wearing a German belt buckle. On the table is a sun helmet showing the red castle worn from May 1916 for a year when yellow was unavailable.

During the Somme battles a yellow rectangle was worn on the small pack.

Companies were identified by coloured bands on the shoulder straps: from left – W, X, Y and Z Companies.

72 Badges of the Regular Infantry, 1914–1918

The replacement shoulder title issued from late 1916 onwards.

A tropical issue version of the standard cloth title.

All ranks in the 1st Battalion wore a red band on their shoulder straps; other ranks also wore a shoulder title.

The 2nd Battalion near the end of the war with only titles and cap badges visible.

The Prince Albert's (Somerset Light Infantry)

All three battalions – two active and one reserve – wore a common cap badge, with officers having collar badges and enlisted men wearing metal shoulder titles – **SOMERSET** – below a separate bugle; by the end of the war it was a one-piece title. The regimental headquarters was at Jellalabad Barracks, Taunton.

1st Battalion

Moving from Colchester to Harrow as part of the 11th Brigade, 4th Division, it landed in France on 22/8/14 and spent the war on the Western Front with the division.

Badges: information from the CO states that signs were adopted on 23/2/17; all ranks wore a yellow horizontal cotton bar, 3¼" × 1", at the top of both sleeves. In correspondence with the writer in 1988, Privates Lowman and Luxton, who served with the battalion between mid-1916 until the end of the war, clearly recalled wearing the yellow bar. It was also worn on both sides of the steel helmet; yellow being the brigade colour. However, a staff order issued by the 31st Division on 20/6/16 informed its attacking troops that the 1st Battalion Somerset Light Infantry would be wearing the sign on the helmet cover during the forthcoming offensive.

74   Badges of the Regular Infantry, 1914–1918

2nd Battalion

The battalion remained at Quetta in India throughout the war.

Badges: NWM correspondence states that no badges were worn, ignoring the pre-war pagri flash that was still in use.[25]

3rd (Reserve) Battalion

As a home service battalion, after moving from Taunton to Devonport it went to Ireland; first to Londonderry, then Belfast.

Badges: regulation cloth and metal.

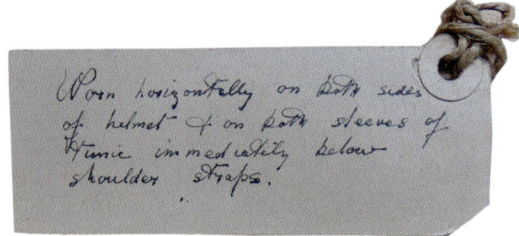

The yellow bar worn by the 1st Battalion and accompanying tag with details of wear.

A less faded 1st Battalion badge.

A private in the 2nd Battalion in India just before the war.

---

25. IWM photo 56281 shows a square badge – green – on the right side with the regimental badge – yellow – superimposed.

The Prince Albert's (Somerset Light Infantry) 75

The 2nd Battalion served in India throughout the war and wore a pagri patch on the right side.

Soldiers of the 2nd Battalion behind a barricade in India.

The 2nd Battalion in the field during the war. The pagri patch is clearly visible in the original photograph.

As a light infantry regiment the cloth shoulder titles were produced in pairs like the metal titles.

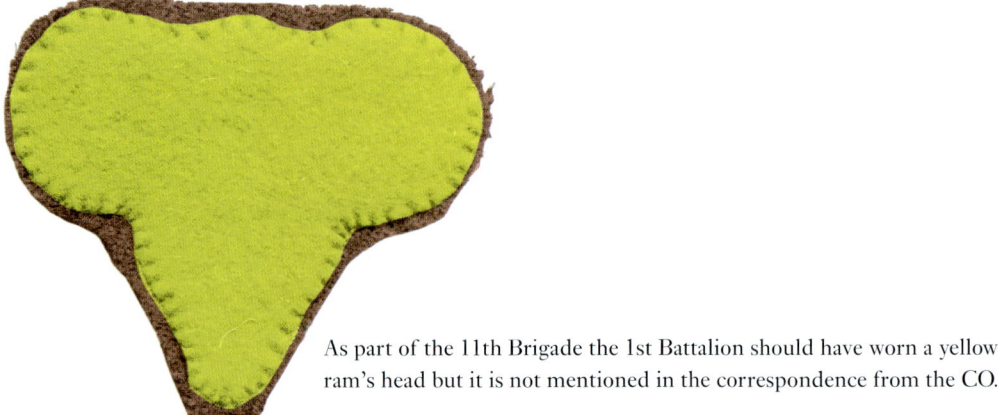

As part of the 11th Brigade the 1st Battalion should have worn a yellow ram's head but it is not mentioned in the correspondence from the CO.

The Prince of Wales's Own (West Yorkshire Regiment)

The Regimental Depot, Imphal Barracks in York, was the base for the reserve and extra reserve battalion when the war broke out; both regular battalions where on different garrisons in England and Malta. All ranks wore a common cap badge, officers wore collar badges and other ranks wore a curved shoulder title – **W.YORK**.

1st Battalion

The battalion moved from Lichfield to Dunfermline and Cambridge within ten days of the start of the war. It landed in France on 10/9/14 as part of the 18th Brigade, 6th Division, and stayed on the Western Front with the division until the armistice.

Badges: conforming to the divisional system, the battalion only wore helmet markings. From October 1916 a patch of regimental colours, maroon/old gold/maroon, was worn on the right side. In July 1917 a white horse was painted on the front; it was replaced by a maroon shield with old gold saltire worn between June 1918 and May 1919 – position, size and style unknown. The helmet badges were worn by all ranks.

2nd Battalion

Stationed in Malta, the battalion joined the 23rd Brigade, 8th Division, in England and landed in France on 5/11/14. It served throughout the war with the division on the Western Front.

Badges: a maroon curved cloth bar, 3″ × 1″, with 1″ central buff section, was worn on both sleeves ½″ below the shoulder seams; it was adopted in March 1917. At the same time a white horse on a maroon oval was worn on the steel helmet by all ranks. This replaced the original helmet sign: a horizontal rectangle painted on the left side in maroon/old gold/maroon and worn by all ranks; stopped in autumn 1916. Bandsmen and drummers wore the 'bandsmen's badge on the sleeve above the right elbow and for parades, playing out, etc. square white pouches' were worn, 'slung over left shoulders – brass fittings, the "White Horse of Hanover" in brass on the pouch flap'. Bandsmen and drummers wore the Prince of Wales's plume with motto 'Ich Dien' on their collar points in service dress. Drummers also wore a green plaited cord fastened to the top jacket button, passing under the right arm; the cords separated over the head with the tassels hooking on the left shoulder. Officers did not wear the regimental collar badge on service dress and their horses had buff head bands and rosettes with buff head ropes.

3rd (Reserve) Battalion

As a home service battalion it formed part of the Tyne Garrison throughout the war.

Badges: regulation cloth and metal.

4th (Extra Reserve) Battalion

Moving From York to Falmouth, in December 1915 it moved to Redcar. In April 1916 it formed part of the Tees Garrison, based in West Hartlepool.

Badges: regulation cloth and metal

The maroon/old gold/maroon badge of the 1st battalion was only worn on the right side of the helmet.

In the 8th Division, infantry badges showed the brigade by shape and the battalion by colour. This badge was worn by the 2nd Battalion on both arms.

The Prince of Wales's Own (West Yorkshire Regiment)

The officer on the right is wearing the 2nd Battalion badge but no collar badges.

A cloth title was authorised in mid-1916 to replace the metal titles.

In June 1918 a maroon shield with gold saltire was adopted for wear on the front of the helmet.

A soldier of a reserve battalion showing his cap badge and shoulder titles.

The East Yorkshire Regiment

The Reserve Battalion was at the Beverley Depot when the war started; one regular battalion was close by, the other abroad. All ranks wore a common cap badge with officers wearing collar badges and other ranks a curved shoulder title – **E.YORK**.

1st Battalion

In York at the start of the war the battalion was part of the 18th Brigade, 6th Division. It landed in France on 10/9/14 and on 26/11/15 transferred to the 64th Brigade, 21st Division, with which it served for the duration.

Badges: writing on 4/8/17, Captain Green recorded that all ranks wore 1″ dark green squares on both sleeves 1″ below the shoulder strap and on the back of the tunic, 1″ below the collar; they were adopted on 15/6/16. On 19/4/17 a brigade order specified that all NCO rank badges were to be worn on the back with the rank touching the collar with the battalion badge in the V; CQMS crown was worn on the angle of the chevrons; it was not successful and the badges returned to their normal position.

Helmets were covered using sandbags for the men and a finer material – similar to horse rubber fabric – was used for officers. When covers were discontinued in early 1918 the helmets were painted service colour and sanded and a ½″ green line painted round the helmet crown. Officers wore a standard lanyard 'over the right shoulder and under the right arm, with clasp knife in right top pocket of tunic'. Puttees were worn 'without any twist in the garment'.

2nd Battalion

On arrival in England from India, the battalion joined the 83rd Brigade, 28th Division. After fighting in France from January 1915 it moved to Egypt in November and Salonika in December 1915 were it stayed for the duration.

Badges: officers and warrant officers wore, 2″ below the collar, a 1½″ red cloth circle with a small regimental button in the centre. This was confirmed by Lieutenant Colonel Hopkins, the Battalion CO, on 3/9/17. In common with other units in the 28th Division, a ½″ red tape strip was worn across the base of both shoulder straps.

3rd (Reserve) Battalion

The battalion moved from Beverley to Hedon immediately after the declaration of hostilities. In April 1916 it became part of the Humber Garrison based in Withernsea for the duration.

Badges: regulation cloth and metal.

The commanding officer of the 1st Battalion pictured just before the war showing the cap and collar badges worn by officers.

A green square was worn on the shoulders and back from 15/6/16.

82 Badges of the Regular Infantry, 1914–1918

Other ranks wore a metal shoulder title at the beginning of the war.

In mid-1916 the metal title was replaced by a cloth title.

All ranks of the 2nd Battalion wore the red divisional sign on their shoulder straps but officers and warrant officers were further identified; on their back, 2" down from the collar, they wore a small regimental button in a red cloth circle.

All ranks of the battalion wore a red band on their shoulder straps; other ranks also wore a shoulder title.

A soldier of the reserve battalion showing his cap badge and shoulder titles.

The Bedfordshire Regiment

When the war began the regular battalions were serving in Ireland and South Africa. The reserve and extra reserve battalions were both based in Kempston Barracks, Bedford. All ranks wore a common cap badge, officers wore collar badges, and other ranks wore a curved shoulder title – **BEDFORD**.

1st Battalion

After leaving Mullingar, Ireland, the battalion joined the 15th Brigade, 5th Division, landing in France on 16/8/14. In December 1917 it moved with the division to Italy, returning to France in April 1918.

Badges: writing on 13/9/18, Major General Ponsonby, CO of the 5th Division, indicated that, conforming to the divisional system the battalion wore no markings on the tunic. However, a painted vertical rectangle 1½″ × 1¼″ divided horizontally into three equal ½″ sections of amber/black/amber, was painted on the helmet, although this was sometimes replaced by a bar in yellow and black. Major Skates in 1988 recalled wearing the vertical sign on his helmet. An official chart of the badges used by the 5th Division, dated 2/8/18, is slightly different: horizontal rectangle black over yellow over black, 1¼″ long with each strip ½″ wide. On 5/11/16 the CO wrote that 'it is considered rather a distinction not to wear them'.

2nd Battalion

The battalion sailed from South Africa, arriving in England on 19/9/14. As part of the 21st Brigade, 7th Division, it landed at Zeebrugge on 7/10/14. On 19/12/15 the 21st Brigade was transferred to the 30th Division and the battalion joined the 89th Brigade; on 11/2/18 it moved to the 90th Brigade. In May 1918 the battalion transferred to the 54th Brigade, 18th Division and absorbed the 7th Battalion.

Badges: the badge worn in the 30th Division is thought to be a green arc which was certainly worn by the battalion in the 18th Division.

3rd (Reserve) Battalion

The battalion moved from Bedford to Felixstowe where for the duration it formed part of the Harwich Garrison.

Badges: as a draft finding unit only regulation cloth and metal badges were worn.

4th (Extra Reserve) Battalion

After serving with the 3rd Battalion it joined the 190th Brigade, 63rd Division, in France on 25/7/16, serving there until the end of the war.

Badges: regulation cloth and metal until the battalion moved abroad. In France the battalion adopted a cloth bar, $3⅝'' \times 1''$, worn horizontally on the upper sleeves, divided vertically into three equal sections – black/yellow/black. Company squares were worn on both arms below the battalion sign: red – A Company; dark blue – B Company; yellow – C Company; green – D Company: they were not always worn. Private Wells, writing in April 1987, clearly remembered wearing the black/yellow/black bar on his tunic and recalled a black and yellow sign on the side of his helmet, which was also recalled by Major Skates. Neither recalled wearing a company square.

The Bedfordshire Regiment 85

In the 18th Division the 2nd Battalion adopted the badge worn by the 7th Battalion.

Company signs in red, dark blue, yellow or green were worn under what is recorded as a horizontal bar in three equal sections, but the example sent to the NWM has a smaller central section.

In the 30th Division the divisional sign was worn on both shoulders.

During mid-1916 cloth titles were adopted to economise on metal.

A member of the 3rd Battalion clearly showing regulation badges.

Two members of the 1st Battalion, one is wearing the cloth title, the other has no title.

The Leicestershire Regiment

At the beginning of the war, the reserve battalion was based in the depot at Glen Parva Barracks near Leicester. The two regular battalions were in India and Ireland. All ranks wore a common cap badge, officers wore collar badges and other ranks wore a curved shoulder title – **LEICESTER**.

1st Battalion

Leaving Fermoy for Cambridge it formed part of the 16th Brigade, 6th Division, landing in France on 10/9/14. On 17/11/15 it became part of the 71st Brigade – a Kitchener Brigade transferred in to the division. It fought with the division for the duration.

Badges: in September 1917 the CO confirmed that no special badges were worn but one was worn on the steel helmet; no details were provided. Private F. Dixon, a pre-war regular who served with the battalion for most of the war, was adamant they did not wear any coloured badges: 'we had no time for any special cloth signs'.

2nd Battalion

As part of the Garhwal Brigade, Meerut Division, it landed at Marseilles, moving within days to Egypt where it joined the 28th Indian Brigade, 7th Indian Division. It fought in the Middle East for the remainder of the war.

Badges: one of the first battalions to wear a cloth badge, it adopted a black, 1½″ cloth diamond in October 1914. It was worn on the left collar point until November 1915. In Mesopotamia all ranks wore a black cloth vertical diamond, 1½″ × 2¾″, on the left side of the pagri. This was confirmed by Lieutenant Colonel Brock on 16/9/17, who also confirmed the re-introduction of the black collar patch on arrival in Egypt on 22/1/18.

3rd (Reserve) Battalion

After moving from Leicester to Portsmouth, in May 1915 it became part of the Humber Garrison where it stayed for the duration. It was a draft finding unit for the regular battalions.

Badges: while the badges were regulation, the puttees were worn with two 'V's in the back starting at the lower portion of the calf of the leg finishing with the end pointing outwards. At the start of the war some new recruits were issued with the blue uniform usually provided to the Kitchener battalions.

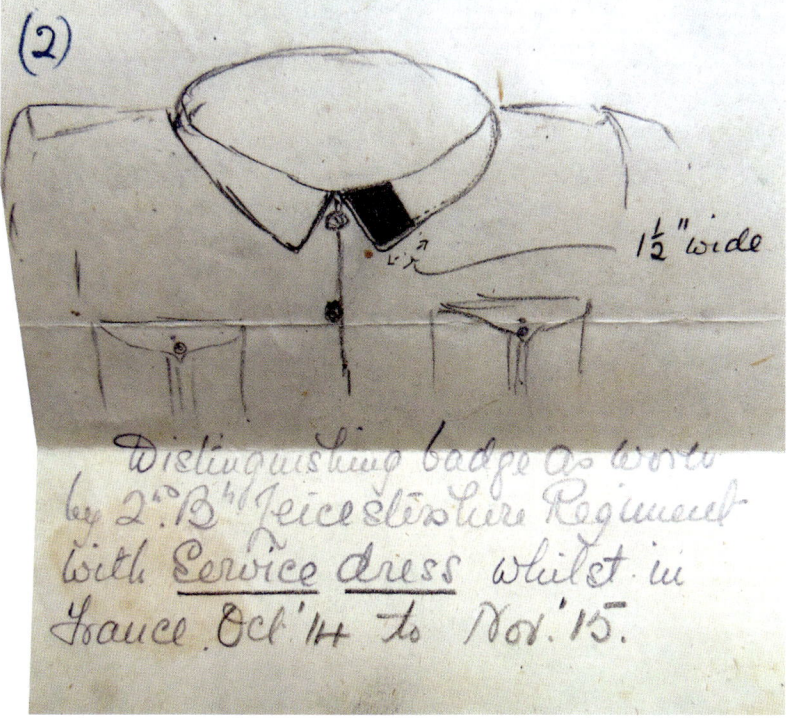

From October 1914 to November 1915 other ranks in the 2nd Battalion wore a black diamond on the left collar. This is the original drawing from the battalion to the NWM.

88 Badges of the Regular Infantry, 1914–1918

A soldier's photo to his wife. The black diamond can be clearly seen on the sun helmet.

Like other regiments the metal title was replaced by a cloth one.

The artwork also included a drawing of the badge adopted for use on the pagri in the Middle East.

The Royal Irish Regiment

As part of the Haldane reforms the battalion formed an extra reserve battalion with a different function to the Reserve Battalion; it was to act as equivalent to the Territorial Force on the mainland with the reserve providing drafts for the front; the 3rd was in Kickham Barracks, Clonmel, and the 4th in Kilkenny. The 1st Battalion was at Nasirabad, the 2nd at Devonport. All ranks wore a common cap badge, officers wore collar badges with a shoulder title – **RI**, and other ranks wore a curved shoulder title – **ROYALIRISH**.

1st Battalion

Arriving at Devonport from India in November 1914, the battalion became part of the 82nd Brigade, 27th Division, landing in France on 20/12/14. After serving on the Western Front it moved to Salonika in December 1915. In November 1916 it joined the 30th Brigade, 10th (Irish) Division, serving with the division in Palestine from September 1917 until the end of the war.

Badges: regulation badges were worn on the Western Front but in Salonika a yellow ½" tape was worn across the base of both shoulder straps. On transfer to the 10th (Irish) Division this was replaced by a green strip for all ranks.

2nd Battalion

One of the first battalions to cross to France as part of the 8th Brigade, 3rd Division, it became Army Troops serving on the Lines of Communication (LoC). in October 1914. In March 1915 it joined 11th Brigade, 4th Division, and in July was part of the 11th Brigade, 4th Division. It joined the 22nd Brigade, 7th Division, in May 1916 and the 49th Brigade, 16th (Irish) Division, in October 1916. From late April 1918 it fought with the 188th Brigade, 63rd Division.

Badges: no badges were worn before joining the 16th (Irish) Division when a green shamrock was worn on both upper sleeves with no badge on the back. From May 1918 in the 63rd Division a horizontal rectangle 2½″ × 1½″ divided vertically into three equal sections of blue/red/green – the regimental colours – was worn on both upper arms. Below this was a 1½″ cloth square indicating the wearer's company: A Company – red; B Company – blue; C Company – yellow; D Company – green; HQ Company – no square. There were no markings on the steel helmet until the battalion joined the 63rd Division when the regimental colours, 2½″ × 1½″, were painted on the left side of all steel helmets. Covers were made of sandbags cut to closely fit the helmet until the practice was forbidden.

3rd (Reserve) Battalion

The battalion spent most of the war in Ireland: Clonmel, Dublin, Templemore, returning to Dublin. In April 1918 it was serving in the Irish Reserve Brigade at Larkhill, Wiltshire.

Badges: regulation cloth and metal.

4th (Extra Reserve) Battalion

Like the 3rd it spent much of the war in Ireland with a spell in Gosport from May to September 1915. It also became part of the Irish Reserve Brigade at Larkhill from April 1918.

Badges: regulation cloth and metal.

The Royal Irish Regiment 91

An example of the yellow/khaki band worn by the 1st Battalion in Salonika.

When the 1st Battalion moved to the 10th (Irish) Division in 1916 it adopted the standard divisional sign of a green band on the shoulder straps.

The Melton cloth title adopted from mid-1916 onwards.

One of the numerous styles of shamrock worn by the 16th Division which the 2nd Battalion fought with.

The 2nd Battalion joined the 63rd Division in April 1918 and adopted their system of badges: a battalion badge in regimental colours above the company sign.

When the 2nd Battalion first joined the 63rd Division it would appear from this photograph that the first badge worn was a shamrock over the company colour, or that in the 16th Division it wore a badge under the shamrock.

In the 27th Division all ranks wore a yellow band on their shoulder straps; other ranks also wore a shoulder title.

When the 1st Battalion transferred to the 10th Battalion it adopted the divisional badge of a green band on the shoulder straps.

The Alexandra, Princess of Wales's Own (Yorkshire Regiment)

Like most British regiments, the 3rd Reserve Battalion was based at the home depot, Richmond Barracks, Richmond; the two regular battalions were in Guernsey and India. All ranks wore a common cap badge, officers wore collar badges and other ranks wore a curved shoulder title – **YORK**.

1st Battalion

Stationed at Bariam in the Punjab, the battalion stayed in India for the duration.

Badges: throughout the war all ranks wore the standard pre-war badges on uniform and a single green band at the top of the pagri.

2nd Battalion

Returning to England from Guernsey it landed in Belgium on 6/10/14 as part of the 21st Brigade in the 7th Division. On 21/12/15, the brigade transferred to the 30th Division and on 11/5/18 the battalion absorbed the 6th battalion in the 32nd Brigade, 11th (Northern) Division, where it remained for the duration.

94 Badges of the Regular Infantry, 1914–1918

Badges: no badges were worn with the 7th Division. In the 30th Division, a green horizontal bar, ¾″ × 2½″, was worn on both sleeves just below the seam by all ranks. This sign was recalled in 1917 by Private Basil Farrer, a pre-war regular who also remembered his brass shoulder titles being replaced with a cloth slip-on. The same-sized sign was also worn on the left side of the steel helmet. In the 11th (Northern) Division, the badges of the disbanded 6th Battalion were adopted: a red cloth horizontal rectangle 1½″ × 3″ with two black vertical bars in the centre, 1″ × ¼″: it was worn on the back of the collars.

3rd (Reserve) Battalion

On mobilisation it moved from Richmond to West Hartlepool where it formed part of the Tees Garrison for the war.

Badges: regulation cloth and metal.

From mid-1916 other ranks were issued with cloth shoulder titles.

A green rectangle was worn by all ranks of the 2nd Battalion when with the 30th Division.

An unusual title was adopted by the 2nd Battalion.

The Alexandra, Princess of Wales's Own (Yorkshire Regiment)

On absorbing the 6th Battalion in the 11th Division it adopted its badge.

When the 30th Division adopted a cloth sign, it was worn on both shoulders by all ranks. It was worn in facing pairs with bird facing forward.

Only regulation badges are in evidence in this photograph of a 3rd Battalion soldier.

A youthful officer showing his cap and collar badges.

The Lancashire Fusiliers

Both the Reserve and Extra Reserve battalions were based at the home depot, Wellington Barracks, Bury, at the start of the war. One of the regular battalions was in India, the other in England. All ranks wore a common cap badge, officers wore collar badges, and other ranks wore a shoulder title – **LF** below a separate grenade. After 1916 this changed to **LgrenadeF** which was worn by officers and men.

1st Battalion

The battalion proceeded to England via Aden in October 1914. On arrival in England it became part of the 86th Brigade, 29th Division. The battalion fought in Gallipoli and moved to France in March 1916 where it served for the rest of the war.

Badges: according to the 1916 Lancashire Fusiliers Annual, company flags were used on leading boats at Gallipoli: A Company, green over white diagonal bottom left to right; B Company, red over white diagonal bottom left to right; C Company, black (top right and bottom left) and yellow squares; D Company, black (top left and bottom right). On the steel helmet a yellow hackle was painted on the left side. A diagonally-bisected 2″ square in yellow and red was worn on the back in different directions to indicate the wearer's company: a square, top left bottom right yellow/red – HQ Company; a diamond red left, yellow right – A Company; a diamond red over yellow – B Company; diamond yellow over red – C Company; diamond yellow left, red right – D Company. On 1 July 1916 officers wore other ranks tunics with rank straps and an inverted cardboard triangle on their back.

2nd Battalion

Based in Dover at the start of the war, it was part of the 12th Brigade, 4th Division, landing in France on 20/8/14. It spent the entire war on the Western Front with the division, apart from 4/11/15 to 3/2/16 when the 12th Brigade was exchanged for a brigade in the inexperienced 36th (Ulster) Division.

Badges: for the Somme offensive the battalion was allocated a vertical red rectangle $3'' \times 1''$ to be worn on the helmet. This was later changed to a $2'' \times 1''$ horizontal rectangle of regimental ribbon vertically bisected in three equal parts – crimson/yellow/crimson – worn on both sleeves. In 1918 a rectangle of red cotton $3'' \times 1''$ was worn on both sides of the steel helmet.

3rd (Reserve) Battalion

Moving from Bury to Hull and then Withernsea, it formed part of the Humber Garrison during the war.

Badges: as well as regulation cloth and metal badges, a horizontal rectangle divided into three equal sections or dark red/yellow/dark red was painted on the helmet, position unknown.

4th (Extra Reserve) Battalion

Like the 3rd Battalion, it remained in the country, eventually forming part of the Severn Garrison.

Badges: regulation cloth and metal.

98   Badges of the Regular Infantry, 1914–1918

In this 1 July 1916 photograph, taken shortly before the Somme attack, the helmet marking is obvious on the helmet on the right, and on the back of the soldier next to him the C Company badge is clearly visible – yellow over red diamond.

All ranks wore company colours on their backs. From top left: HQ, A, B, C and D Company.

The Lancashire Fusiliers 99

All ranks of the 1st Battalion wore the red divisional sign on both arms while on the Western Front.

On Gallipoli and in the Middle East all ranks wore a pagri patch of a grenade above LF on a vertical red rectangle.

This crimson/yellow/crimson badge was worn on both sleeves by all ranks of the 2nd Battalion.

A simple patch was worn on both sides of the steel helmet by all of the 2nd Battalion.

100 Badges of the Regular Infantry, 1914–1918

As a fusilier regiment the cloth title incorporated a grenade in the design.

This badge showed the division by shape and the brigade by colour: 4th Division, 12th Brigade. It was worn above the 2nd Battalion badge.

During the Gallipoli landings a company flag was flown on the leading boat: A Company – green over white; B Company – red over white; C Company – black and yellow; D Company – black and white.

A youthful new recruit showing his shoulder title.

The Royal Scots Fusiliers

The battalion had two regular battalions, one in Gosport, the second in Gibraltar. A third battalion was based at the home depot in Ayr. The cap badge worn by all was similar but more intricate for officers. Officers and senior NCOs wore collar badges, other ranks wore a shoulder title – grenade above **RSF**.

1st Battalion

The battalion landed at Le Havre on 14/8/14 as part of the 9th Brigade, 3rd Division. It remained with the division on the Western Front for the duration.

Badges: officers wore a 3½″ × 3″ fringed patch of universal tartan and all ranks wore company colours on both arms: A Company – 2″ red square; B Company – 2″ red triangle; C Company – red 1⅜″ sided diamond, 1½″ across; D Company – 2″ red circle.[26] HQ Company – 2″ red eight-point star. The steel helmet was painted on the left side with a 3″ × 3½″ patch of regimental tartan.

2nd Battalion

On arrival from Gibraltar the battalion joined the 21st Brigade, 7th Division, landing at Zeebrugge about 6/10/14. In December 1915 the brigade moved to the 30th Division, the battalion joining the 90th Brigade. On 7/4/18 it formed part

---

26. IWM photo Q6506 Hinges, 11/4/18.

of the 120th Brigade, 40th Division. From 26/4/18 it was in the South African Brigade, 9th (Scottish) Division, and from 13/9/18 it fought with the 28th Brigade, 9th (Scottish) Division.

Badges: only steel helmet markings are recorded. In early 1917 a grenade similar to an officer's cap badge but with thistle on bomb was painted on the right side. In July a diamond of tartan was sewn to the right side of the sandbag cover. When the covers were discarded in December 1917 a black grenade with white thistle was painted on the right side; worn by all ranks.

3rd (Reserve) Battalion

As a home service battalion it defended the Clyde area throughout the war.

Badges: regulation cloth and metal.

The officers' cap badge was very similar but more intricate.

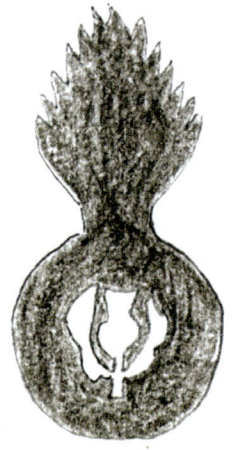

From December 1917 all ranks had a white thistle on a black bomb painted on the right side of the helmet.

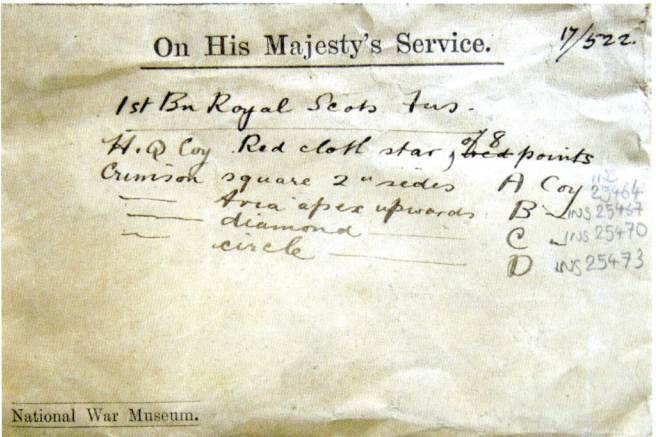

Badges received from units were placed in a standard envelope and the details recorded.

The Royal Scots Fusiliers 103

As a fusilier regiment, it had a grenade added to its cloth title to mimic the metal one.

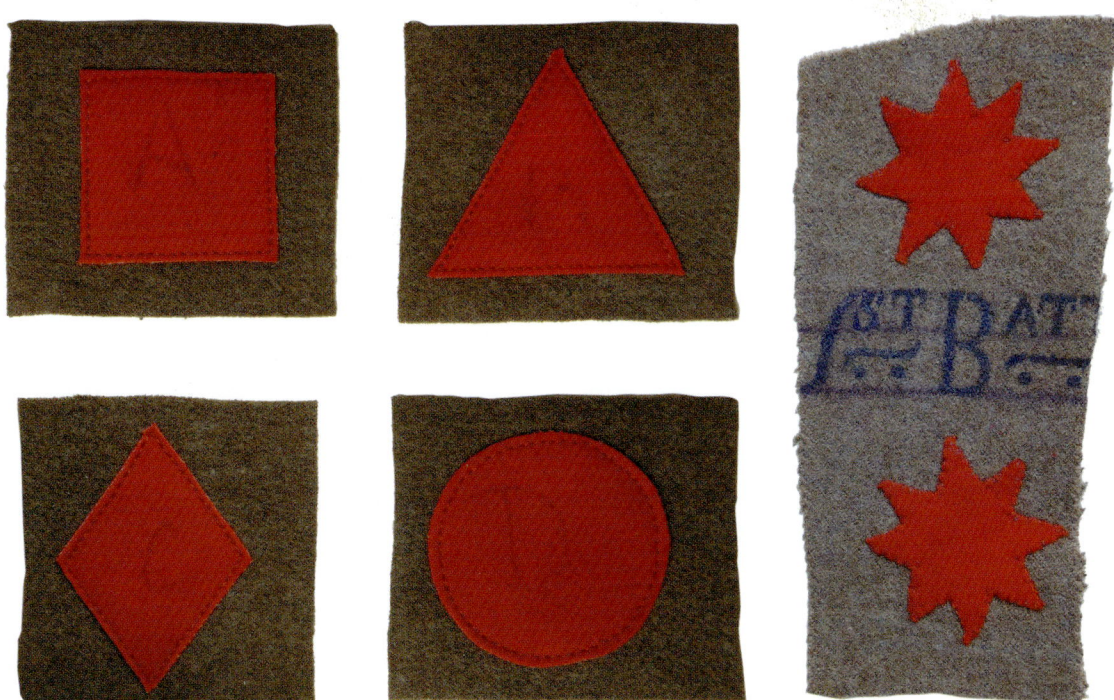

In the 1st Battalion companies were identified by different red shapes: from left, A, B, C, D and HQ Company.

Officers wore a fringed patch of universal tartan as well as their company patch.

One of the many variations of the 9th Division badge that can be found.

A left shoulder badge worn when the battalion was in the 30th Division.

A young fusilier of the 1st Battalion on leave in Edinburgh. On both arms he is wearing the red diamond of C Company.

An unknown private late in the war wearing a tam-o'-shanter with cap badge and metal shoulder titles.

The Royal Scots Fusiliers 105

A photograph that tells an interesting story. A lance corporal in the 2nd Battalion, his badges provide a considerable amount of information about his service: wounded four times, marksman, lance corporal, Lewis gunner, and 9th (Scottish) Division. Unusually he is wearing collar badges, suggesting the image was taken at the end of the war.

Two soldiers from the 1st Battalion; neither is wearing their company colour. On the right is Private Henry Stafford 11590, a very early volunteer who fought in France from 3/8/15 until his discharge.

The Cheshire Regiment

Although the regiment raised over thirty battalions during the war it consisted of just three battalions before August 1914: two regular battalions in Ireland and India with a reserve battalion in Chester Castle. All ranks wore a common cap badge, officers wore collar badges and other ranks wore a curved shoulder title – **CHESHIRE**.

1st Battalion

From Londonderry, the battalion landed in France on 16/8/14 as part of the 15th Brigade, 5th Division. Apart from a period in Italy – December 1917 to April 1918 – it fought on the Western Front with the division.

Badges: following the divisional system, only regulation badges were worn on the tunic. A green cloth oak leaf on a white cotton background, 2″ × 3½″, was adopted in 1917 and worn on the front of the helmet cover. The Battalion CO explained why the badge had only just been taken into use: it was 'considered that as a Regular Battalion such badges were not needed.'

2nd Battalion

On arrival from Jubbulpore, India, it trained as part of the 84th Brigade, 28th Division, landing in France in January 1915. In October it moved to Egypt and in November to Salonika. The 1st Manx (Service) Company joined the battalion in Salonika during January 1916 after training with the 16th King's Liverpool and the 3rd Cheshires.

The Cheshire Regiment 107

Badges: in January 1915, when the battalion landed in France, officers wore a dark green oak leaf, 3¼″ × 1¼″, on the back of the tunic, point of leaf to left. It was short-lived and not replaced when worn out. In Salonika all ranks wore a red ½″ tape across the base of the straps. On joining the battalion, the 1st Manx Service Company became A Company. The Governor of the Isle of Man, Lord Raglan, had obtained permission from the War Office for the company to be kept separate and to wear the Manx coat of arms on the shoulder straps; a circular brass badge above the **CHESHIRE** shoulder title.

3rd (Reserve) Battalion

The battalion was part of the Mersey Defences until December 1917 when it moved to the north-east. There it was absorbed into the Tees Garrison.

Badges: regulation cloth and metal.

A green oak leaf on white cotton was the only badge worn by the 1st Battalion.

This is a variation on the oak leaf on white worn on the helmet.

As the centre of the cap badge is an acorn and oak leaf it is not surprising that both regular battalions adopted the oak leaf as their badge. This was worn when the 2nd Battalion landed in France.

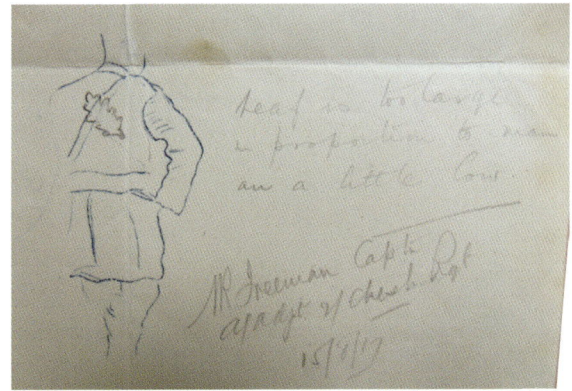

As well as an example, the 2nd Battalion sent a diagram to show its position of wear.

The 7th (Isle of Man) Volunteer Battalion in August 1914, the only surviving volunteer battalion after the 1908 changes, was attached to the West Lancashire TF Division. A service company joined the 16th King's in March 1915 and in October was transferred to the 3rd Battalion Cheshire Regiment becoming the 1st Manx (Service) Company. On joining the 2nd Battalion in Salonika it became A Company and wore a special badge above the shoulder title.

The standard cloth title was worn from mid-1916.

A 1st Battalion man showing cap badge and shoulder title. Incredibly, not only is he in the transport section – spurs on his boots – but he is also a Lewis gunner and signaller.

In the 28th Division all ranks wore a red band on the shoulder straps; other ranks wore a shoulder title.

When the Manx Company joined the 2nd Battalion they wore a special identifying badge above the shoulder title.

The Royal Welsh Fusiliers

Recruiting mainly in the north of Wales, the battalion had two regular and a reserve battalion based in Malta, Portland and Hightown Barracks, Wrexham, respectively. All ranks wore a common cap badge, officers wore collar badges and other ranks wore a shoulder title – **RWF** below a grenade.

1st Battalion

Arriving from Malta on 3/9/14 it landed at Zeebrugge on 7/10/14. As part of the 22nd Brigade, 7th Division, it fought on the Western Front until November 1917. From then until the end of the war it served in Italy.

Badges: correspondence with the Battalion CO dated 1/8/17 states that only regulation badges were worn. The 'flash' was worn on the back by officers, warrant officers and staff sergeants.

2nd Battalion

The battalion was in France within eight days of the declaration of hostilities as LoC troops. On 22/8/14 it joined the 19th Brigade at Valenciennes, which became part of the 6th Division on 12/10/14. The brigade was attached to the 27th Division on 31/5/15 and the 2nd Division on 19/8/15. Three months later the brigade was in the 33rd Division, and on 6/2/18 it was in the 115th Brigade, 38th Division, where it remained.

Badges: correspondence from the Battalion CO dated 29/7/17 states that no badges other than regulation ones had been worn. The wearing of only regulation badges was confirmed in July 1987 by Sergeant E. Turner who was certain that such things were only worn by brigade and divisional staff. However, on joining the 38th Division the divisional sign was worn on the left shoulder and a red square on the right. Second Lieutenant F. Molz, serving with the 1st Middlesex, recalled that officers of the Royal Welsh Fusiliers wore a black flash on the backs of their service jackets, sewn under the collar and hanging loose.

3rd (Reserve) Battalion

After a short period guarding Pembroke Docks, it went to Litherland, via Wrexham, and in November 1917 to Ireland. At the end of the war it was in Limerick.

Badges: the 'flash' was worn by officers, warrant officers and sergeants and a grenade was worn on the front of officers' steel helmets. Otherwise only regulation cloth and metal badges were worn. All of this was remembered by an anonymous correspondent in 1990.

The back flash worn by the regiment, a distinction granted by King William IV. This is an officer's quality flash.

Company Sergeant Major Barter VC served with the 1st Battalion. He is not even wearing shoulder titles.

The Royal Welsh Fusiliers

With a shortage of uniforms at the start of the war new recruits to the 3rd Battalion were issued with a lapel badge.

The cloth shoulder title authorised in mid-1916 to replace the metal title.

On transfer to the 38th (Welsh) Division, the 2nd Battalion conformed to the divisional system of badges and put up a Welsh Dragon badge on the left upper sleeve.

The divisional sign was worn by all ranks in the battalion.

On joining the 115th Brigade it was the most senior battalion and adopted the badge worn by the 17th Battalion – a light red square.

The South Wales Borderers

A standard three-battalion regiment in 1914, with one regular battalion in England, the other in China. The reserve battalion was at the home depot in Brecon, which was simply called The Barracks. All ranks wore a common cap badge, officers wore collar badges, and other ranks and officers wore a shoulder title – **SWB**.

1st Battalion

After leaving Bordon, the battalion went to France on 13/8/14. It fought on the Western Front throughout the war as part of the 3rd Brigade, 1st Division.

Badges: no battalion identifier was worn; instead specialists in the battalion were identified by coloured rectangles, 2″ × ¼″: red – bombers; black - grenadiers; dark green – riflemen; yellow – Lewis gunners. Steel helmets painted khaki with regimental badge in green and white on the front were adopted in January 1917; worn by all ranks. Puttees were worn with two consecutive twists forming two 'V's in the centre of the leg with the tape of the puttee wound round and fastened 1″ below the knee cap with the trouser folded over to cover the top fold of the puttee. When the battalion left England, officers wore 'Stohwasser' pattern leggings, but that died out and long trench boots were generally worn.

2nd Battalion

This was the only battalion to fight with the Japanese at Tsingtao, being stationed nearby at Tientsin. On arrival in England it sailed, after training, with the 8th Brigade,

29th Division, for Gallipoli. On 15/3/16 it arrived in France where it fought with the division on the Western Front.

Badges: 'no badges other than the ordinary numerals were worn by this battalion at TSINGTAU or GALLIPOLI.' However, a white patch was worn on the topee to differentiate them from the Germans. A dark green ½" stripe – introduced May 1917 – was worn on the base of the shoulder strap with a cloth shoulder title sewn directly below and above the 29th divisional red isosceles triangle introduced in March 1916 – correspondence from the CO, Lieutenant Colonel Raikes, dated 23/8/17. The divisional sign was stencilled on the front of the sandbag helmet covers with two green horizontal bars on the left side.

3rd (Reserve) Battalion

As a Home Service battalion it remained in the UK throughout the war serving at Pembroke Dock, Edinburgh and Liverpool.

Badges: regulation cloth and metal.

The only identifiers used by the 1st Battalion were specialism badges: horizontal bars in red, black, dark green and yellow for bombers, grenadiers, riflemen and Lewis gunners respectively.

114   Badges of the Regular Infantry, 1914–1918

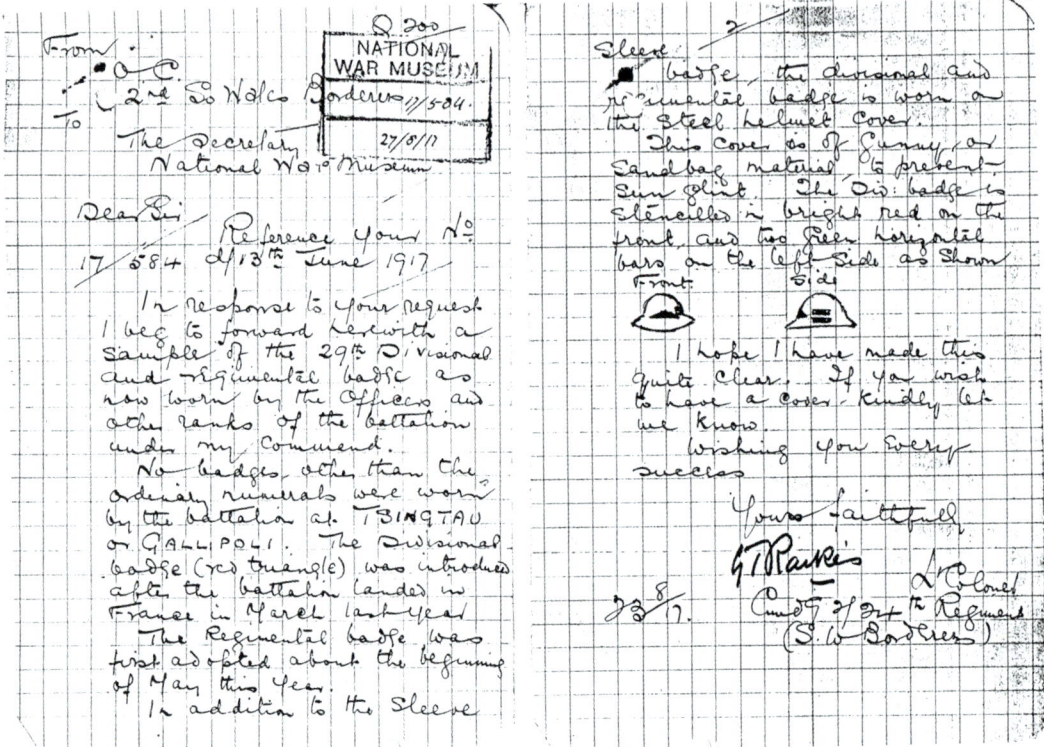

In August 1917 the 2nd Battalion CO wrote to the NWM providing information about the badges his men wore and included two drawings to clarify the helmet badges.

The sandbag helmet cover sent by the battalion to the NWM showing the divisional sign on the front and battalion sign on the side.

The 2nd Battalion adopted badges when the division arrived in France. Each member of the battalion wore the divisional sign and shoulder title. A green band was worn on the straps from May 1917. This is an actual cut down tunic sent to the NWM by the CO of the battalion; the original metal title holes can be clearly seen.

The South Wales Borderers

The soldier second from the right is from the 2nd Battalion and his triangle and metal shoulder strap title are easy to spot.

The example sent by the battalion had a cloth badge below the green band which is slightly different in colour to the example produced by the ACD in mid-1916.

The King's Own Scottish Borderers

Three battalions existed before the war: two regular in Lucknow and Dublin and a reserve at Ravensdowne Barracks in Berwick-on-Tweed. All ranks wore a common cap badge, officers wore collar badges, and other ranks wore a shoulder title – **KOSB**.

1st Battalion

The battalion arrived in England on 28/12/14 and in March 1915 sailed for Gallipoli with the 87th Brigade, 29th Division. From late March 1916 until the end of the war it fought on the Western Front with the division.

Badges: Lieutenant Colonel Welch, the Battalion CO, in July 1917 informed the NWM that in Gallipoli a 3″ square of Leslie tartan, introduced during the South African War, was worn on the left side of the pagri. The divisional red triangle, worn on both upper sleeves, was recalled by Private William Watson and Private John Plaskett and both were certain they wore no other signs on their tunics. It was painted on the steel helmet cover with a simplified version of the cap badge in red – both introduced in May 1916.

2nd Battalion

The battalion left Ireland to form part of the 13th Brigade, 5th Division, landing in France on France 14/8/14. It fought on the Western Front with the division throughout the war except for five months in Italy – December 1917 to April 1918.

Badges: no tunic badges were worn by infantry units in the 5th Division but they were permitted on the helmet. In December 1916 a diamond of Leslie tartan, privately purchased initially, was sewn to the helmet cover and in August 1918 yellow numerals – **XXV**, ¾″ high with ¼″ between figures – were added front and back. A khaki rosette behind the cap badge was worn on the tam-o'-shanter; officers wore glengarries. As a lowland regiment the pipers wore a brown leather sporran with regimental badge on the lapel of the pocket and khaki drill apron over Royal Stewart tartan kilt. No badges were worn on the pagri in Italy.

3rd (Reserve) Battalion

A very mobile battalion; it served in the West Country (Portland and Weymouth), Scotland (Edinburgh) and finally Ireland (Templemore and Claremorris).

Badges: regulation cloth and metal.

On Gallipoli the 1st Battalion wore a tartan square on the left side of the pagri.

In France all ranks wore the divisional sign: a red triangle.

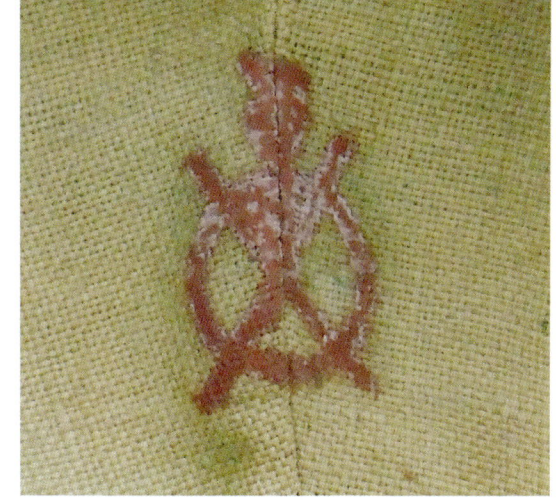

A close-up of the battalion sign sign stencilled on the helmet cover.

Other ranks wore a metal shoulder title when they landed in France; it was later replaced by one in cloth.

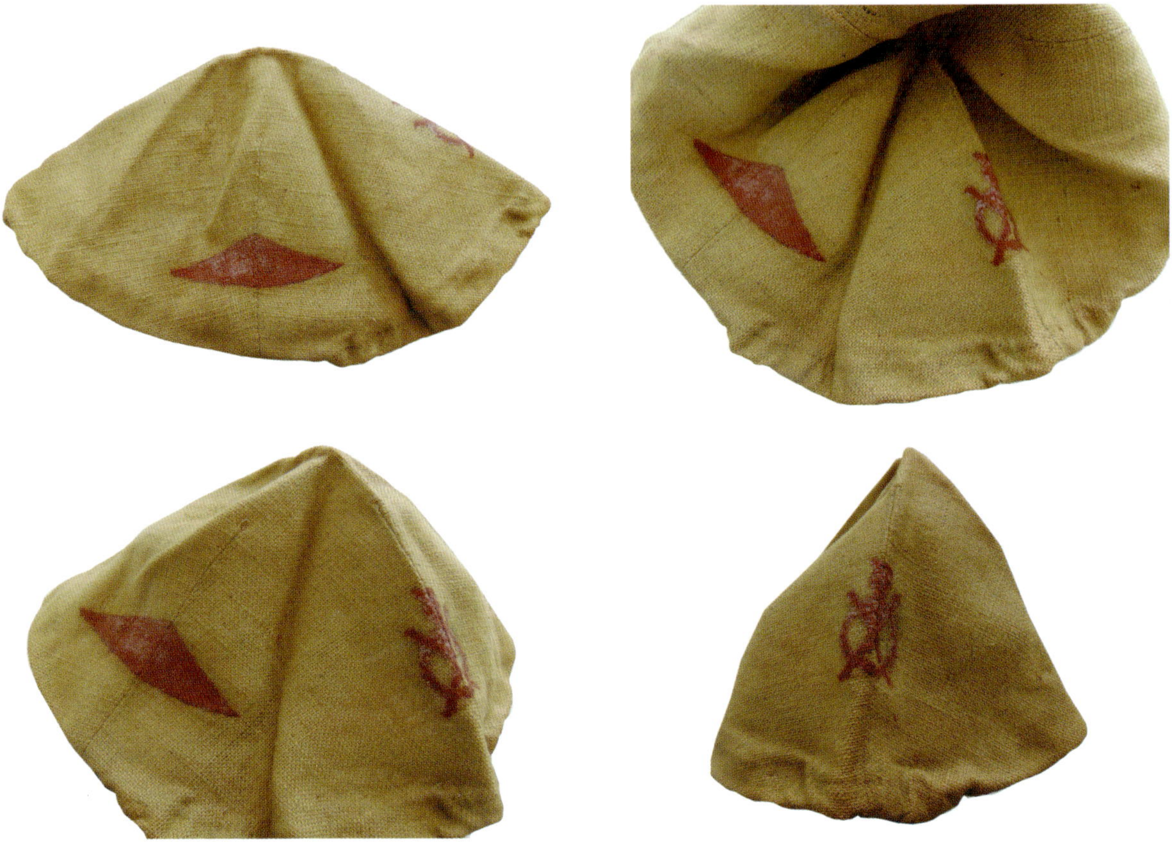

118 Badges of the Regular Infantry, 1914–1918

Four views of a helmet cover showing the positioning of the divisional sign and the battalion badge, both in red.

An officer's collar badge.

The Cameronians (Scottish Rifles)

A four battalion regiment with regular troops in Glasgow and Malta; the Home Service battalions, a reserve and extra reserve were based in Hamilton and remained in Scotland for the duration. All ranks wore a common cap badge, officers wore collar badges, and other ranks wore a blackened brass shoulder title – **SR**.

1st Battalion

Based in Glasgow at the start of the war it landed in France on 15/8/14 as LoC troops for a week before joining the 19th Brigade. It stayed on the Western Front as part of the Brigade in the 6th, 27th, 2nd and 33rd Divisions.

Badges: initially a 1¼″ Douglas tartan diamond with a white cross was on the helmet cover on the left side from the introduction of the steel helmet. From July 1916 regimental colours were painted on both sides – blue/black/green, probably a horizontal rectangle in three equal vertical sections. No other badges were used during the war; this was confirmed by the 1921 questionnaire. Regulation tam-o'-shanters and balmorals were worn without rosette or hackle. Officers wore black lanyards under the collar, short puttees and Douglas tartan hose tops. Puttees were rolled inwards finishing off inside the knee, showing only one thickness of tape. Black glengarries were worn until early 1915 and officers carried swords until September 1914.

2nd Battalion

Stationed in Malta, the battalion landed in France on 22/9/14 as part of the 23rd Brigade, 8th Division. It remained with the division until 3/2/18 when it joined the 59th Brigade, 20th (Light) Division.

Badges: a curved bar of three equal vertical sections – green/black/blue – 3″ × 1″, was worn at the top of each arm by all ranks; the colours are reversed in the divisional history published in 1926. In 1918 all ranks wore a black circle above a single horizontal black bar on both arms.

3rd (Reserve) Battalion

A home service battalion, it formed part of the Cromarty Garrison throughout the war.

Badges: regulation cloth and metal.

4th (Extra Reserve) Battalion

Remained in Scotland throughout the war. During 1917 it was on coastal defences in East Lothian and in June 1918 formed part of the Forth Garrison.

Badges: regulation cloth and metal.

An officer's collar badge.

A tartan diamond was the first badge worn by the 1st Battalion.

The Cameronians (Scottish Rifles)

In the 8th Division the shape informed the brigade, the colour the battalion.

The metal shoulder title worn by other ranks until the cloth version replaced it.

A sergeant in the 1st Battalion having his photo taken when out of the lines. He has seen considerable service as he has Boer War ribbons on his chest.

At home on leave, a sergeant of the 2nd Battalion poses with his dogs. On his right shoulder it is possible to make out the battalion arc. He is a long-serving regular with Boer War ribbons on his chest.

The Royal Inniskilling Fusiliers

As an Irish regiment it raised two regular battalions, a reserve battalion based at the RHQ, St. Lucia Barracks Omagh, and an extra reserve battalion at Enniskillen. All ranks wore a common cap badge, officers wore collar badges, and other ranks wore a curved shoulder title – **RINNISKILLING**.

1st Battalion

The battalion was in Trimulgherry, India, at the outbreak of war, arriving in England on 10/1/15. In March 1915 it sailed for Gallipoli with the 87th Brigade, 29th Division. From March 1916 the battalion fought on the Western Front with the division until 5/2/18 when it was transferred to the 109th Brigade, 36th (Ulster) Division.

Badges: on Gallipoli a painted green vertical rectangle 2″ × ½″ was worn on the left side of the pagri. From May 1915 warrant officers and NCOs discarded badges of rank on the sleeve, replacing them with equivalent signs on the shoulder straps but in indelible pencil. On the back of the tunic collar all ranks wore a dark green rectangle 2″ × ½″, vertical for officers and horizontal for other ranks. The badge was continued on arrival in France but it was worn horizontally by all ranks. From June 1916 a red triangle was worn on both sleeves, and from their issue until September 1916 the green rectangle was also added to the left side of the helmet – painted – or on the helmet cover – cloth. The helmet was painted bright brown after September 1916.

When the battalion was transferred to the 36th (Ulster) Division it adopted the badge of the disbanded 11th Royal Inniskilling Fusiliers: blue $2'' \times \frac{1}{2}''$ horizontal rectangle, worn at the top of both sleeves by all ranks. In November 1988, Major Sir H. Stewart confirmed the wearing of the green bar and red triangle

2nd Battalion

Stationed in Dover, the battalion was part of the 12th Brigade, 4th Division, the battalion landed in France on 22/8/14. On 6/12/14 it became GHQ Troops and on 26/1/15 transferred to the 5th Brigade, 2nd Division; six months later they became Third Army Troops. On 18/11/15 they were part of the 14th Brigade, 5th Division, and five weeks later joined 96th Brigade, 32nd Division. In February 1918 it was transferred to the 109th Brigade, 36th (Ulster) Division.

Badges: before joining the 32nd Division, only regulation badges were worn. The 32nd Division used a system of badges that clearly identified the division (red), the brigade (shape) and the regimental seniority (number of bars below the brigade sign). All ranks wore a red cotton $1\frac{3}{4}''$ equilateral triangle above four red bars. During 1917 the four bars were used to show the wearer's company: A Company – red; B Company – light green/turquoise; C Company – yellow; D Company – light blue; HQ Company – black.

In the 36th (Ulster) Division, for a short while the colours of the disbanded 10th Battalion were worn: a horizontal rectangle split vertically into equal parts blue and orange. This was replaced in August 1918 by a horizontal red rectangle $2\frac{1}{2}'' \times 1''$ that was worn at the top of both sleeves. The same patches were painted on the left side of the steel helmet during the time the battalion served in the 32nd and 36th (Ulster) Divisions. Helmet covers were not worn in either division. During raids, identity discs were taken off and a special numbered disc issued bearing no name or regiment.

3rd (Reserve) Battalion

After $3\frac{1}{2}$ years in Ireland it absorbed the 4th and 12th Battalions and moved to Oswestry.

Badges: regulation cloth and metal for all ranks except the battalion pipers who wore a Kilmarnock bonnet with crest on the side: grenade and castle with a wreath of shamrock and a grey feather. Officers could wear a blue side cap with a unique badge:

grenade with star of St. Patrick on the ball. The unsigned 1920s IWM questionnaire provides a wealth of detail about the pipers' uniform. 'The Irish Pipers of the Battalion marching wear black tunic with silver regt. buttons silver 1 in lace on collar, grenade and castle, and INNISKILLINGS in silver on shoulder strap. Saffron Kilt, green hose. Khaki spats and boots (shoes with silver buckles full dress) green garters. Belt 2 in. brown leather with large silver buckle. Cross belt brown leather with silver ornaments. Green shawl over left shoulder. Kilmarnock bonnet (black with badge at side and grey feather). Sporran. Brown leather, ornamented with silver and grenade in centre.'

4th (Extra Reserve) Battalion

The battalion remained in Ireland until absorbed by the 3rd battalion when it moved to Oswestry.

Badges: shortly after the war an ex-CO, Major Beales, recorded that only the usual badges of the regiment were worn. Once again pipers were mentioned. In the 4th they wore kilts, a shaped coat, and a bonnet with a feather, all in khaki. Colour was provided by a green cloak and silver ornaments.

A green rectangle was worn by all ranks in the 1st Battalion: vertical for officers, horizontal for other ranks.

On joining the 36th (Ulster) Division the 1st Battalion adopted the sign of the disbanded 11th Battalion.

A corporal poses for a keepsake photograph for those at home. On his shoulder is the 29th Division triangle.

The Royal Inniskilling Fusiliers

The 29th Division sign was worn by all ranks.

Lieutenant Colonel Sherwood-Kelly after his VC investiture. He was acting CO of the 1st Battalion; the divisional sign is visible on his upper sleeve.

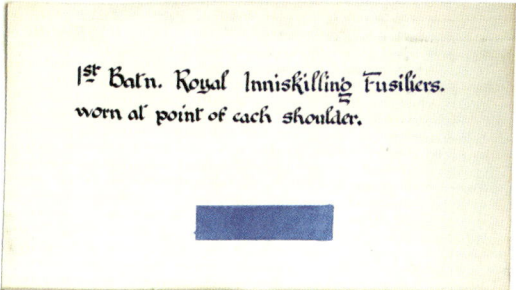

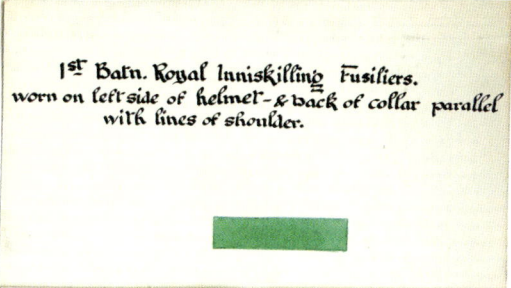

Two record cards completed by the NWM detailing the badges worn by the 1st Battalion.

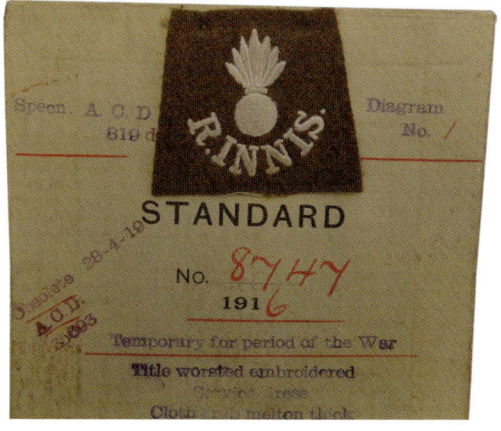

The cloth shoulder title authorised in mid-1916 was classed as obsolete on 28/4/19.

Badges were often made of any available material. This is made of different cloth and is on a different backing to the examples in the IWM. This is the badge worn by A Company, 2nd Battalion.

126 Badges of the Regular Infantry, 1914–1918

The A Company example sent by the 2nd Battalion to the NWM in 1917.

Another variation sent by the battalion.

B Company used four green bars as an identifier.

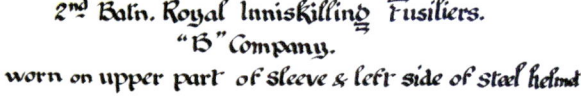

A contemporary piece of artwork detailing the badges of B Company and details of wear.

The badges of C Company, four yellow bars under the brigade triangle; red was the divisional colour.

Some of the badges have faded over the last century. This is the bright red triangle and light blue bars of D Company.

The Royal Inniskilling Fusiliers

2nd Batn. Royal Inniskilling Fusiliers.
"D" Company.
worn on upper part of sleeve & left side of steel helmet.

Another contemporary illustration of the badges worn by D Company.

Four black bars identified Battalion HQ personnel.

On transfer to the 36th (Ulster) Division it replaced the 10th Battalion and adopted its colours.

In August 1918 the 2nd Battalion adopted a new sign – a horizontal red rectangle worn on the sleeves and painted on the helmet.

The Gloucestershire Regiment

A three battalion regiment at the beginning of the war with the reserve battalion at the home depot in Bristol – Horfield Barracks, one regular battalion in China, the other at Bordon. All ranks wore a common cap badge, officers wore collar badges, and other ranks wore a curved shoulder title – **GLOSTER**. Unusually, as a battle honour the regiment wore a small version of the cap badge in a circular laurel wreath on the rear of the service cap, to commemorate an honour won by the 28th Regiment when it fought in two ranks back to back at the Battle of Alexandria in 1801.

1st Battalion

The battalion landed at Le Havre on 13/8/14 and served throughout the war with the 3rd Brigade, 1st Division, on the Western Front.

Badges: no battalion marks were worn, just regulation badges. However, a soldier's specialism was clearly identified by a coloured ⅝″ diamond on the back of the collar: yellow – Lewis gunners; red – bombers; black – rifle grenadiers; green – riflemen. Officers wore no patches. The back badge was brazed on the back of the steel helmet. Major T.H. Barnard, then a young second lieutenant, joined the battalion in April 1918; he had very strong memories of the period when he wrote in January 1988. He is certain that by 1918 the use of the collar badges had fallen into disuse and only regulation badges were worn. However, the Back Badge was soldered on the back of the helmet for all ranks. As the Intelligence Officer, he was in Company HQ and recalled that the Battalion HQ and the transport lines where identified with a board painted with the Back Badge. Helmet covers were made from sandbags.

2nd Battalion

Like the 2nd SWB, the battalion was in Tientsin but was not involved in the Tsingtao operations. The battalion arrived in Southampton on 8/11/14 joining the 81st Brigade, 27th Division. It landed in France on 18/12/14, moving at the end of November 1915 to Salonika where it remained.

Badges: following 27th Divisional practice, the battalion wore a ½″ khaki strip at the base of the shoulder straps. It also wore a vertical red stripe ½″ × 2½″ on the right side of the pagri with the 'back badge' sewn on appropriately. When the slouch hat was worn the cap badge was worn the left side and the 'back badge' on the back of the pagri. Puttees were wound straight round with no crossing. Steel helmets were covered in khaki material with sun shades at the back; no badges were worn on the helmet. Ordinary pattern shorts were worn in 1916 but from 1917 they were replaced by a Salonika pattern. Puttees were wound straight round with no crossing.

3rd (Reserve) Battalion

After moving from Bristol to Woolwich, Gravesend and Sittingbourne it finally settled in the latter as part of the Thames and Medway Garrison for the duration.

Badges: Private Took, later Major, who served with the battalion for a year, recalled only wearing regulation cloth and metal badges.

The Back Badge – worn to commemorate the back-to-back fighting in Egypt on 21 March 1801 against the French – was worn on the cap and helmet by all ranks of the battalion.

The 1st Battalion did not wear a battalion badge but specialists were identified by different coloured diamonds on the back of their collar: red – bombers; black – rifle grenadiers; green – riflemen; yellow – Lewis gunners.

A cloth shoulder title was authorised in mid-1916 and was for wartime use only; it was obsolete by October 1919.

After the war the 2nd Battalion provided details of the badges on the slouch hat worn in Salonika and how the men wore their equipment.

An example of the 27th Division shoulder strap band, khaki rather than yellow.

The Gloucestershire Regiment

A private in the 2nd Battalion in late 1918. On the table is his cap, clearly showing the badge, and on his shoulder strap is the yellow/khaki band worn round the base.

A lieutenant colonel of the reserve battalion.

A newly commissioned officer of the 1st Battalion. His only identifying badge is on his collar.

In the 27th Division all ranks wore the divisional sign on their shoulder straps: a yellow band. Other ranks also wore a shoulder title.

A vertical red band was worn on the right side of the pagri.

The Worcestershire Regiment

The home depot in Norton Barracks just outside Worcester was the home for the 5th and 6th Reserve Battalions. Two of the regular battalions were abroad and two in England. The 1st was in Cairo, the 2nd at Aldershot, the 3rd at Tidworth and the 4th in Meiktila in Burma. All ranks wore a common cap badge, officers wore collar badges, and other ranks wore a curved shoulder title – **WORCESTERSHIRE**.

1st Battalion

On arriving in Liverpool from Egypt the battalion formed part of the 24th Brigade, 8th Division, landing in France on 6/11/14. In October 1915 the brigade moved to the 23rd Division, returning to the 8th Division in July 1916. It fought throughout on the Western Front.

Badges: Private R. Finch who served with the battalion in 1915/16 confirmed that only regulation badges were worn during that period. In February 1917 a 2″ vertically bisected circle white/green was adopted for wear on both sleeves 1″ below the seam, by all ranks – correspondence from Captain Stone, 27/6/17. The wearing of the circle, its colours, green to the front, and size, were recalled by Private F. Ashman in 1988 who served with the battalion in 1916/18. He also recalled runners wore a red armband on the sleeve.[27] The 1926 divisional history has the colours reversed. Shoulder titles were not worn in the line and no markings were worn on the helmet.

---

27. IWM photo Q310 taken at Doullens on 29/3/18 has the circle horizontally bisected, white over green; possibly a company marking.

2nd Battalion

The battalion landed in France as part of the 5th Brigade, 2nd Division, on 14/8/14. On 20/12/15 it transferred to the 100th Brigade, 33rd Division, with which it remained for the rest of the war.

Badges: according to the CO, in August 1917 only regulation badges were worn – clearly shown in August 1918, photo of Captain Crowe receiving the VC from the King. The wearing of only regulation badges was confirmed in July 1987 by Sergeant E. Turner who was certain that such things were only worn by brigade and divisional staff. However, in 1918 the divisional sign in black and white a double three domino was worn on the left side of the helmet and scouts, observers and snipers wore a fleur-de-lis to show their function; runners wore a red band.

3rd Battalion

The battalion landed at Rouen on 16/8/14 as part of the 7th Brigade, 3rd Division, moving with the brigade to the 25th Division on 18/10/15. On 10/11/17 it transferred to the 74th Brigade, 25th Division, and on 22/6/18 joined the 57th Brigade, 19th (Western) Division.

Badges: all units in the 25th Division wore identifying badges: the divisional sign – a red horseshoe, a brigade bar (billet) and a unit marking where appropriate. The battalion wore a red horseshoe on the back enclosing a red or blue bar, 1¾″ × ½″, 7th and 74th Brigade respectively. In August 1917 Lieutenant Colonel Whalley informed the NWM that the battalion had recently adopted a unique shoulder title, white on dark green, 4⅞″ × 2″, **WORCESTERSHIRE** above "**FIRM**". Private Johnson, in December 1987, recalled wearing the title when he was transferred to the battalion after the 10th Battalion was reduced to cadre. On green painted helmets a white painted regimental badge was worn from 1916 until about December 1917 when it was replaced by a soldered-on cap badge; this was also recalled by Private Johnson.

Members of the drums wore a brass valise star on the white pouch. During the last eighteen months of the war all battalion horses wore green and white brow bands. Lieutenant Colonel Whalley of the regiment recorded that 'instead of the coloured brassards ordered to be worn by various specialists, and which were untidy and difficult to see, coloured shoulder straps were adopted in the Battn. about January 1918. Red for runners, green for scouts and observers, and blue for signallers.'

4th Battalion

In February 1915 the battalion landed at Avonmouth from Burma and became part of the 88th Brigade, 29th Division. It fought in Gallipoli between April 1915 and mid-January 1916. After a brief rest in Egypt it moved to the Western Front and from March 1916 until the end of the war was on the Western Front with the division.

Badges: in France, from 20/3/16, the Adjutant reported that the battalion wore the divisional sign on both upper sleeves and it was painted on the front of the helmet cover; a green eight-pointed star, 2″ diameter, was painted on both sides of the helmet cover.[28] Company signs, diamonds 2″ sides × 3″ high, in green and white were worn on the back of the jacket: W Company – green (left)/white; X Company – white over green; Y Company – white (left)/green; Z Company – green over white. These were clearly recalled by Drummer J.C. Blaber who served with the regiment from 1911 to 1920. He also remembered that on Gallipoli the only badges worn were the regimental cap and shoulder titles. Lance Corporal E.E. Hoskins also recalled wearing in France a company sign on his back in X Company.

5th & 6th (Reserve) Battalion

The two battalions served together in Plymouth initially and then from 1917 in the Harwich Garrison.

Badges: the regimental museum confirmed that only regulation cloth and metal badges were worn.

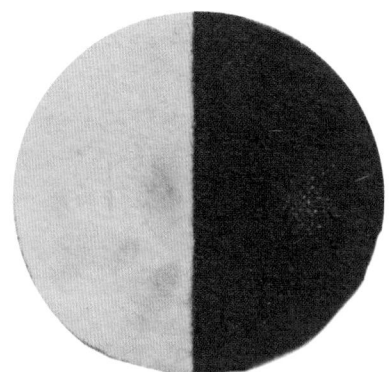

From February 1917 all ranks wore a vertically bisected white/green circle on both upper sleeves.

On 7 December 1918 the King visited the 8th Division in Tournai. The 1st Battalion are seen flanking the King. For some reason the badge is reversed.

---

28. Q717 28/6/16 at Acheux painted on front.

The Worcestershire Regiment 135

A typical runner's armband.

A red bar and horseshoe were worn on the back when the battalion was in 7th Brigade, 25th Division.

Two versions of the unique 3rd Battalion badge exist. This is the most common.

In the 74th Brigade all ranks wore a blue bar and red horseshoe.

A second version of the 3rd Battalion sign uses different lettering and is a rectangle.

Two soldiers of the 4th Battalion at the end of the war. The divisional sign is clearly visible and is in line with the top of the pocket as ordered.

This is believed to be how specialists in the 3rd Battalion were identified: coloured shoulder straps, in this case a signaller.

136   Badges of the Regular Infantry, 1914–1918

The 29th Division sign was always worn. It is easily visible on these 4th Battalion men on their way to the front. The purpose of the white band is uncertain but probably to help identify NCOs at a distance.

The 4th Battalion wore a company indicator on their backs: W Company, X Company, Y Company and Z Company.

An example of the 29th Division badge.

A green eight-pointed star was painted on the front of the 4th Battalion helmets.

A photograph of a platoon of the 5th or 6th Battalion soldiers taken in Plymouth

The 4th Battalion during the Somme battle. Although a poor quality image, the divisional sign is visible on the second soldier from the left.

The East Lancashire Regiment

Fulwood Barracks, Preston, was the Regimental Depot and home of the reserve battalion. There were two regular battalions: the 1st at Colchester, the 2nd at Wynberg in South Africa. All ranks wore a common cap badge, officers wore collar badges, and other ranks wore a curved shoulder title – **ELANCASHIRE**.

1st Battalion

The battalion landed at Le Havre on 22/8/14 as part of the 11th Brigade, 4th Division, until 1/2/18 when it joined the 103rd Brigade, 34th Division. On 26/5/18 it transferred to the 183rd Brigade, 61st Division.

Badges: the CO informed the NWM on 4/8/17 that all ranks wore a vertical 3″ × 1″ yellow rectangle 2″ below the shoulder seam on both sleeves. It was also painted on both sides of the helmet from June 1916 and worn on covers; to this was added a yellow ram's head worn above the battalion flash. In the 34th Division this was changed to a yellow triangle that was removed in June 1918 and a gilt transfer of the regimental badge was applied to the front of the helmet. It was worn by all ranks. Puttees were worn with three folds in front of the leg. Buglers' lines were worn hanging from the left shoulder with the tassel resting on the left shoulder, and band members had a regimental cap badge on the front of their pouch. In the 183rd Brigade all ranks wore a yellow triangle.

2nd Battalion

Sailing from Cape Town, the battalion became part of the 24th Brigade, 8th Division. It landed in France on 6/11/14 and remained with the division until 18/10/15 when the brigade joined the 23rd Division, returning to the 8th Division on 15/7/16. It transferred to the 25th Brigade on 3/2/18. It served throughout the war on the Western Front.

Badges: in the 24th Brigade a 2″ vertically divided red/white circle, white to the front, was worn on both arms between February 1917 and February 1918. Worn 1″ below was the divisional sign, a red square in a ¾″ white square; this indicated a mention in divisional orders. In the 23rd Division the circle became a 2″ square; white to the front, worn on both arms and painted on the right side of the helmet. It was worn until May 1919. The steel helmet was painted a mud colour.

Officers wore a red lanyard over the right shoulder. Puttees were crossed to show two 'V's on the shin and finished to fasten outwards. Band members wore a white buff pouch with a special badge: the number 59 circled by laurel and crown. Along with the standard precautions taken for a raid, false identity discs were issued.

3rd (Reserve) Battalion

After moving to Plymouth just a few days after the start of the war it moved to Saltburn in the summer of 1917 as part of the Tees Garrison.

Badges: Private A. Birtwhistle, later a CSM at 20 years of age, served in the battalion in early 1915 and recalled only wearing regulation metal badges.

All ranks of the 1st Battalion wore a vertical yellow rectangle on both sleeves.

On transfer to the 34th Division, the 1st Battalion wore a yellow triangle. The same badge was also worn in the 61st Division, as is shown in this September 1918 photo.

Following the 8th Division system, the 2nd Battalion wore a circular badge to show the brigade, and the two colours the battalion, in this case red and white.

The 2nd Battalion sign worn in the 24th Brigade is clearly visible; white to the front.

In February 1918 the 24th Brigade circle became a square.

The specimen ACD card for the East Lancashire Regiment cloth shoulder title was authorised in 1916; it acknowledged that it was temporary for the war.

A photo taken in Plymouth of a private in the 3rd Battalion, showing only regulation badges.

In the 11th Brigade the 1st Battalion wore a yellow ram's head above the yellow battalion badge.

The East Surrey Regiment

A four battalion peace-time regiment, with a reserve and extra reserve battalion billeted at The Barracks in Kingston-upon-Thames, the Regimental Depot. Both regular battalions were serving outside England; the 1st in Dublin, the 2nd at Chaubatia, India. All ranks wore a common cap badge, officers wore collar badges, and other ranks wore a curved shoulder title – **ESURREY**.

1st Battalion

Moving from Dublin, the battalion joined the 14th Brigade, 5th Division, in France on 15/8/14. On 12/1/16 four battalions were exchanged with the 95th Brigade and the battalion was transferred to the new brigade, remaining with the division. It served on the Western Front, except between December 1917 and April 1918 when it was in Italy.

Badges: correspondence from the 5th Division states that the battalion only wore regulation badges. This is confirmed by the Battalion CO in July 1917: 'no special badges or marks of distinction have been worn by this Battalion during the Campaign, other than the Official Badge.'

2nd Battalion

Leaving India in November 1914 on arrival in England on 23/12/14, it formed part of the 85th Brigade, 28th Division. It landed In France on 19/1/15 and after nine months on the Western Front it moved to Salonika for the remainder of the war.

Badges: during service on the Western Front, officers wore a 2″ sides, 3″ high, red diamond on their back, 1″ down from the collar, from March to November 1915. According to the Battalion CO in August 1917, 'no other badges have been worn by them, nor have any regimental badges been worn by the men of this Battalion at any time.' In Salonika all ranks wore the 28th Divisional ½″ red tape at the base of the straps. A yellow diamond was worn on the left of the topee.

3rd (Reserve) Battalion

The battalion served throughout the war with the Dover Garrison.

Badges: Lieutenant Colonel Shipley, writing from Grand Shaft Barracks in Dover on 2/8/17, told the NWM that apart from a cap badge and cloth or metal shoulder titles, 'no other distinguishing badges have been worn by this Battalion.'

Issued from mid-1916, the cloth title for the East Surrey regiment was obsolete by October 1919.

To economise on metals, after 1916 most other rank cap badges were made from one metal. This is the economy version of the cap badge.

The East Surrey Regiment 143

An illegal photograph of 1st Battalion officers in the front line (cameras were forbidden for all ranks on active service); only regulation badges are being worn.

In common with most battalions on the Western Front, armbands were worn on the left forearm to show function.

Between March and November 1915 officers of the 2nd Battalion were identified by a large red diamond on their backs.

In Salonika, as well as the divisional band on the straps, all ranks wore a yellow diamond on the left of the topee.

In the 28th Division all ranks wore the divisional sign on their shoulder straps – a red band; other ranks also wore a shoulder title.

The Duke of Cornwall's Light Infantry

Victoria Barracks in Bodmin was the Regimental Depot and housed the reserve battalion. Both regular battalions were not in England; the 1st was at the Curragh in County Kildare, the 2nd was in the Far East. All ranks wore a common cap badge, officers wore collar badges and other ranks wore a curved shoulder title – **CORNWALL** under a bugle with the mouthpiece facing front.

The shoulder title worn by other ranks was in facing pairs.

1st Battalion

After leaving the Curragh, it joined the 14th Brigade, 5th Division, and proceeded to France, landing on 15/8/14. Like the 1st East Surrey Battalion, it served in the 95th Brigade and was in Italy between December 1917 and April 1918 returning to the Western Front for the remainder of the war.

Badges: no distinguishing badges were worn on the tunic. Correspondence from the 5th Divisional CO in September 1918 states that helmets were marked with three $1\frac{1}{2}'' \times \frac{1}{2}''$ horizontal bars with a $\frac{1}{2}''$ gap between: dark red over white over green – the regimental colours; position of wear unknown.

2nd Battalion

Although in Hong Kong at the outset of the war, it did not fight at Tsingtao but was recalled to England. On arrival it joined the 82nd Brigade, 28th Division, landing in

The Duke of Cornwall's Light Infantry   145

France on 21/12/14. After nearly a year on the Western Front it was sent to Salonika for the rest of the war.

Badges: apart from the ½" red tape at the base of the shoulder straps, no other badges were worn. This was confirmed by Second Lieutenant Warwick who served with the battalion in 1917/18.

3rd (Reserve) Battalion

After nine months guarding Falmouth the battalion became part of the Portsmouth Garrison. It remained on the Isle of Wight for the duration.

Badges: regulation cloth and metal.

The only badge worn by the 2nd Battalion was the 28th Division sign on the base of the shoulder straps.

The standard dress of a soldier in training with the reserve battalion.

When the cloth shoulder title was introduced from mid-1916 they were made in pairs.

In the 5th Division only the helmet showed the battalion. The 1st Battalion wore red over white over green.

The Duke of Wellington's (West Riding Regiment)

Although the potential recruiting area was large and populous the regiment consisted of only three battalions in August 1914. The Regimental Depot was Wellesley Barracks, Halifax, and home to the reserve battalion; the 1st Battalion was in India and the 2nd at Dublin. All ranks wore a common cap badge, officers wore collar badges and other ranks wore a curved shoulder title; initially **W.RIDING**, replaced in 1915 by **DUKE/OF/WELLINGTON'S**.

1st Battalion

Stationed in Lahore in August 1914, the battalion continued to serve in India throughout the war.

Badges: regulation badges were worn on the uniform and the pre-war pagri flash was worn on the topee.

2nd Battalion

The battalion landed in France on 16/8/14 as part of the 13th Brigade, 5th Division. On 16/8/14 it moved to the 12th Brigade, 4th Division, and on 10/2/18 to the 10th Brigade. It fought throughout the war on the Western Front with the 4th Division.

Badges: the first sign, a 2″ red cotton square, was worn in action for the first time on 1/7/16 on either side of the cover on the steel helmet. A month earlier the covers

The Duke of Wellington's (West Riding Regiment)

had been dyed dark brown using Condy's fluid. When covers were discontinued on 1/10/16, the sign was painted on both sides of the helmet. Correspondence from the CO on 6/8/17 states that the red square was adopted for wear, on both sleeves, 2″ below the shoulder seams, from March 1917: officer's badge was in scarlet cloth, other ranks in red twill. From 10/5/18 officers and the RSM wore a specially made khaki drill cover with a four-fold pagri with the red square sewn on both sides; the red square was painted on other ranks' helmets. Canvas covers for other ranks were introduced at the same time and the badge was painted on. The green ram's head, worn above the battalion sign, was introduced around the same time. From November 1918 a green ram's head – 10th Brigade – was painted above the red square on the helmet for other ranks; the ram for officers and warrant officers was white with a green border; the use of covers was discontinued. The badges were discontinued on arrival back in the UK on 8/6/19. Puttees were worn with two figure 8s in the centre. Drummers wore the elephant collar badge on the collar of the service dress jacket.

3rd (Reserve) Battalion

From August 1914 until the end of the war the battalion formed part of the Tyne Garrison.

Badges: regulation cloth and metal.

The pre-war pagri flash was worn by the 1st Battalion in India throughout the war.

In the 10th Brigade all ranks should have worn the brigade sign above the battalion badge. This is the brigade sign – it was not always worn.

A soldier of the 2nd Battalion wearing just the battalion badge.

On transfer to the 12th Brigade all ranks should have worn a red ram's head.

An RSM of the 3rd Battalion who has seen overseas service – note MM ribbon above his pocket.

A red square was worn by the 2nd Battalion from 1 July 1916.

In common with all other units, a cloth title was adopted from late-1916.

A junior officer in the 3rd Battalion; the photo was taken at Whitley Bay.

From November 1918 a ram's head was painted on the helmet; green for other ranks and white with green outline for warrant officers and officers, both above a red square.

The Border Regiment

A three-battalion regiment with the reserve battalion at the Regimental Depot, Carlisle Castle, the 1st Battalion stationed in Maymyo, Burma, and the 2nd at Pembroke Dock. All ranks wore a common cap badge, officers wore collar badges, and other ranks of the 1st Battalion wore a curved shoulder title – BORDER; the 2nd Battalion wore a straight version.

1st Battalion

On arrival from Burma on 10/1/15 the battalion joined the 87th Brigade, 29th Division, landing in Gallipoli on 25/4/15. After a brief spell in Egypt in early 1916 the battalion moved to France in March where it remained for the duration.

Badges: on arrival in Gallipoli all ranks wore a red rectangle $2\frac{1}{2}'' \times 1\frac{3}{4}''$ on the left side of the topee: horizontal for officers, vertical for other ranks. They were removed on 20/5/15 and moved to the back of the tunic collar; this rectangle, which measured $2'' \times \frac{1}{2}''$, was worn until the end of the war. In France the divisional sign, a red isosceles triangle – 4″ base, 1¼″ high, introduced 21/4/16, was worn with the base of the triangle in line with the top of the breast pocket on both arms. Both signs were also worn on the helmet or cover: centre front – stencilled red triangle – both sides centrally, a red rectangle – horizontal for officers and vertical for the men. A metal badge of honour was worn in the centre of the divisional sign on the right arm only, by all ranks who had received the Divisional Commander's parchment certificate for gallant conduct and devotion to duty in the field.

In about June 1917 the Corps of Drums was formed and green buglers' lines were worn over the left shoulder. 'The battalion from the beginning of the war wore the great coat with the front skirts looped up in the French manner, this afterwards became universal for the whole army... In Gallipoli and on the 1st July 1916 in France the Battn. wore pieces of bright tin on the back with a view to showing how far the attack had progressed, these were afterwards superseded by the use of flares.'

2nd Battalion

The battalion landed at Zeebrugge on 6/10/14 as part of the 20th Brigade, 7th Division. It fought for three years on the Western Front until November 1917 when it was sent to Italy where it remained until the armistice.

Badges: a bright pink cotton cloth patch 11″ × 10″ compete with holes for buckles was worn on the back of the small pack during the July 1916 offensive. In Italy during the summer months a flash was worn on the left side of the topee – colour unknown but probably pink.

3rd (Reserve) Battalion

After spending time in Shoeburyness, Conway and Barrow, the battalion finished the war near Liverpool as part of the Mersey Garrison.

Badges: the Battalion CO sent the NWM details of the badges worn by five battalions of the regiment but did not mention those worn by his. From this it is safe to assume that only regulation cloth and metal badges were worn. The 1921 questionnaire did not mention anything other than regulation badges. Captain A. Fulton, then a private, trained with the battalion in 1915 and told the writer he only wore regulation badges during that time.

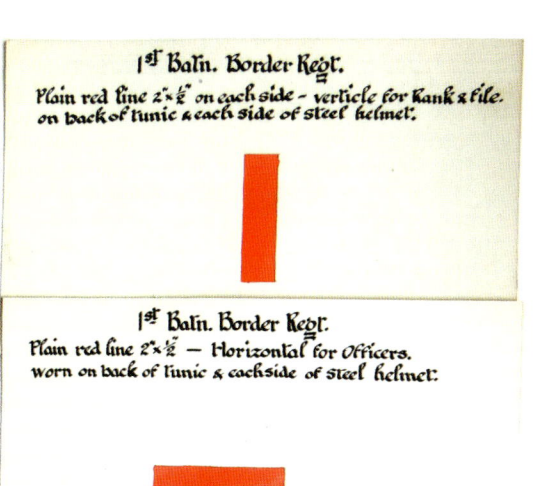

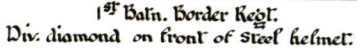

Three NMW cards detailing the badges worn by the 1st Battalion with position of wear.

Cloth shoulder titles were introduced in mid-1916 to replace and save metal.

Shortly after arrival in France the battalion wore the divisional sign, a red triangle.

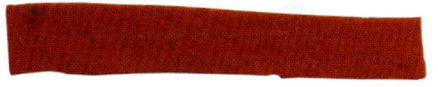

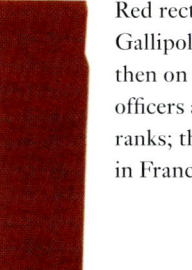

Red rectangles were worn in Gallipoli, firstly on the pagri and then on the back: horizontal for officers and vertical for other ranks; they continued to be used in France and Belgium.

In the 7th Division, badges were not always worn and some were difficult to class as a badge but were very effective as battalion markings. During the Somme battles the battalion wore a pink cloth on the small pack. The images show the cloth, now faded, spread out, showing the holes for buckles and it folded and stuck to the NWM card.

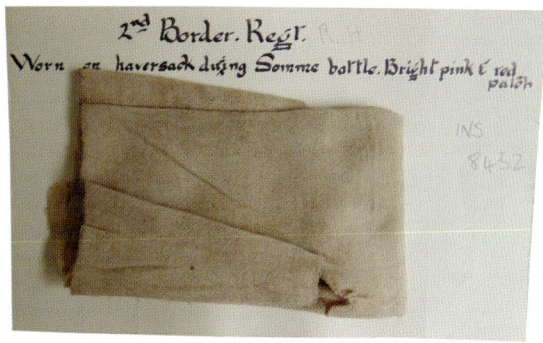

An assortment of men from the 20th Brigade, 7th Division: 2nd Borders, 8th Devons and 2nd Gordon Highlanders. The soldier sitting at the left is from the Border Regiment; on his sun helmet is a dark coloured patch – colour unknown.

A typical private of the reserve battalion.

An officer of the Border Regiment showing the badges worn.

The Royal Sussex Regiment

Roussillon Barracks in Chichester was the Regimental Depot and home for the reserve battalion. Just over forty miles north, the 2nd Battalion was stationed in Woking; the 1st was at Peshawar were it remained for the duration. All ranks wore a common cap badge, officers wore collar badges, and other ranks wore a curved shoulder title – **ROYALSUSSEX**.

1st Battalion

The battalion remained in India throughout the war.

Badges: a red horizontal rectangle, embroidered **ROYAL/SUSSEX** in white, was worn on the left side of the ten-fold pagri. Some photos also show a dark square with a cap badge on the front or on the left side of the topee. Officers' forage cap badges were a special pattern in silver and enamel. Bandsmen's pouches had the cap badge on the front.

2nd Battalion

After landing in France in August 1914 the battalion served on the Western Front with the 2nd Brigade, 1st Division, throughout the war.

Badges: a diamond of regimental colours, blue/orange/blue, in equal sections, was adopted in late 1916. Specialists were identified by a horizontal bar on the back of the collar: red – bombers; black- rifle grenadiers; green – riflemen; yellow – Lewis gunners. Private W.E. Grover in 1987 recalled wearing the green bar on his collar with the diamond below.

3rd (Reserve) Battalion

After nine months service in Dover the battalion became part of the Newhaven Garrison for the duration.

Badges: regulation cloth and metal.

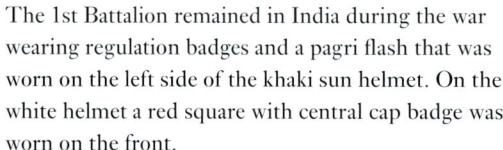

The 1st Battalion remained in India during the war wearing regulation badges and a pagri flash that was worn on the left side of the khaki sun helmet. On the white helmet a red square with central cap badge was worn on the front.

The Royal Sussex Regiment   155

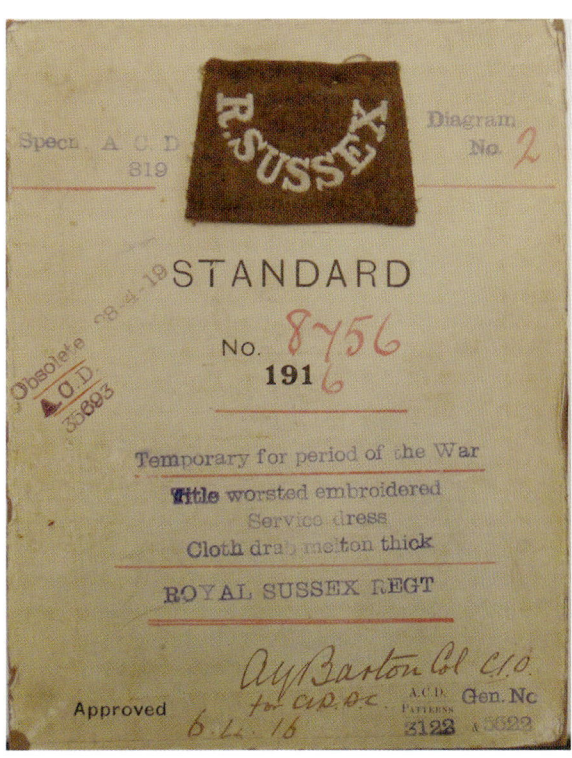

The standard metal title worn by other ranks and its cloth replacement.

Specialists in the 2nd Battalion were identified by horizontal bars on the back of the collar: red – bombers; black – rifle grenadiers; green – riflemen; yellow – Lewis gunners.

The 1st Division only wore regulation badges so it is almost certain that the badge adopted by the 2nd Battalion was worn on the helmet.

156 Badges of the Regular Infantry, 1914–1918

A private in the 2nd Battalion wearing the newly adopted wound badge and shoulder title before the battalion wore a battalion badge.

Carefully modelled by an RSM of the reserve battalion; only regulation badges are in use.

The Hampshire Regiment

Winchester was the regimental town for the regiment with the 3rd Battalion based in the Lower Barracks, Southgate Street; the 1st Battalion were at Colchester, the 2nd at Mhow in India. Officers and men wore different cap badges, officers wore collar badges and other ranks wore a curved shoulder title – **HANTS**.

1st Battalion

The battalion landed in France on 23/8/14 with the 11th Brigade, 4th Division. It served with the division on the Western Front for the duration.

Badges: between 28/5/16 and 31/7/17 a 2″ square of yellow cotton was worn directly below the shoulder seams on both arms and on both sides of the steel helmet. On Minden Day – 1/8/17 – the yellow square was replaced by a 2½″ × 1½″ khaki patch with a yellow tiger 1⅞″ × 1⅛″ sewn on. This was worn below the yellow ram's head for 11th Brigade, but it was not always worn. Private T. Broach, who served with the battalion in 1917/18, said he did not wear the divisional sign but did wear the yellow lion (sic) on each shoulder.

2nd Battalion

On arrival from India on 22/12/14 the battalion became part of the 88th Brigade, 29th Division. It remained with the brigade throughout the war fighting in Gallipoli between April 1915 and January 1916, and on the Western Front from March 1916.

Badges: no signs were worn on the topee at Gallipoli. From spring 1916 the divisional sign – a red 29th Division triangle – was worn on both arms and on the front of the dark green steel helmet: company signs were painted on both sides with a white border to the sign. Yellow and black 1½″ squares, all worn as diamonds, were worn on the back of the jacket to show the wearer's company: W Company – yellow top right over back; X Company – yellow bottom right; Y Company – yellow bottom left; Z Company – yellow top left; HQ yellow over black. Private W. Hodge remembered wearing these when corresponding with the writer in 1992.

The battalion band wore bleached/scrubbed PH helmet satchels as musician's pouches with the divisional sign on the flap. Officers of the battalion did not wear collar badges. Puttees were folded over twice in succession commencing at the completion of the third turn from the boots. Buglers wore green dress cords.

3rd (Reserve) Battalion

After a brief spell of duty at Parkhurst the battalion moved to Gosport as part of the Portsmouth Garrison.

Badges: in a letter dated 2/2/20, Lieutenant Colonel Spencer-Smith, commanding the Regimental Depot, informed the IWM that as the battalion did not serve overseas 'no special badges, articles of dress, deviations from the scale, or method of wearing equipment, were introduced during the time the Battalion was stationed at the Isle of Wight and at Gosport throughout the war.' Private W. Hodges wore regulation badges when he served with them in 1914/15.

An officer's badge was in bronze and completely different.

The first badge worn by the 1st Battalion was a yellow square – shown here with a handwritten label from the battalion describing the position of wear.

The Hampshire Regiment   159

On 1/8/17, Minden Day, the yellow square was replaced by a tiger.

An unknown officer wearing the divisional/brigade sign above the battalion badge.

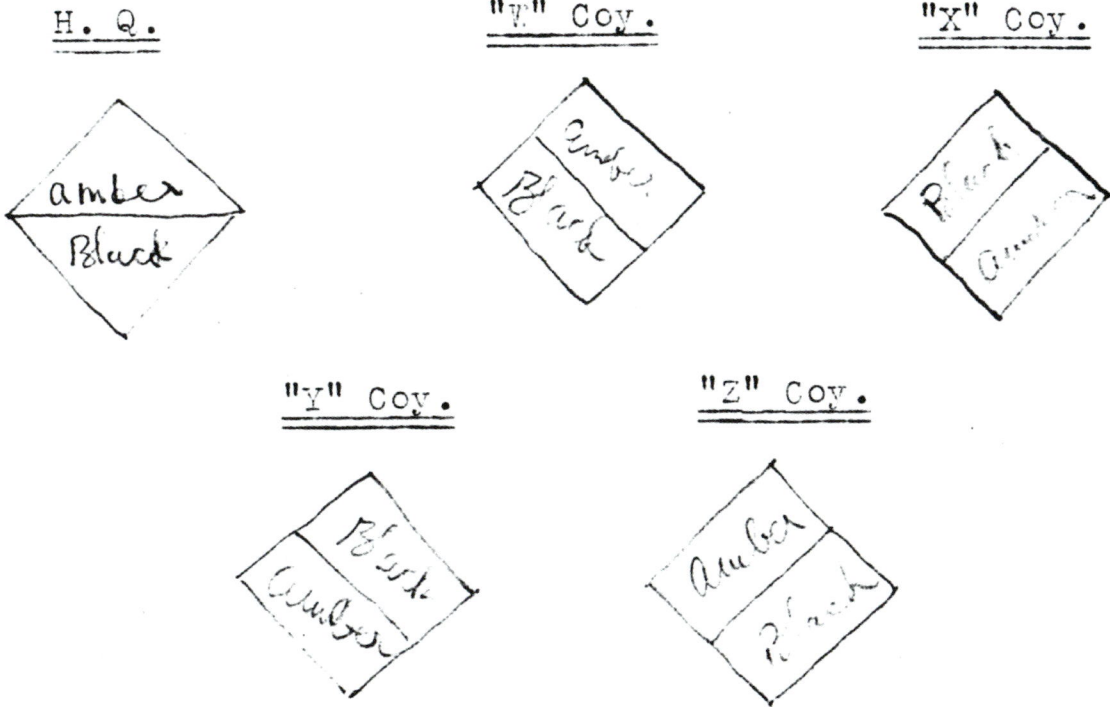

The 2nd Battalion wore company badges on the back as well as the divisional sign on the sleeves. This is from the original artwork done by Haswell-Miller for the IWM in 1921/2.

160   Badges of the Regular Infantry, 1914–1918

In the 29th Division some battalions wore company signs on their back; the 2nd Battalion used black and yellow squares – HQ, W, X, Y, and Z respectively.

Six officers from the 2nd Battalion pictured in 1918. Four of the most junior officers have a number of years' service at the front suggesting that they are promoted other ranks; supporting this, the officer on the left has the MM ribbon on his chest.

The Hampshire Regiment 161

A private in the 2nd Battalion. His divisional sign is in line with his top pocket as specified.

All ranks of the 29th Division wore a red triangle.

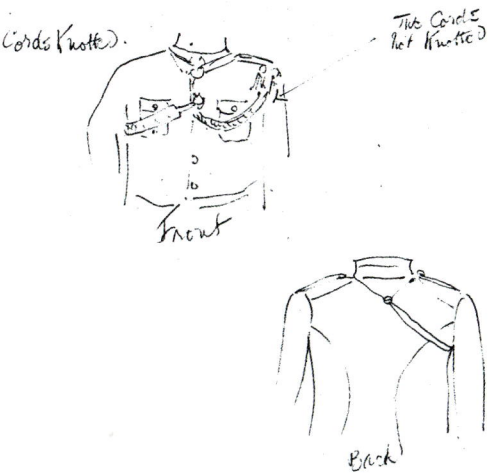

A Haswell-Miller drawing for the IWM showing how the battalion's buglers wore their dress cords.

The cloth title issued to the battalions in mid-1916.

Although all the infantry brigades should have worn the divisional sign in brigade colours it was not strictly enforced and many did not wear it. The yellow ram's head signified the 11th Brigade.

The South Staffordshire Regiment

Whittington Barracks near Lichfield was home to both the reserve and extra reserve battalions; the 1st Battalion was at Pietermaritzburg and the 2nd in Aldershot. All ranks wore a common cap badge; officers wore collar badges, as did other ranks in the 1st Battalion. Other ranks wore a curved shoulder title – **SSTAFFORD**.

1st Battalion

From South Africa, the battalion moved to England to join the 22nd Brigade, 7th Division, landing at Zeebrugge on 7/10/14. In December 1915 it became part of the newly transferred 91st Brigade. It served on the Western Front until November 1917 when it moved to Italy.

Badges: Lieutenant Colonel Beaumont, the Battalion CO, told the NWM in August 1917 that from 14/7/16 the battalion wore a pink cotton 1½″ circle on the right arm mid-way between the shoulder and elbow. From about January 1917 a white Stafford knot on blue was worn on the helmet, and when canvas covers were worn a black Stafford knot was painted on the front. In Italy a blue cloth circle was worn on the left side of the pagri by all ranks; it was also worn on both sleeves 8″ below the seam. All ranks wore gilt Staffordshire Knot collar badges.

Puttees were folded with two cross folds, three-quarters of the way up the leg in the centre over the shin bone. Buglers' cords were made of coloured silk in the regimental colours, green/yellow/black. The cord hung around the neck, draped over the front of the jacket, and finished up with two large tassels hanging from the left shoulder. Bandsmen wore a large gilt regimental badge on their pouches.

2nd Battalion

As part of the 6th Brigade, 2nd Division, the battalion landed in France on 13/8/14. It fought with the division on the Western Front until the end of the war.

Badges: correspondence from 29 July 1917 clearly states that only regulation badges were worn on the tunic. 'The official cap badge of the South Staffordshire Regiment is the only distinctive mark worn by all ranks of this Battalion. No cloth badges have been worn, either on the sleeve or on the back of the Service Dress jacket, throughout the Campaign.' However, when steel helmets were issued the regimental badge was painted on the front – colour not stated.

Puttees were crossed twice. Green bugler lines were worn from the right shoulder. Bandsmen wore a white cross-belt with gilt badge on red cloth on the pouch. Officers wore collar badges of the same pattern as the cap badge – a crown and scroll.

3rd (Reserve) Battalion

Serving briefly in Plymouth it moved to Sunderland and Newcastle where it became part of the Tyne Garrison.

Badges: in April 1920, the Battalion CO, Captain Adams, confirmed that 'no special distinctive markings were adopted by' the unit.

4th (Extra Reserve) Battalion

After a period as a home service battalion it landed in France in October 1917 joining the 7th Brigade, 25th Division. It was transferred to the 50th Division in June 1918 and moved to the 116th Brigade, 39th Division, in July. The battalion was disbanded on 6/11/18.

Badges: regulation cloth and metal until the battalion moved to France. In the 25th Division, all ranks wore the divisional sign – a horseshoe – on the back and a blue brigade bar above it on the collar. The cap badge in white and yellow was worn on the front of the steel helmet and red bands were worn on the shoulder straps. Private Illingworth served briefly with the battalion during the German 1918 offensive. Arriving in late March 1918 as a Notts and Derby soldier he was transferred to the North Staffs and then the 4th South Staffs in just a matter of days and by 11 April he was a PoW. Even though he was with them just over a week he still found time to put up his horseshoe and bar. No badges are recorded during service with the 50th and 39th Divisions; however, it is probable that they wore the golden horseshoe with the latter division.

From 14/7/16 the 1st Battalion wore a pink circle on both sleeves.

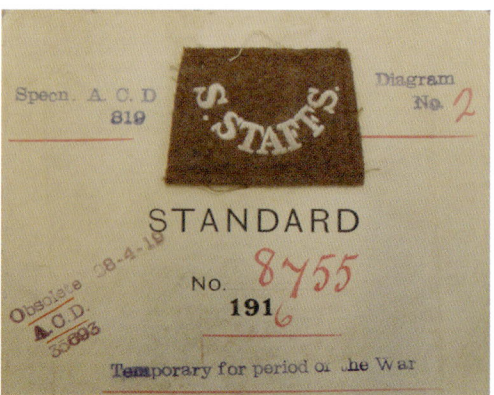

Obsolete less than three years after it was authorised, the cloth title was a replacement for the metal title.

The cloth title was also produced in a different form.

According to the IWM questionnaire all ranks of the 1st Battalion wore gilt Staffordshire knots on their collars.

On joining the 25th Division in 1917 all ranks wore the red horseshoe – divisional sign – and the brigade badge; there is no record of a battalion sign being worn.

In the 39th Division all ranks wore a golden horseshoe; there is evidence that a battalion badge was worn.

The South Staffordshire Regiment 165

A newly commissioned officer of the 3rd Battalion.

Only regulation badges were worn in the 3rd Battalion, as shown by this private.

Although badges were supposed to be worn in a specified way, they were often not. A private in the 1st Battalion wearing the pink circle less than eight inches from the seam.

In Italy a blue circle was worn on the pagri. Although the IWM questionnaire gives the position of the badge as the left side, here it is being worn on the right.

The Dorsetshire Regiment

Dorchester was the regimental home town of the regiment where the 3rd Battalion were trained at The Keep. Both regular battalions were out of the country; the 1st was in Belfast, the 2nd at Poona. All ranks wore a common cap badge, officers wore collar badges and other ranks wore a curved shoulder title – **DORSET**.

1st Battalion

The battalion landed in France on 16/8/14 with the 15th Brigade, 5th Division. It transferred to the 95th Brigade, 32nd Division, at the end of 1915 becoming 14th Brigade, 32nd Division, a few days later. It fought with the division on the Western Front for the remainder of the war.

Badges: a 'Brass Title Shoulder badge (sic) worn by the Battalion on proceeding to France August 1914.' The first badge was introduced in April 1915 by Major Cowie, CMG, DSO, commanding the battalion at the time. A shoulder title in red silk embroidered on pale grey cotton (Cash's title) was worn on both sleeves directly below the shoulder seams: **1st DORSET**; it was worn throughout the war. In the 14th Brigade all ranks wore a red 1⅝″ diamond on each upper arm, infantry battalions were identified by bars underneath to show regimental seniority. This was painted on the left side of the helmet from about June 1916; the single bar under the diamond was ½″ × 1¼″. As the most senior regiment they wore a single red 2⅛″ × ″ bar from February to August 1916 when a Royal Scots battalion joined the brigade; they then became the second senior regiment and wore two red bars. In 1917 the two bars were used to identify the company by their colour: red – A Company; green – B Company; yellow – C Company; blue – D Company; black – HQ Company. From June 1916 the red diamond, $1¼'' \times 1¼''$, was painted above a single red bar, $1¼ \times ½''$, on the left side of the helmet. This was changed to two bars in August and in 1917 to company colours.

The battalion wore its puttees to show two 'V's in front with the trousers pulled down over puttees the width of the band from the knee-cap. Collar badges were worn by the RSM and bandmaster. Band members wore the lyre badge.

2nd Battalion

Serving in India, the battalion went to the Persian Gulf in November 1914 and fought in Mesopotamia. It was captured at Kut-al-Amara on 29/4/16 and a composite battalion of Dorsets and Norfolks was formed from drafts and recovered wounded. The battalion was reconstituted in July 1916 as part of the Tigris Corps. In January 1917 it joined the 9th Brigade, 3rd Indian Division, serving in Palestine.

Badges: in September 1917 the battalion was commanded by a captain who informed the NWM about the battalion badges. 'This Battalion, beyond the Official Cap Badge, has no other special badges or marks of distinction, except a green band of ribbon between the 3rd and 4th folds of the puggrees (sic) of the topee worn in tropical countries'; this had been sanctioned on 29/8/12. Officers' lanyards were of green cord and worn on the left shoulder. Puttees were crossed in the 3rd and 4th folds from the bottom.

3rd (Reserve) Battalion

It formed part of the home defences serving in the Portland Garrison.

Badges: only regulation badges worn.

168　Badges of the Regular Infantry, 1914–1918

A sergeant gymnastics instructor of the 1st Battalion showing off his badges. The metal title was replaced by a cloth tape with the battalion details above the brigade sign over the battalion badge and company indicator.

A late 1915/early 1916 photograph, using the PH bag as a reference, of a soldier in the brigade headquarters. Interestingly he is wearing a Kitchener unit leather belt.

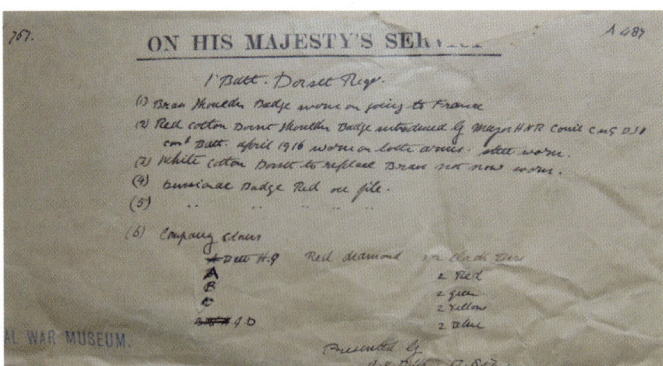

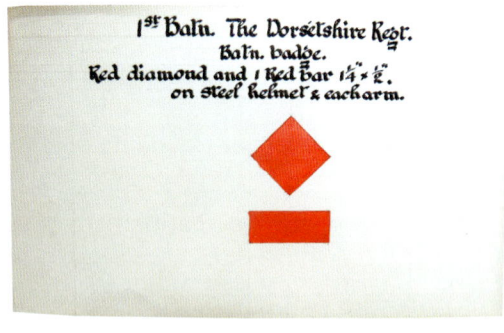

The envelope detailing the badges worn by the 1st Battalion received by the NWM on 13/8/17.

Original artwork detailing the 1st Battalion badge before company badges were introduced and when the battalion was the most senior in the brigade.

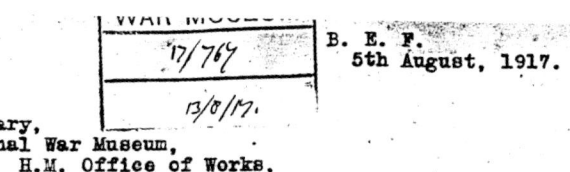

B. E. F.
5th August, 1917.

The Secretary,
   National War Museum,
      H.M. Office of Works,
         Westminster.

Sir.,
   Ref your No.17/767 D.13/6/17. I have the honour to forward the Badges worn by the 1st Battalion Dorsetshire Regiment during the War.
They are numbered 1 to 6.

(1) The Brass Title Shoulder badge worn by the Battalion on proceeding to France August 1914.

(2) The Red Cotton "1st Dorset" badge introduced by Major. H.N.R. Cowie, C.M.G., D.S.O., commanding the Battalion in April 1915. - worn on both arms below the Shoulder Strap. This badge is still worn.

(3) White Cotton Dorset - to replace brass title - not now worn.

(4) The 32nd. Divisional Badge in Red.
   Each Brigade in the Division having a separate pattern - 14th Infantry Brigade, to which the Battalion belonged on joining this Division in January 1916, by a Diamond Shaped Red Patch - each Battalion having Bars below in accordance with seniority of Regiment. The 1st. Dorset Regiment being Senior Regiment wore one Bar and Brigade Badge below the Red Cotton "1st Dorset."

(5) August 1916, the Battalion became the Second Senior Regiment and wore the Diamond and two Bars.

(6) As it was necessary to distinguish Companies etc, the colour of the Seniority Bars were changed in 1917, so that each Company of any Battalion in the Division would always be known in addition to the Regiment and Brigade.

            Battalion Headquarters; Red Diamond & 2 Black Bars.
            "A" Company.   "   "   " 2 Red Bars.
            "B" Company.   "   "   " 2 Green Bars.
            "C" Company.   "   "   " 2 Yellow Bars.
            "D" Company.   "   "   " 2 Blue Bars.

   These Badges are at present worn by the Battalion with the Red Cotton "1st. Dorset" above them.

         I have the honour to be,
            Sir,
               Your obedient servant

                        Major
5. 8. 17.   Commanding 1st Dorset Regiment.

On 5/8/17 the CO of the Battalion sent details of the badge worn, dating the Sergeant Gymnastic Instructor photograph sometime after August 1916.

170 Badges of the Regular Infantry, 1914–1918

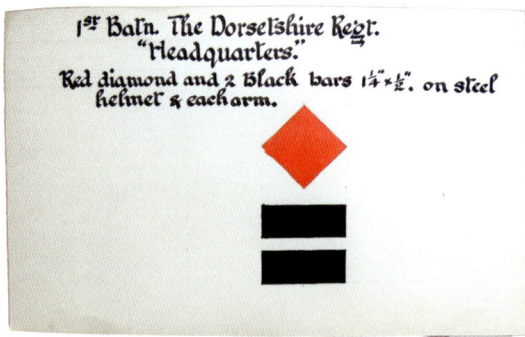
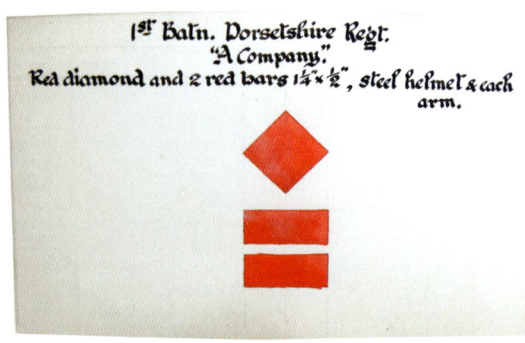
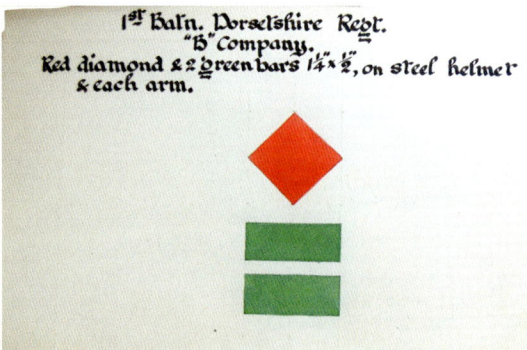
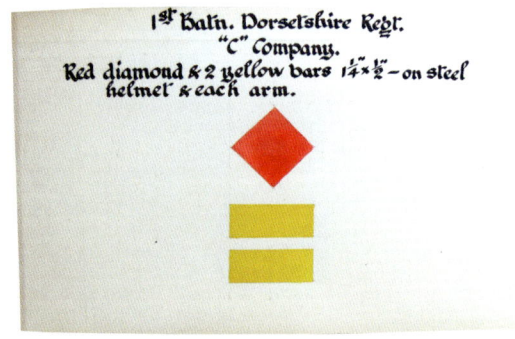
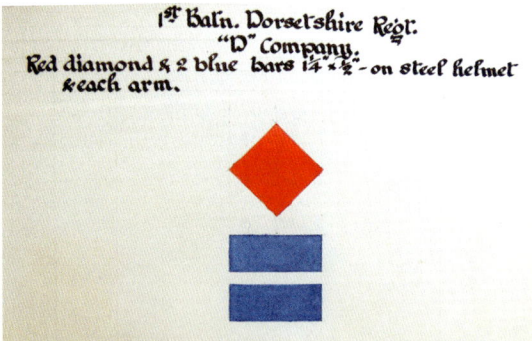

Original NWM artwork detailing the badges worn by the 1st Battalion.

HQ Company, 1st Battalion.

The Dorsetshire Regiment

1st Battalion, A Company.

B Company, 1st Battalion.

1st Battalion, C Company – the yellow has faded.

D Company, 1st Battalion.

The complete set of battalion/regimental badges worn by the 1st Battalion.

From February to August 1916 the battalion was the senior regiment in the brigade and wore one bar below the brigade sign.

The sergeant with a moustache on the left is in the 1st Battalion but is not wearing a battalion title.

172   Badges of the Regular Infantry, 1914–1918

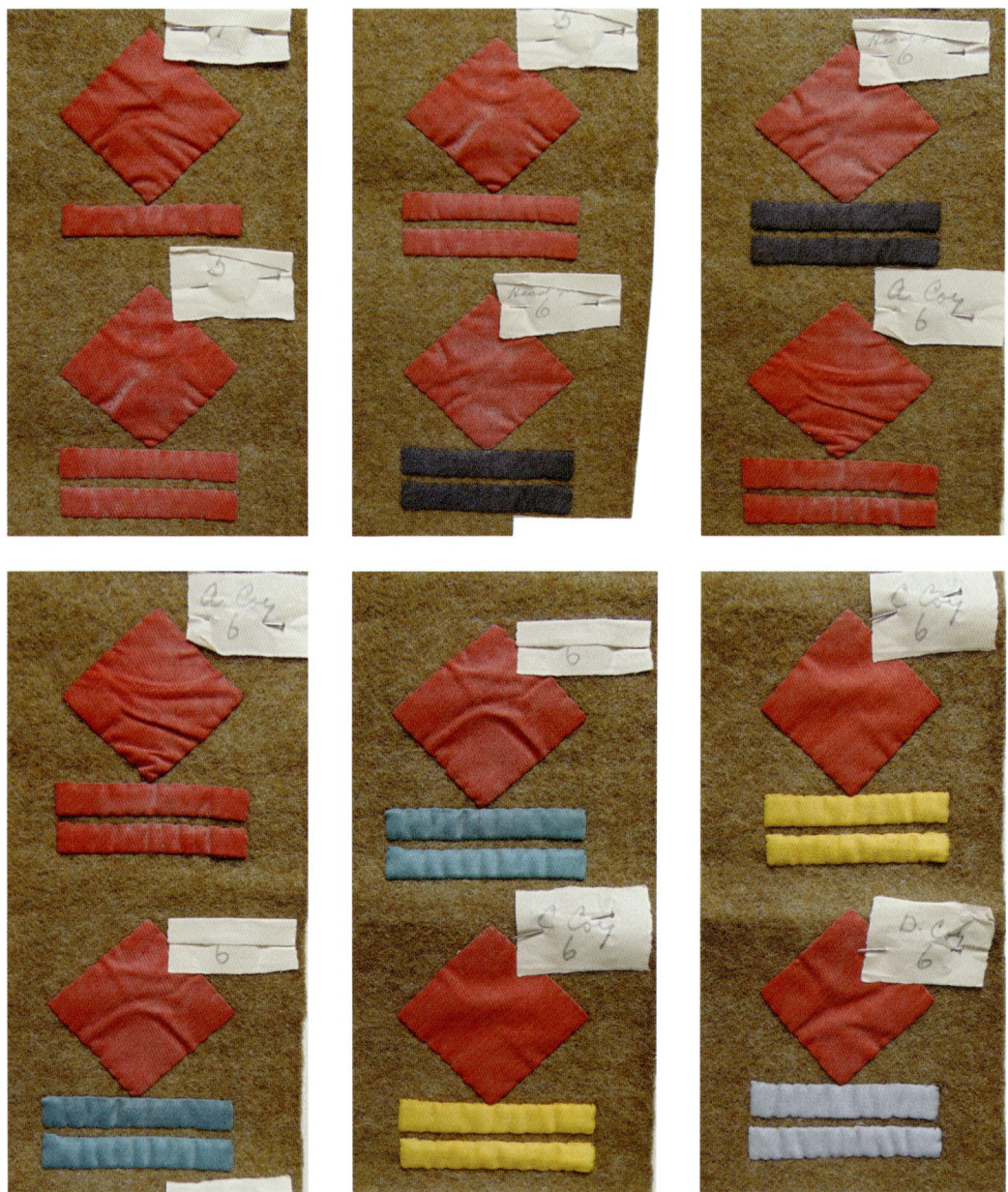

All the badges sent by the battalion were on one long piece of khaki uniform with HQ at the top and D Company at the bottom.

The Prince of Wales's Volunteers (South Lancashire Regiment)

The home depot for the regiment was Peninsula Barracks in Warrington where the 3rd Battalion trained. Quetta was the overseas station for the 1st Battalion; the 2nd were at Tidworth. All ranks wore a common cap badge, officers wore collar badges, and other ranks wore a curved shoulder title – **S.LANCASHIRE**.

1st Battalion

The battalion remained in India throughout the war.

Badges: a white vertical rectangle 2⅝" × 2" with the central part of the cap badge above **S.LAN.R** embroidered in red was worn on the left side of the pagri by all ranks. Hose-tops were khaki coloured. Buglers wore a green dress cord with two plaits, one on the left breast and a large one coming from under the right arm up to the first button of the tunic. Officers wore their rank on the shoulder straps on campaign. Steel helmets were not worn. Officers did not wear collar badges on the field service tunic.

2nd Battalion

Landing in France on 14/8/14 as part of the 7th Brigade, 3rd Division, the brigade joined the 25th Division in October 1915. Days later the battalion moved to the 75th Brigade, 25th Division, and in June 1918 to the 64th Brigade, 21st Division, and nine days later to the 89th Brigade, 30th Division.

Badges: no badges were worn with the 3rd Division, but on joining the 25th Division it adopted the divisional system: a brigade sign on the back of the collar – a green bar (lozenge) for the 75th Brigade – above a red horseshoe – the divisional sign – about ½″ below the collar. Interestingly the diagram sent to the IWM after the war by the CO has the horseshoe inverted. The 2nd Battalion had its origins in the 82nd Regiment of Foot raised in 1783 and adopted its number in white on a red oval 1″ × 1⅜″ as the battalion identifier. In 1920 Lieutenant Colonel Herbert, Battalion CO, explained this was 'to distinguish the Battalion from the Service Battalions serving in the same Brigade'. It was worn on the upper left arm just below the shoulder. The wearing of this badge was recalled by Second Lieutenant J. Adamson who served with the battalion in 1917. A white stencilled 82, 1½″ high, was painted on the front of the steel helmet and worn by all ranks. In June 1918 the 30th Division sign was worn on both arms just below the shoulder seams with the oval white on red 82 badges, worn in the centre of the back just below the collar. Red cloth was worn behind the cap badge.

Puttees were worn in the spiral manner; crossing over was not permitted.

3rd (Reserve) Battalion

A home service battalion that served in Warrington, Crosby and Barrow-in-Furness.

Badges: the Battalion CO forwarded a number of battalion badges, from units serving overseas, to the NWM on 22/8/17 and regretted that he could not send more but this was because the officers had returned to their units. As he did not mention his own battalion's badges it is safe to assume that only regulation cloth and metal badges were worn. Private J.A. Pollitt recalled only wearing a cap badge and metal shoulder titles when he was with the battalion.

In India the 1st Battalion wore regulation metal badges and a pagri flash. The sun helmet on the right belongs to a 1st Battalion soldier.

The Prince of Wales's Volunteers (South Lancashire Regiment)

Part of a company of the 1st Battalion just before the outbreak of the war. The sun helmet on the ground in the front centre of the photograph shows the battalion flash.

The battalion sent in a diagram of their flash to the IWM and right is an image of the flash provided in the 1980s.

The cloth title authorised for all battalions in 1916 was obsolete by April 1919.

A red backing was worn behind the other ranks' cap badge by the 2nd Battalion.

2nd BATTN. THE P. of W.V. SOUTH LANCASHIRE REGT.

1. Western Front. 13th August 1914 to Armistice. Active Operations. and from Armistice to May 1919. training and special duty at Boulogne.

2. '82' stencilled on front of Steel Helmet, same for all Ranks. Size of figures about 1½ inches.

3. None worn.

4. None worn.

5. Not applicable.

6. Piece of Red Cloth worn under Cap Badge.

7. Same pattern for all Ranks. Officers bronzed, other ranks polished.

8. Up to September 1915, the Battn. were with the original formation of the 7th Brigade, 3rd Division, In that month was transferred to serve with the "New Armies" and joined 75th Infantry Brigade, 25th Division. Here first instructions of special marks on Service Dress Jackets took place and the following were adopted.

    Divisional Sign. Red Horse Shoe   Red Cloth worn in
    (25th Division) centre of back about ½ inch below the edge
                     of the collar.

    Brigade Sign
    (75th Inf.Bde.) Green Lozenge   green cloth, worn
                     on collar immediately above Divisional Mark.

    Battalion Sign. "82" embroidered -white on red- 82 - in
                    circular form worn on upper left arm of
                    Jacket just below shoulder.

    About June 1918 the Battalion was transferred to 30th Division when the following signs were taken into wear in place of those mentioned above.

    Divisional Sign Lord Derby's Crest, embroidered white on
    (30th Division). Black worn on both upper arms of Service
                     Jacket, just below shoulders.

    Brigade Sign.   Nil.
    (89th Bde.)
    Battalion Sign. Same pattern as in 25th Division but worn in
                     centre of back just below collar of Jacket.

Information provided by the 2nd Battalion to the IWM about the badges and uniform worn during the war.

The Prince of Wales's Volunteers (South Lancashire Regiment)

In the 75th Brigade the 2nd Battalion wore a red horseshoe and green bar on their back.

To differentiate the battalion from the service battalions in the division the 2nd Battalion adopted a red oval with the number of their original line regiment.

In the 30th Division the battalion badge was worn in the centre of the back and the divisional sign on both arms.

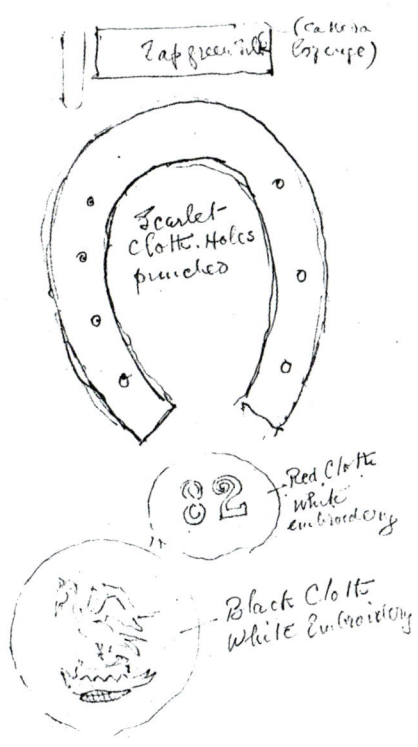

The CO of the 2nd Battalion sent the IWM a diagram to explain the badges used. For some reason he drew the horseshoe upside down.

The Welsh Regiment

Maindy barracks in Cardiff was the Regimental Depot and home of the 3rd Battalion at the beginning of the war; it was used by the American army later in the war. The 1st Battalion was at Chakrata and the 2nd in England. All ranks wore a common cap badge, officers wore collar badges, and other ranks wore a curved shoulder title – **WELSH**.

1st Battalion

After arrival from India on 22/12/14 the battalion became part of the 84th Brigade, 28th Division. It served on the Western Front for ten months from 18/1/15 and then went to Salonika via Egypt. It finished the war north of Lake Doiran in Macedonia.

Badges: on arrival in France a white 3″ square was worn on the back of officers' tunics. It was withdrawn as unsatisfactory in January 1915 and replaced by scarlet Prince of Wales's feathers 3½″ × 3″ that was worn for the rest of the war. When slouch hats were issued experimentally in Salonika in summer 1916, all ranks wore a smaller version 1¾″ wide × 1½″ high on the turned up side; when the hats were withdrawn the badge was discontinued. From October 1915 a red strip was worn across the base of the shoulder straps by all ranks in the 28th Division, but this is not mentioned by the Battalion CO in his letter dated 15/8/17. Officers had a cap badge painted on the front of the steel helmet in gold and silver.

2nd Battalion

Stationed at Bordon, it formed part of the 3rd Brigade, 1st Division. It landed in France on 13/8/14 and remained on the Western Front with the brigade.

Badges: apart from regulation badges the only distinguishing marks worn were those to identify specialists. An isosceles triangle, 1″ sides × 1¼″ base, was worn on the back of the collar: bombers – red; rifle grenadiers – black; Lewis gunners – yellow; rifleman – green. The badges were no longer in use by 1918. Lieutenant J. Stileman served with the battalion during 1916/17; in 1990 he told the writer that no battalion badges were worn: 'In the 1st Division we didn't wear a flash and despised other units who did as mere New Comers.' In 1988, Private Ivor Watkins recalled swapping his red dragon and green disc when he left the 15th Welsh for a white/red/green cloth bar when he joined the battalion in August 1918. It was worn on both arms below the seams.

A scarlet Prince of Wales's feathers was worn by officers on their back from January 1915.

3rd (Reserve) Battalion

The battalion served in Cardiff until June 1916 when it moved to Barry, followed by a move in October to Kinmel. In May 1917 it moved to Redcar as part of the Tees Garrison where it stayed.

Badges: regulation cloth and metal.

180   Badges of the Regular Infantry, 1914–1918

The officers' back badge was larger than the badge worn by all in Salonika.

The slouch hat badge worn by all ranks in Salonika.

Only regulation badges were worn by the 2nd Battalion but specialists were identified by triangles worn on the back of the collar: red – bombers; black – rifle grenadiers; yellow – Lewis gunners; green – riflemen.

In 1988 ex-Private Ivor Watkins sent the writer this piece of ribbon to illustrate the badge he had worn serving with the 2nd Battalion in late 1918.

The cloth title adopted in 1916 was obsolete by October 1919.

Although the stretcher bearer's badge was officially obsolete from 1901 it continued to be used. This 3rd Battalion soldier is showing only regulation badges and an unofficial cloth badge.

All ranks of the 1st Battalion wore the divisional sign – a red band – on their shoulder straps; other ranks also wore a shoulder title.

Headquarters staff of the 2nd Battalion somewhere in France after 1916. Only regulation badges are being worn.

The Black Watch (Royal Highlanders)

Perth was the home of the regiment with the 3rd Battalion at Queen's Barracks. The 1st were in Oudenarde Barracks, Aldershot, the 2nd were overseas in Bareilly, India. All ranks wore a common cap badge, officers wore collar badges and other ranks wore a shoulder title – **BW**.

1st Battalion

As part of the 1st Brigade, 1st Division, the battalion landed in France on 14/8/14, serving with the division on the Western Front throughout the war.

Badges: only regulation badges were worn throughout the war apart from specialist 1½″ square colour patches: red – bombers; black – rifle grenadiers; yellow – Lewis gunners; green – riflemen. A red hackle was painted on the left side of the helmet in 1918. Corporal Frank MacFarlane MSM and French MM, a pre-war regular (joined 20/2/12) who served with the battalion throughout the war, recalled, in December 1987, wearing R.H. in brass on his shoulder straps and a red hackle on his helmet. As a signaller he wore a blue band on the bottom of his left sleeve below brass crossed flags. In 1914 the glengarry was worn, replaced in 1915 by a blue Balmoral and in 1916 by a tam-o'-shanter – worn until the end of the war. The standard regimental badge was worn on the glengarry, a red hackle without badge or rosette with the Balmoral. The tam-o'-shanter was worn as issued without tails, except by officers who usually wore tails. 'Some of the officers and senior N.C.Os of the 1st Bn. wore a badge with a "42" in lieu of a St. Andrew's cross.' Short puttees and khaki hose tops were worn. The kilt and apron were worn without the sporran. 'Pipers wore ordinary regulation dress,

Royal Stewart Kilt, khaki hose tops, skeleton web equipment, etc. Sporrans of ordinary pipers and sergeants pattern were worn from 1917 onwards… Dirks were carried.'

2nd Battalion

The Bareilly Brigade, Meerut Division, left Karachi for France on 21/9/14. After a year on the Western Front it embarked for Mesopotamia. On arrival the brigade became the 21st Indian Brigade, 7th Indian Division. After heavy casualties it formed, in February 1916, the Highland Battalion with the 1st Seaforth Highlanders in the 19th Brigade, 7th Indian Division, resuming its identity in the 21st Brigade five months later. In January 1918 the division moved to Palestine and Tripoli.

Badges: a red hackle was worn from 1916 on the left side between the top turn of the pagri and on the steel helmet; unfortunately, as there was great difficulty in getting hold of them in Mesopotamia, Lieutenant Colonel Stewart, the Battalion CO, was unable to send the NWM a specimen, but helpfully suggested they contact the 1st Battalion for one. From 10/10/18 a red hackle was fixed to the left side of the ordnance issued helmet cover. All ranks below sergeant wore a khaki tam-o'-shanter without tails with a red hackle on the left side of the bonnet. Sergeants and all ranks above wore a blue Balmoral with tails and red hackle on the left side. No identification badges were worn on the tunic and officers did not wear collar badges.

'Short puttees were always worn with the kilt and also khaki Hose-tops. In Palestine, long trews and short puttees were worn daily after 18.00 hrs. in order to lessen the probability of mosquito bites. Shorts worn with khaki Hose tops – short puttees and garters. Puttees worn with four folds, ¼" between each fold and finishing on the inside of the ankle.' Pipers wore Royal Stewart tartan kilts. Bandsmen had a 'regimental badge on pouches and belt.'

3rd (Reserve) Battalion

After three years in Scotland the battalion moved to Ireland for the duration.

Badges: writing from Nigg on 10/8/17, the Battalion CO informed the NWM 'that no badges or marks of distinction are worn on the sleeve or the back of the S.D. Jackets of the men under' his command. Only regulation cloth and metal badges were worn. The tam-o'-shanter was worn with a small red hackle but no cap badge. Collar badges were not worn by officers. When wearing a kilt, short puttees were worn with Tullibardine hose tops. Pipers wore Royal Stewart tartan kilts.

The soldier on the right, resplendent in a kilt, has just been released from hospital in Alexandria. The studio photograph shows a hackle in the pagri, a lack of shoulder titles, and the short puttees and khaki hose tops mentioned in the IWM questionnaire.

An officer of the 1st Battalion wearing a hackle and an unusual small version of the cap badge.

Old affiliations die hard and some officers in the 1st Battalion wore the badge of the 42nd (Royal Highland) Regiment of Foot which dated back to the pre-Childers Reforms of 1881.

Other ranks wore a metal RH shoulder title until it was replaced in 1916 by a cloth title.

A soldier's function in the 2nd Battalion was identified by a small square on the back of the collar: red – bombers; black – bombers; yellow – Lewis Gunners; green – riflemen.

Men of the 2nd Battalion somewhere in Mesopotamia; the hackle, short puttees and khaki hose tops are clearly visible.

A 1914/15 photograph of the 3rd Battalion soldier wearing spats over his shoes. Like so many soldiers he is not wearing shoulder titles.

The 2nd Battalion Tug-of-War Team in 1919 when serving with the Egyptian Expeditionary Force. None of the officers have collar badges, the officer on the left is not wearing a hackle and the other two officers are wearing tam-o'-shanter without a badge but one has a hackle as does the RSM.

The Oxfordshire & Buckinghamshire Light Infantry

At the start of the war the 3rd Battalion was based in the home depot of the regiment, Bullingdon Barracks, Cowley; the 2nd Battalion was close by at Aldershot, the 1st Battalion was at Ahmednagar, India. All ranks wore a common cap badge, officers and men in the 1st Battalion wore collar gorgets, officers in the 2nd Battalion wore collar badges. Other ranks wore a curved shoulder title – **OXF&BUCKS** below a bugle.

1st Battalion

The battalion landed in Mesopotamia in late November 1914. It was captured at Kut on 29/4/16 but later reformed as a provisional battalion. It became the 1st Battalion again on 19/10/17. Until the end of the war it was part of the 50th Brigade, 15th Indian Division.

Badges: while serving in the Middle East, Major Whitall, the Battalion CO, informed the NWM in September 1917 that the battalion wore a pagri patch in silk for officers and cotton for other ranks: red 2″ × 2″ diamond embroidered in white with stringed bugle and **OXFORD**. The Field Service cap was Austrian Pattern; green with silver bugle for other ranks, plain khaki with small khaki rosette on front for officers. All ranks wore an unusual collar arrangement: a gorget button and khaki cord on each collar. Ranks from sergeant upwards wore small regimental buttons and officers wore the title **OXFORD** on the shoulder straps of the khaki drill tunic. Lanyards were not worn; a leather whistle strap was buttoned on to the top button of the jacket. The top of the puttee was turned down over the puttee strings. Bandsmen wore brown pouches with gold bugles and bugler's lines were worn over the right shoulder – colour not known. Officers wore metal dics (sic) on their shoulder straps.

2nd Battalion

As part of the 5th Brigade, 2nd Division, the battalion landed at Boulogne on 14/8/14 and fought on the Western Front for the entire war with the division.

Badges: only regulation badges were worn on the uniform. This was confirmed by the Battalion CO on 6/10/17: 'We have not had to wear any special badges of the kind you mention, so that I have nothing I can send.' However, distinctive markings were permitted on the helmet which he did not mention. In July 1916, on the left of the helmet cover all ranks wore a horizontal 1″ piece of regimental ribbon in proportions: dark blue (⅓)/gold (⅙)/red (⅙)/dark blue (⅓). Second Lieutenant E. Simmons (later Lieutenant Colonel) served with the battalion from mid-1918 and was certain that he only wore regulation badges on his tunic but there was a patch of regimental colours on the sandbag cover of his helmet. The IWM 1922 questionnaire adds that officers wore a silver cap badge on the front of the helmet.

3rd (Reserve) Battalion

After three years serving in Portsmouth, the battalion moved in October 1917 to Dover for the remainder of the war.

Badges: writing from Fort Purbrook, Cosham, the Battalion CO sent the NWM a detailed diagram of the regiment's badges but did not include his own battalion in the record. It is safe to assume that none were worn except regulation cloth and metal badges. Further correspondence with the battalion elicited a detailed response. 'On shoulders straps of NCOs and men Bugle (mouthpiece to the front) and Oxford & Bucks numerals. WOs: Gorget Buttons and string on collar, nothing on shoulder straps. Officers: Gorget Buttons and Strings. Badges of Rank (brass) on shoulder straps.' Second Lieutenant H.M. Gray served with the battalion for a few months in mid-1917 and recalled that only regulation badges were worn. Similarly, Second Lieutenant E. Simons who served in early 1918 with the battalion was certain only regulation metal badges were worn.

188   Badges of the Regular Infantry, 1914–1918

All ranks of the 1st Battalion wore a red diamond pagri flash but the quality differed; this is embroidered on felt and was for other ranks.

A studio portrait that clearly shows the unique collar patches worn by the 1st Battalion.

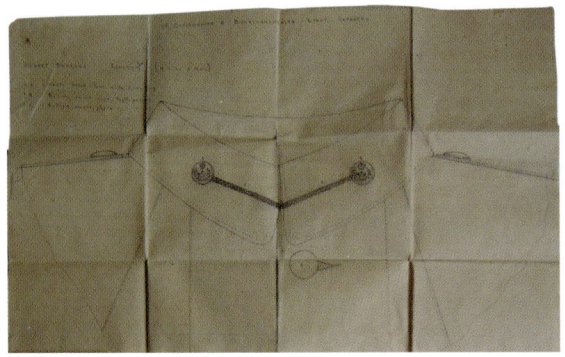

Two diagrams showing how the gorget button and khaki cord were worn on a soldier's tunic.

In 1916 the metal title was replaced by a cloth version worn in facing pairs.

A lighter cloth title was worn by troops in hot climates.

The Oxfordshire & Buckinghamshire Light Infantry

Two studio portraits that show the regulation cap badge and the shoulder title worn by other ranks in the third battalion.

In the 2nd Division few non-regulation badges were worn but some wore helmet badges. The 2nd Battalion wore a rectangle of regimental colours.

The Essex Regiment

Warley Barracks near Brentford was the home of the 3rd Battalion while the 1st Battalion was overseas and the 2nd at Chatham. All ranks wore a common cap badge, officers wore collar badges and other ranks wore a curved shoulder title – **ESSEX**.

1st Battalion

Arriving from Mauritius in December 1914, the battalion was part of the 88th Brigade, 29th Division, when it left for Gallipoli. From mid-March 1916 it served on the Western Front with the division until February 1918 when it joined the 112th Brigade, 37th Division.

Badges: no badges are recorded during service on Gallipoli. From May 1916 a red 2″ square diamond was worn 3″ below the collar on the back with the 29th Division sign on the arms. The divisional sign was worn on the front of the steel helmet with the red diamonds on both sides from July 1916. In December 1917 the red diamond was replaced by a vertical black diamond, 1½″ sides, with horizontal ¼″ yellow stripe. On joining the 37th Division a yellow horseshoe was worn on both sleeves 1″ above a red square with a red triangle on the back of the collar. Companies were identified by ½″ bands on the base of the shoulder straps: blue – W Company; red – X Company; mauve – Y Company; green – Z Company. Buglers lines were stated to have been worn but no detail was provided.

2nd Battalion

The battalion landed at Le Havre on 24/8/14 as part of the 12th Brigade, 4th Division. In November 1915 the brigade was transferred to the 36th (Ulster) Division and attached to 109th Brigade. It returned to the 4th Division and fought for the remainder of the war with the division.

Badges: the first badge was a red 2″ square diamond worn on both upper arms, with a smaller version worn on the helmet which contradicts a 31st Staff Order of 20/6/16 that states the helmet badge size as 2″ and that it was worn before the arm badge. This was changed to a 2″ × 1½″ horizontal rectangle, divided vertically, in regimental colours – violet/yellow/black – worn on the helmet and 3″ below the seams on both arms below a red ram's head. The wearing of the latter two badges in April 1918 to the end of the war was recalled by Lieutenant J. Harford (later Sir James) in May 1988; he even sent me his badges.

3rd (Reserve) Battalion

Part of the Harwich Garrison, it did not serve abroad.

Badges: Second Lieutenant Solly (later Lieutenant Colonel) served with the battalion in 1917 and informed the writer that only regulation cloth and metal badges were worn.

The original artwork provided for the badges worn by the 1st Battalion providing colour and position of wear.

192   Badges of the Regular Infantry, 1914–1918

Original examples of the badges sent by the 1st Battalion to the NWM in 1917.

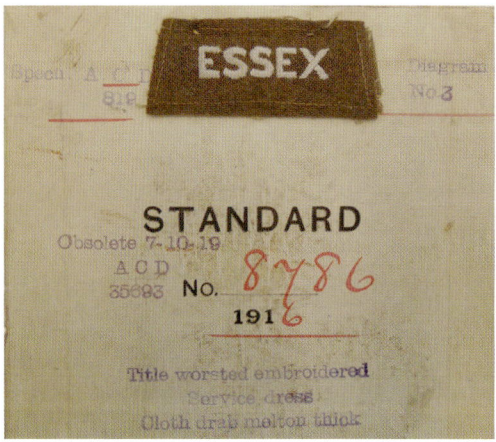

From late 1916 all battalions of the regiment adopted a cloth shoulder title; it was obsolete three years later.

These badges were worn by Sir James Harford, then a lieutenant when he served in the 2nd Battalion from April 1918 to the end of the war.

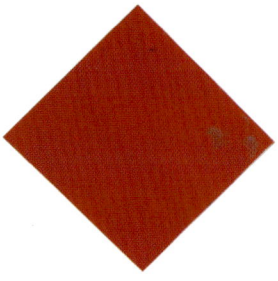

An original 2nd Battalion badge and artwork from late 1917.

The Essex Regiment

Newly commissioned Second Lieutenant Tebbutt portrays the perfect example of an officer serving with the 3rd Battalion while waiting an overseas posting during 1915.

A transport officer of the 3rd Battalion with his dogs later in the war; his rank is no longer on the sleeve.

A private in the Harwich Garrison; even at home shoulder titles were not always worn.

On transfer to the 39th Division, the 1st Battalion followed the divisional system and wore the golden horseshoe and company bars on the shoulder straps: blue – W Company; red – X Company; mauve – Y Company; green – Z Company.

The Sherwood Foresters
(Nottinghamshire & Derbyshire Regiment)

The 3rd Battalion was at the home depot, Normanton Barracks, Derby, in August 1914 and the regular battalions were in Bombay – 1st Battalion, and Sheffield – 2nd Battalion. All other ranks and officers of the 2nd and 3rd Battalion wore a common cap badge; officers of the 1st Battalion wore the badge without the scroll. Officers wore collar badges and other ranks wore a curved shoulder title – **NOTTS/AND/DERBY**.

1st Battalion

Arriving from India on 2/10/14 it joined the 24th Brigade, 8th Division. For nine months in 1915/16 the battalion was part of the 23rd Division before returning to the 8th Division for the remainder of the war.

Badges: adopted in February 1917, Private R.F. Hughes recalled wearing, in 1918, a 2″ maroon (front) and Lincoln green vertically bisected circle on the sleeves 1″ below the shoulder seam. Officers had a unique helmet cover: dark khaki drill with a four-fold pagri, the 5th fold dark green with the cap badge at the front and a small regimental button on the top. A green round weave lanyard was worn from the right shoulder by officers; they also wore the regimental cap badge without the scroll underneath. The regimental badge was fixed on the front of bandsmen's pouches. Officers wore 'Hill's pattern lace up gaiters'.

2nd Battalion

The battalion was part of the 18th Brigade, 6th Division, which landed at St. Nazaire on 11/9/14. In October 1915 it was transferred to the 71st Brigade which had joined the division. It remained with the 6th Division until the end of the war.

Badges: in July 1917 the Battalion CO informed the NWM that the only badges worn were regulation: 'I beg to inform you that this Battalion has never yet worn any of the badges referred to.' This was confirmed in 1920 in the IWM questionnaire completed by the battalion and recalled by Privates N. Clayton and T. Fidler in 1987. However, in 1916 a chocolate brown Maltese Cross was painted over the top of the helmet and when canvas covers were adopted in 1917 a green cloth band was worn around the crown. When no cover was worn the helmet was painted chocolate brown with a green band. Like the 1st Battalion, officer's covers had a pagri with the fifth fold in green. This was to a certain extent a continuation of the pagri worn on the Foreign Service helmet, with other ranks wearing the top fold green and officers the top three. It was made by Messrs. Hawkes in London.

There was no battalion lanyard but some officers wore a green whistle cord over the right shoulder. Puttees were worn spiral. Green buglers' lines were worn out of the line. While not related to badges, it is interesting to note that battalion horses wore chocolate and green brow bands with rosettes.

3rd (Reserve) Battalion

At the start of the war the battalion moved to its war station at Plymouth and in May 1915 moved to Sunderland where it remained.

Badges: regulation cloth and metal.

4th (Extra Reserve) Battalion

The battalion's war station was Sunderland where it was joined by the 3rd Battalion forming part of the Tyne Garrison.

Badges: only regulation cloth and metal badges were worn, recalled an anonymous veteran.

196 Badges of the Regular Infantry, 1914–1918

Following the 8th Division system the 1st Battalion adopted a vertically bisected circle badge: maroon (front) and Lincoln green. It was worn by all ranks on both shoulders.

Officers wore a unique helmet cover: dark khaki drill with a four-fold pagri, the fifth fold was dark green with the cap badge at the front and a small regimental button on the top. This is not visible on the specimen sent by the battalion in 1917.

Officers wore a green round weave lanyard from the right shoulder.

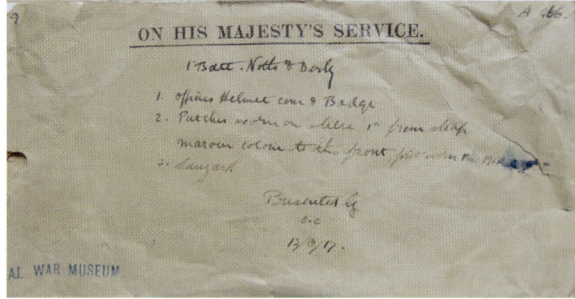

The badge, lanyard and helmet cover were sent by the battalion CO in August 1917 according to the envelope with the articles.

```
    2nd BATTN. THE NOTTS & DERBY REGIMENT.
    THE SHERWOOD FORESTERS.


1.    Western Theatre. France and Belgium.
      7.9.14 - 13.4.19.

2.    Steel Helmets issued painted Service Colour 1916.
      First markings ordered by Brigade in Chocolate     1917.
      then Regimentally covered with canvas 1917, with a green
      cloth band-afterwards painted chocolate with a green band 1918.
      Officers had a special helmet cover made by Messrs. Hawkes,
      London. Service Colour cloth with puggaree of same colour
      and a green fold at top.

3.    A green band on top of puggaree on the Wolseley Helmet.
      Officers 3 narrow green folds on top.
```

A section of the 1921 IWM questionnaire completed by the CO of the 2nd Battalion detailing the unusual steel helmet markings.

The Sherwood Foresters (Nottinghamshire & Derbyshire Regiment)

A private in the 3rd Battalion showing the badges worn: metal cap and shoulder titles. The lanyard is probably an affectation as there are no records of other ranks using them.

A newly commissioned officer displaying the standard badges worn by the regiment.

In 1916 metal titles were replaced by a standardised Melton cloth title. However, there were many variations: this is a painted version.

The Loyal North Lancashire Regiment

Fulwood Barracks, Preston, the Regimental Depot, was home to the 3rd Battalion. The 1st Battalion were in Tournay Barracks, Aldershot, the 2nd were in Bangalore. All ranks wore a common cap badge, officers wore collar badges and other ranks wore a curved shoulder title – **NLANCASHIRE**.

1st Battalion

The battalion landed at Le Havre on 13/8/14 with the 2nd Brigade. On 7/2/18 during the divisional reorganisation it was transferred to the 1st Brigade where it remained.

Badges: no unit-identifying badges were worn, only those sanctioned by the regulations. The battalion adjutant, Lieutenant Lindsell, informed the NWM of two methods employed by the battalion to identify a man's role: coloured squares worn on the centre on the back collar, and armbands. They were adopted in April 1917. A $1\frac{1}{4}''$ square on the back collar: green – riflemen section; red – bomber's section; black – rifle grenadier section; yellow – Lewis gunner's section; and a $17''$ long × $1\frac{1}{2}''$ wide armband with buckle, worn above the elbow on the left arm: red – orderlies; green – scouts; blue – signallers; white – mopping-up parties; yellow – carrying parties. Green canvas covers were worn on the helmet; there were no badges on it. Puttees were folded with three turns.

2nd Battalion

As part of the 27th Indian Brigade it landed at Tanga in German East Africa on 3/11/14 moving immediately to Mombasa. Between May and August 1915 it was in

South Africa due to the ill health of the battalion. In December 1916 it moved to Egypt as LoC troops becoming part of the 75th Division in April 1917. The battalion transferred to France in late May 1918 joining the 94th Brigade, 31st Division, and then in June the 101st Brigade, 34th Division.

Badges: in Africa and Palestine a badge was worn on the left side of the topee – **LOYAL/NORTH/LANCASHIRE** in white on a red half-circle – part of the red shoulder strap – sanctioned for wear on 29/8/12; recalled by Second Lieutenant H. Tunnadine in 1990. The cap badge was also often worn on the front. When supplies ran out, evidence suggests an inverted red circle was worn in its place. No markings were worn on the steel helmet. In the 34th Division a red (battalion colour) horizontal bar (brigade badge) was worn below the divisional sign on both arms by all ranks. There were no markings on the steel helmet. Puttees were worn with two turns in front. Bandsmen wore a double sized cap badge on the front of the pouch.

3rd (Reserve) Battalion

Within days of the start of hostilities the battalion moved to its war station, Felixstowe, where it stayed for the duration.

Badges: Second Lieutenant H. Tunnadine served in the battalion and recalled only seeing regulation cloth and metal badges.

1st Batn. L.N. Lancs. Regt.
Rifle Grenadiers - Black patch worn on back of collar.

Coloured squares worn on the back of the collar were used to identify a soldier's function: green – riflemen; red – bombers; black – rifle grenadiers; yellow – Lewis gunners.

Badges of the Regular Infantry, 1914–1918

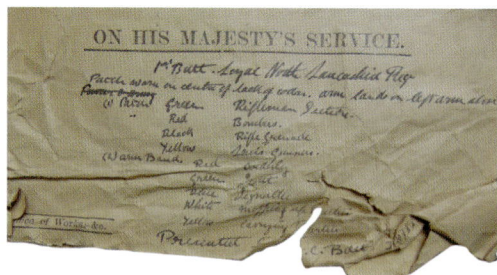

A rather battered envelope detailing the badges sent by the CO of the 1st Battalion in August 1917.

The 2nd Battalion wore part of the shoulder strap of the red tunic worn for ceremonial duties. When supplies ran out it was replaced by a red half-circle.

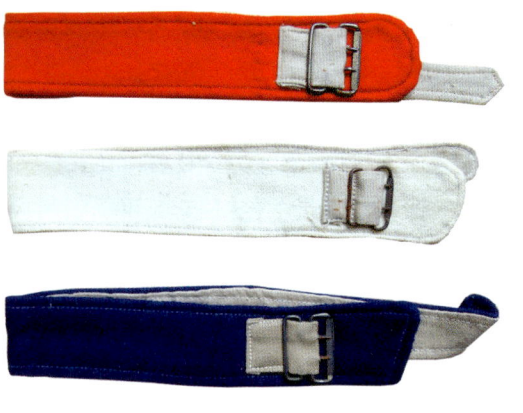

Armbands were also worn by the 1st Battalion to show a wearers function: red – orderlies; white – mopping-up parties; blue – signallers; green – scouts; yellow – carrying parties.

A Section of the 2nd Battalion with cap badge on the front of the pagri but no pagri flash visible.

The Loyal North Lancashire Regiment   201

A lieutenant of the 1st Battalion showing only regulation collar badges.

To conserve metal, cloth titles were introduced in late 1916. That for the North Lancashires did not last three years.

In the 34th Division all ranks wore a red vertical bar under the divisional sign.

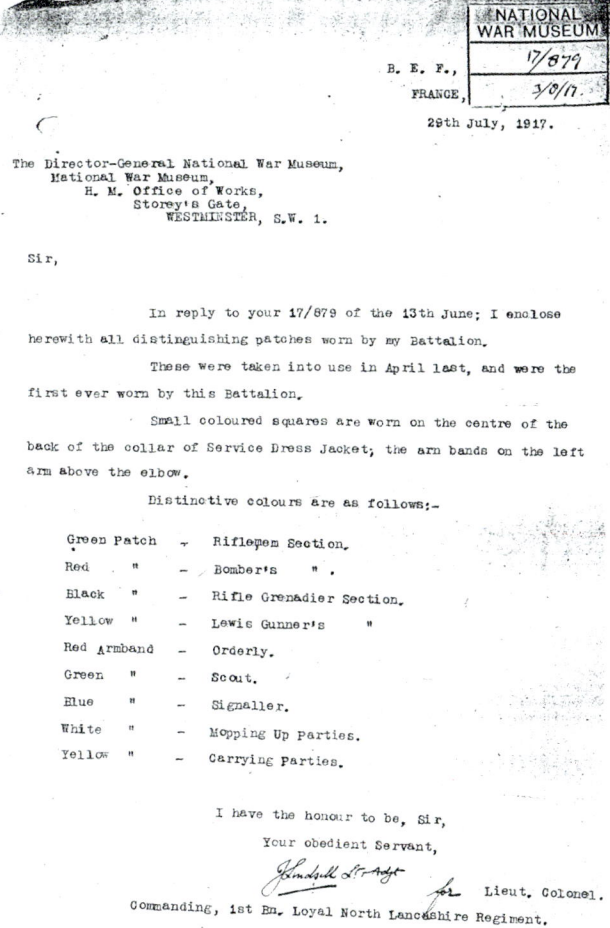

The letter sent by the 1st Battalion on 29/7/17 detailing the distinctive badges and armbands the battalion wore.

The half-circle was worn on the left side and photographic evidence shows that a vertical red bar and cap badge was also sometimes worn on the right side.

The noticeboard reads in French, Service Medical. These are the stretcher bearers of the 1st Battalion.

All ranks of the 34th Division wore the divisional sign on both arms.

Even when at home recuperating from wounds, soldiers did not always wear regulation badges. The only identification as to his unit is the cap badge.

Christmas 1914 and two youthful recruits in the 3rd Battalion pose for a keepsake. As in so many cases, one soldier is not wearing shoulder titles. Both, however, have a cap badge.

The Northamptonshire Regiment

The 3rd Battalion was at the home depot, Gibraltar Barracks in Northampton, the 1st Battalion were at Blackdown, Aldershot, and the 2nd Battalion were in Alexandria. All ranks wore a common cap badge, officers wore collar badges, and other ranks wore a curved shoulder title – **NORTHAMPTON**.

1st Battalion

Arriving in France from Aldershot on 13/8/14, the battalion served throughout the war in the 2nd Brigade, 1st Division.

Badges: for much of the war no cap badges were worn so the only battalion identifiers were the regulation badges on the tunic. However, specialists were identified. They wore an isosceles triangle, apex upwards, 2″ base with 1½″ sides on the back of the collar: green – riflemen; red – bombers; black – rifle grenadiers; yellow – Lewis gunners. Steel helmets were canvas covered and had no badges on them. During his service with the battalion, 21/7/16 to 12/12/17, Private B. Whayman was certain that the only badges he wore were his shoulder titles, and as a signaller crossed flags on his left arm; he was also a bomber and did not wear the red triangle on his collar but an inverted bomb. This possibly suggests that the coloured specialism badges were dying out in 1917; see other 1st Division battalions.

2nd Battalion

On arrival from Egypt in October 1914 the battalion joined the 24th Brigade, 8th Division. It landed in France on 5/11/14 and served with the division on the Western Front until the end of the war.

Badges: a 2″ red and black vertically bisected circle was worn on both sleeves from February 1917. A painted version, painted both sides of the helmet, red to the front, was adopted in early 1918 for wear by all ranks. From October 1917 to the end of the war, officers wore black whistle cords. Puttees were worn rolled outwards with two crosses in the centre of the shin.

3rd (Reserve) Battalion

From its war station in Portland, it went to Gillingham and Stroud, returning to Gillingham in March 1916. In March 1918 it became part of the Thames and Medway Garrison.

Badges: replying to the request for information about badges the Depot CO, Major Roberts, informed the IWM that the battalion 'was employed as a Training Battalion in England'. From the reply it is safe to assume that only regulation cloth and metal badges were worn.

As well as regulation badges the battalion wore coloured triangles on the back of the collar to show a soldier's function: green – riflemen; red – bombers; black – rifle grenadiers; yellow – Lewis gunners.

The Northamptonshire Regiment

1st BATTN. THE NORTHAMPTONSHIRE REGT.

1. Western 12.8.1914 to 10.5.1919.
2. No distinguishing marks during the War.
   Covered with canvas.
   Officers and men identical.
3. Nil.
4. No.
5. -
6. Nil.
7. No.
8. None.
9. No.
10. No.
11. None.
    Neither.
12. None.
13. No.
14. None.
15. Regulation pattern.
16. Regulation pattern.
17. -
18. -
19. -

The questionnaire completed by the CO of the battalion in 1921 was very brief.

The 8th Division had a very exact system of badges to identify units. In the 24th Brigade battalions wore vertically bisected circles on both arms: red (front) and black.

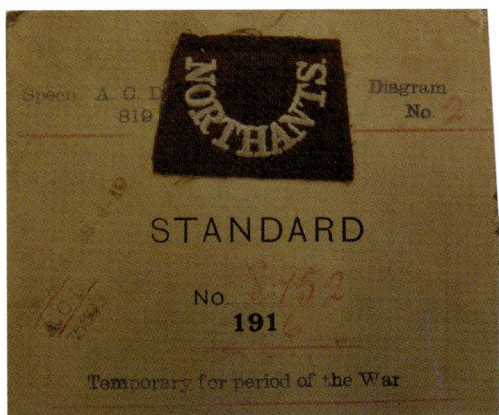

The replacement cloth title was introduced in late 1916 and obsolete on 28/4/19. It differed from the metal title using NORTHANTS instead of NORTHAMPTON or NORTHAMPTONSHIRE.

The Princess Charlotte of Wales's (Royal Berkshire Regiment)

Brock Barracks, Reading, was home to the 3rd Battalion and the Regimental Depot. The 1st Battalion were just over twenty miles away at Mandora Barracks, Aldershot, and the 2nd Battalion were at Jhansi. Other ranks wore a shoulder title - **ROYALBERKS**. Officers and men wore different cap badges.

1st Battalion

The battalion landed at Rouen on 13/8/14 with the 6th Brigade, 2nd Division. In mid-December 1915 it transferred to the 99th Brigade, 2nd Division. It stayed with the brigade for the rest of the war.

Badges: the only badges worn on the tunic were specified in the regulations. However, as most battalions wore a regimental device on the steel helmet it is probable that this was the case in this battalion; almost certainly a painted cap badge dragon on the left.

2nd Battalion

In India at the beginning of the war, it arrived in England on 22/10/14 to become part of the 25th Brigade, 8th Division. It landed at Le Havre on 5/11/14 and fought with the division on the Western Front for the entire war.

Badges: a red dragon, facing right, on a 2″ blue square, was worn on both arms until November 1917. This was replaced, according to the Divisional History in February 1918, by a green 2″ square, with ½″ red diagonal bar, top left to bottom right. Three helmet badges were worn: a painted black dragon on the front and a green 2″ square with a ½″ vertical red stripe on the left. From June 1918 this was replaced by a green square with red diagonal as the tunic badge. Initially the helmet was covered in khaki drill but this wore out quickly and was replaced by sandbag material. For a period when no cover was worn the helmet was covered irregularly with patches of brown and green paint.

On active service, band members wore a pouch with original Royal Berkshire badge on the front and buglers wore bugle strings (Royal) from the left shoulder.

3rd (Reserve) Battalion

Leaving Reading shortly after the start of the war it went to Portsmouth. In November 1917 it moved to Ireland where it remained.

Badges: the 1921 IWM questionnaire indicates that regulation badges were worn. Bugler's lines were 'Royal in the regulation manner' and band members wore the regimental badge on their pouch.

A private in the 1st Battalion with 18 years' service; his medal ribbons show pre-war service. Although officially there was no battalion badge on the tunic he has 1 above ROYAL BERKS.

The first badge worn by the 2nd Battalion was a China dragon on a blue square; it was worn on both arms.

Badges of the Regular Infantry, 1914–1918

A lance corporal of the 2nd Battalion some time in 1916/17. He is wearing a wound badge, two years' good service chevron, lance corporal stripe, battalion badge and cloth shoulder title.

A soldier in the 3rd Battalion who again is not wearing shoulder titles.

In February 1918 the China dragon on blue was replaced by a green square with red diagonal bar.

On the steel helmet the 2nd Battalion wore a dragon (probably red) and a green square with a vertical red stripe, changed in June 1918 to the diagonal red stripe on a green square worn on the tunic.

The Queen's Own (Royal West Kent Regiment)

The home depot of the regiment was Maidstone Barracks, Maidstone, home of the 3rd Battalion. Both regular battalions were out of the country: the 1st in Dublin, the 2nd in Multan. All ranks wore a common cap badge, officers wore collar badges, and other ranks wore a curved shoulder title – **R.W.KENT**.

1st Battalion

As part of the 13th Brigade, 5th Division, it landed in France on 15/8/14. It spent most of the war on the Western Front, apart from four months In Italy during December 1917 to April 1918.

Badges: only regulation badges were worn on the uniform: 'this being a regular Battalion, no mark of distinction has ever been worn on Service Dress. The only mark which has been adopted, is a blue oblong painted vertically on the front and back of the Steel Helmet. This was commenced in January 1917.' Correspondence from the divisional commander in August 1918 confirms that there was a dark blue vertical rectangle 2" × 1" painted on the front and back of the crown 1" from the brim. Specialists wore a coloured band on the lower sleeve: blue – signaller; red – regimental runner; green – sniper.

2nd Battalion

Leaving Bombay on 30/1/15, the battalion arrived in Basra on 6/2/15 as part of the 12th Indian Brigade, with two companies becoming attached to the 30th Brigade, 6th

210   Badges of the Regular Infantry, 1914–1918

Indian Division. On their capture at Kut, the remaining two companies joined the 34th Brigade, 15th Indian Division. In August 1917 the brigade joined the 17th Indian Division for the remainder of the war.

Badges: as well as the regulation metal badges the top fold of the pagri was light blue and the second fold dark blue. Officers and WO1s wore bright metal collar badges. Puttees were worn with two 'V's in front and khaki hose-tops. Steel helmets were not worn by the battalion other than for a very short period of time.

3rd (Reserve) Battalion

After nearly four years at Chatham the battalion moved in the summer of 1918 to Leysdown as part of the Thames and Medway Garrison.

Badges: regulation cloth and metal.

Other ranks wore a cloth shoulder title from late 1916 unless they could obtain a metal version.

An officer's collar badge worn by both regular battalions.

The Queen's Own (Royal West Kent Regiment)   211

Soldiers and families of the 2nd Battalion before leaving India. The two-coloured band in the ribbon is visible in the pagri (see inset).

Specialists in the 1st Battalion wore a coloured band on the left cuff: red – runner; blue – signaller; green – sniper.

In the 5th Division, helmet badges were worn. The 1st Battalion used a vertical blue oblong painted on the front and back of the helmet.

The King's Own (Yorkshire Light Infantry)

The 1st Battalion was in Singapore and the 2nd in Dublin in August 1914; Pontefract Barracks was the home depot of the regiment and housed the 3rd Battalion. All ranks wore a common cap badge, officers wore a curved shoulder title – **YORKSHIRE** with a bugle above.

1st Battalion

Stationed in Singapore, on arrival in England on 9/11/14 the battalion joined the 83rd Brigade, 28th Division, serving on the Western Front from 16/1/15. In October 1915 it moved to Salonika, returning to France in July 1918 to join the 151st Brigade, 50th Division.

Badges: as well as the regulation metal badges, a ½″ red tape – the 28th Division sign – was worn at the base of the shoulder straps. The evidence for the badges of the 50th Division after its reformation is patchy but it is probable that following the divisional system it wore either a blue or red vertical diamond badge on both arms.

2nd Battalion

The battalion left Dublin and landed in France on 16/8/14 with the 13th Brigade, 5th Division. At the end of December 1915 it transferred to the 97th Brigade, 32nd Division; it stayed with the division until the armistice.

Badges: only regulation badges were worn in the 5th Division. After joining the 32nd Division it followed the divisional scheme introduced in April 1916. All ranks wore a red, 2″ circle, at the top of both sleeves above two horizontal red bars, 2″ × ½″ – red for the division, circle for the 97th Brigade and two bars for second senior in the brigade. From May 1917 the bars were worn in different colours to show the wearer's company: red – A Company; mid-green – B Company; dark yellow – C Company; light blue – D Company; black – HQ Company.[29] The CO took the NWM's request for information and examples very seriously sending them dummy sleeves with all the badges on and marked to identify the company.

3rd (Reserve) Battalion

On moving to its war station in August 1914, the battalion spent the war in East Yorkshire becoming part of the Humber Garrison in August 1918.

Badges: regulation cloth and metal.

An economy version of the cap badge.

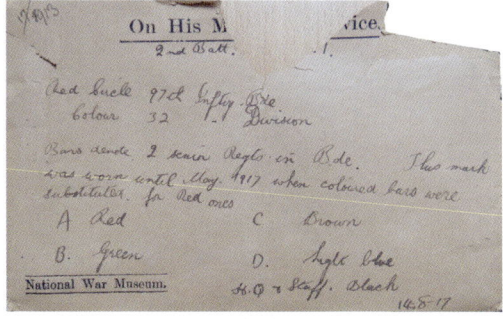

Details of the badges worn by the 2nd Battalion were recorded on an official envelope by the NWM.

On the sleeve the brigade circle and two bars are easily recognisable. On his strap is a metal title and his cap badge is a bi-metal version.

---

29. IWM photo Q9231 Le Bearde 6/8/18.

214   Badges of the Regular Infantry, 1914–1918

The 32nd Division had a rigid system of badges which the 2nd Battalion adopted. The divisional colour was red, the shape showing the brigade and the bars the battalion seniority in the brigade. As the second battalion in the 97th Brigade it wore two bars under a red circle. The bars were in different colours to identify companies: red – A Company; mid-green – B Company; dark yellow – C Company; light blue – D Company; black – HQ Company.

The ACD card for the cloth shoulder title introduced from mid-1916. It was obsolete by 1/4/19.

In 1919 just before they became obsolete a further pattern was produced with the titles being delivered in pairs.

As light infantry they also wore a green-on-khaki title.

The shoulder title worn by most other ranks was a bugle over YORKSHIRE.

A recruit in the 3rd Battalion who is identified only by his cap badge.

An officer with the 3rd Battalion wearing a cap badge and collar badges.

All ranks in the 1st Battalion wore the 28th Divisional sign on their shoulder straps; other ranks wore a shoulder title as well. According to Westlake (1980) this title was not introduced until 1921 but is seen in wartime photographs.

The King's Shropshire Light Infantry

Copthorne Barracks in Shrewsbury was the Regimental Depot and home for the 3rd Battalion; the 1st Battalion was in Tipperary and the 2nd in Secunderabad. All ranks wore a common cap badge, officers wore collar badges, and other ranks wore a shoulder title – **KSLI**.

1st Battalion

As part of the 16th Brigade, 6th Division, the battalion landed at St. Nazaire on 10/9/14. It spent the entire war on the Western Front with the division.

Badges: on 2/8/17 the Battalion CO sent the NWM 'a complete set of metal titles and cap badge which have been worn by this Battalion during the whole campaign' stating that 'the 1st Battalion King's Shropshire Light Infantry has no special Battalion Badges or marks of distinction worn on the sleeve or on the back of the Service Dress Jacket.' However, a rifle green $2\frac{1}{2}'' \times 1\frac{1}{2}''$ diamond was worn on the left side of the steel helmet cover from late 1915 until May 1917 when it was stopped. Helmets were covered in service issue cloth and later with sandbags. Puttees were rolled spirally from ankle to just below the knee with no twists. Rifle green buglers lines were worn when out of the line. The RSM wore officers' collar badges. 'Signallers, Bombers, Lewis Gunners, Trench Mortar personnel wore gilt metal badges (Govt. issue).'

2nd Battalion

On arrival from India in November 1914 it formed part of the 80th Brigade, 27th Division. It fought in France from 20/12/14. On 4/12/15 it went to Salonika where it remained for the rest of the war.

Badges: as well as regulation badges, all ranks wore the 27th Division sign on the base of both straps – a ½″ khaki strip. On the left side of the eight-line pagri was a vertical rifle green rectangle and officers wore a ¹⁄₁₀″ rifle green piping above the pagri. The pagri of all ranks had three pleats, one in front and one on each side. No markings were used on the steel helmet but covers were always worn. When worn, the left side of the slouch hat was turned up and fastened with the regimental badge. Rifle green lanyards were worn by officers, WOs, and sergeants over the left shoulder. Salonika pattern shorts were worn during the summer.

3rd (Reserve) Battalion

In August 1914 it guarded Pembroke Dock, moving to Edinburgh in Mar 1915. It then returned to Pembroke Dock. In December 1917 it was sent to Ireland, first to Cork and later to Fermoy.

Badges: on 13/8/17, writing from Pembroke Dock, the Battalion CO informed the NWM that 'no badges are available in the Battalion under my command', meaning that only the regulation cloth and metal badges were worn. This was confirmed by the adjutant of the Regimental Depot on 11/12/20, adding two details: officers wore a green lanyard and the band wore a star on the front of the pouch. Private E.V.J. Jones recalled having to buy his own shoulder titles when he served with the battalion.

Regular soldiers of the 1st Battalion over the first winter of the war. It is not possible to tell whether they are wearing shoulder titles under their fur jackets.

An ex-other ranks newly commissioned second lieutenant. He has been wounded twice and is wearing the MM ribbon and collar badges.

218 Badges of the Regular Infantry, 1914–1918

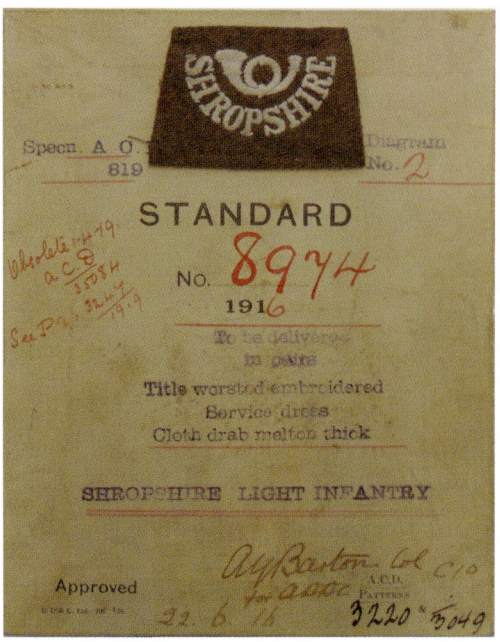

Authorised on 22/6/16, the cloth shoulder title was obsolete on 1/4/19.

Like the KOYLI in 1919 the ACD directed the production of the shoulder titles in pairs.

All ranks in the 2nd Battalion wore a khaki/yellow strip round the base of the shoulder strap.

A KSLI officer, Hugh Stuart Rogers, APM, on brigade or divisional staff. Although he is still a KSLI officer he has changed his collar badges for staff tabs.

The 2nd Battalion wore a vertical rifle green rectangle on the left side of the pagri.

A green diamond was worn on the left side of the steel helmet cover between late 1915 and May 1917.

All ranks in the 2nd Battalion wore a yellow or khaki band to show the 27th Division. Other ranks also wore a shoulder title.

The Duke of Cambridge's Own (Middlesex Regiment)

Situated in the west of London, the recruitment potential meant that the regiment consisted of four regular battalions and two reserve battalions. Inglis Barracks, Mill Hill, was the Regimental Depot and home of the 5th and 6th Reserve Battalions. Two of the regular battalions were in England: the 1st at Woolwich and the 4th at Devonport; and two abroad: the 2nd in Malta and the 3rd in Cawnpore. All ranks wore a common cap badge, officers wore collar badges, and other ranks wore a curved shoulder title – **MIDDLESEX**.

1st Battalion

On landing in France on 22/8/14 the battalion became LoC troops, joining the 19th Brigade when it formed towards the end of August. On 12/10/14 the brigade joined part of the 6th Division. In May 1915 the brigade was transferred to the 27th Division and in August to the 2nd Division and to the 33rd Division in November with the battalion joining the 98th Brigade; it remained with the division for the remainder of the war.

Badges: throughout the war only regulation badges were worn. The wearing of only regulation badges was confirmed in July 1987 by Sergeant E. Turner who was certain that such things were only worn by brigade and divisional staff. In June 1988, Second Lieutenant F. Molz was adamant that no special badges were worn and that officers wore cloth 'pips' on their shoulder straps.

2nd Battalion

On 7/11/14 the battalion landed at Le Havre as part of the 23rd Brigade, 8th Division. It fought with the division on the Western Front until the armistice.

Badges: writing in August 1917, the Battalion CO stated that from 1/2/17 all ranks wore, on both arms, a curved yellow bar 3″ × 1″ close to the seams: the shape indicated the brigade and the colour the battalion. He sent two specially prepared shoulder pieces showing the 'distinctive badge worn by 2nd Battalion Middlesex Regiment since 1st February 1917. No other badges have been worn by this battalion except the normal bombers, Lewis gunners, etc as laid down in general routine orders from time to time.' From November 1917 all ranks wore a vertically bisected diamond, red left and yellow right, on both sides of the helmet; officers were distinguished by a small yellow diamond above the diamond. The lack of a special recognition sign was confirmed by Private R. Weedon, a pre-war regular who served with the battalion until 1/7/16 when he was wounded. When he returned he was sent to the 11th Battalion.

3rd Battalion

On arrival from India in December 1914 it joined the 85th Brigade, 28th Division. After ten months on the Western Front – January to October 1915 – it went to Salonika where it remained for the rest of the war.

Badges: the battalion was quick to recognise the importance of tactical markings, wearing four different badges. In France a yellow 3″ square was worn on the centre of the back below the collar and on the pack when worn. This was replaced by a red 3″ × 2″ diamond. In November 1915 this was replaced by a lemon yellow version which in March 1916 became a yellow isosceles triangle, base 3½″, sides 2¾″. Although not mentioned in the correspondence with Lieutenant Colonel Mellis, the Battalion CO, all ranks should have been wearing a ½″ red band across the base of both shoulder straps.

4th Battalion

The battalion landed in Boulogne on 14/8/14 as part of the 8th Brigade, 4th Division. In November 1915 it joined the 63rd Brigade, 21st Division; the brigade moving to the 37th Division in July 1916. It remained with the 37th Division, fighting on the Western Front for the rest of the war.

Badges: in the 63rd Brigade a 1½″ yellow square was worn on both arms by all ranks. When the brigade was transferred to the 37th Division the sign was retained and worn below the yellow horseshoe of the division and above company indicators: red – A

Company; blue – B Company; mauve – C Company; green – D Company; no bar – HQ Company. The divisional sign was worn three inches from the shoulder seam and was first worn about August 1916. From January 1918 the signs were painted on the right side of the helmet. According to Captain Wootton, the 5th Battalion Adjutant, the square was also worn on the back between the shoulders close up to the back of the collar and also on the helmet. In January 1918 a 2″ × 1″ horizontal rectangle bisected diagonally bottom left to top right – red left and yellow right – was worn by all ranks on the helmet.

Puttees were worn with two 'V's at the back of the calf.

5th (Reserve) Battalion

After twenty months at their war station – Rochester – the battalion moved to Chatham where it joined the 6th Battalion. During 1917 and 1918 it was stationed in Gillingham.

Badges: in 1915 when Second Lieutenant F. Molz served with the battalion only regulation cloth and metal badges were worn.

6th (Reserve) Battalion

Gillingham was the battalion's war station until November 1915 went it moved to Chatham where it remained.

Badges: regulation cloth and metal.

The 2nd Battalion sent the NWM a piece of officers' tunic with an officer-grade badge on.

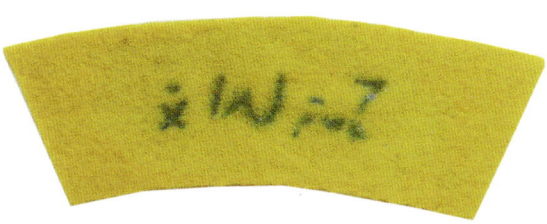

The other ranks badge for the 2nd Battalion was of a felt-like material.

Badges of the Regular Infantry, 1914–1918

A yellow triangle was worn on the back by all ranks of the 3rd Battalion from March 1916.

In the 63rd Brigade the battalion wore a yellow square on both arms. It was also worn when the battalion moved to the 37th Division.

A corporal in the 3rd Battalion. He is wearing a pre-war belt, regimental buttons and the 28th divisional band underneath his shoulder title.

A 1918 studio photograph of a private in the 1st Battalion. His cap has his regimental badge and on his shoulders are metal titles. He has been wounded twice and has two good service chevrons: six years good conduct. On his right arm are overseas chevrons for 1914 (different coloured one at the bottom), 15, 16 and 17. His function in the battalion is revealed by the crossed axes: pioneer – responsible for construction and maintenance.

The Duke of Cambridge's Own (Middlesex Regiment)

In warmer climates a thinner cloth in a different colour was used for the shoulder title.

Produced as an economy measure to save metal, the cloth title was introduced from mid-1916 and was obsolete about three years later.

The 2nd Battalion football team in 1919; those in uniform are still wearing a yellow arc at the top of each sleeve.

All ranks of the 4th Battalion wore the divisional sign above their battalion badge and company bars: red – A Company; blue – B Company; mauve – C Company; green – D Company; no colour – HQ Company.

224   Badges of the Regular Infantry, 1914–1918

From November 1917 all ranks wore a yellow and red vertical diamond on both sides of the helmet; officers were distinguished by a small diamond above the sign.

In 1915 while serving on the Western Front a yellow square was worn on the back and small pack by the 1st Battalion. A smaller version was worn by the 4th Battalion on both arms in the 21st and 37th Divisions.

The large yellow square worn by the 3rd Battalion was replaced by a vertical red diamond; in Salonika in November 1915 it was changed to yellow; followed by a yellow isosceles triangle in March 1916 – see below.

In January 1918 the 4th Battalion adopted a helmet badge: a horizontal rectangle bisected diagonally bottom left to right, red over yellow.

The King's Royal Rifle Corps

As the regiment had no territorial affiliation, recruiting nationally, it had six regular battalions in August 1914. The two reserve battalions were at the Regimental Depot, Upper Barracks, Winchester; the 1st Battalion was at Salamanca Barracks, Aldershot, the 2nd at Blackdown, the 3rd was in Meerut and the 4th Gharial. Officers wore a bugle on a red boss cap badge, other ranks wore a Maltese cross mounted with a crown. Officers did not wear collar badges except on mess dress and all ranks wore a blackened brass shoulder title - KRR.

1st Battalion

The battalion left Aldershot as part of the 6th Brigade, 2nd Division, proceeding to France where it landed on 13/8/14. In mid-December the 99th Brigade joined the division and the battalion was swapped in from the 6th Brigade. It fought with the brigade for the rest of the war.

Badges: Private James Horton, a regular soldier at the start of the war, who was taken PoW at Ypres in 1914, told the writer that only metal badges were worn at that time. The only non-regulation badge was worn on the front of the helmet cover according to the Battalion CO Lieutenant Colonel Watson on 30/7/17: a red and green silk representation of the cap badge over the numerals 1/60 on grey cloth was worn on the canvas cover. This was confirmed by the son of Private Benjamin Harrop, MM, who has an original badge. Officers wore a thick black lanyard on the left shoulder that became double as it went into the pocket, and wore a Sam Browne belt with silver fittings. Band members wore a black patent leather cross belt with black patent leather pouch and silver bugle on back.

2nd Battalion

From 13/8/14 when the battalion landed in France to the armistice, the battalion fought on the Western Front with the 2nd Brigade, 1st Division.

Badges: specialists in the battalion were identified by ½" square diamonds worn on the back of the collar: green – riflemen; yellow – Lewis gunners; red – bombers; black – rifle grenadiers. No other non-regulation badges were worn.

3rd Battalion

The battalion left Mumbai on 16/10/14 and on landing it joined the 80th Brigade, 27th Division at Winchester. It landed in France on 21/12/14 and after eleven months on the Western Front it went to Salonika where it remained.

Badges: as was usual in the 27th Division, apart from regulation badges, the only sign worn was the divisional ½" khaki tape across the base of both straps. No markings were worn on the steel helmets; khaki covers were used and no badges were worn on the pagri. A black lanyard was worn over the left shoulder. Buglers' lines were worn over the left shoulder and looped to the top button of the jacket and band members wore a black cross with a silver bugle on the pouch. Black chin straps were used on the topee.

4th Battalion

Sailing from Bombay with the 3rd Battalion, it arrived in Plymouth on 18/11/14 and also joined the 80th Brigade, 27th Division. It fought alongside its sister battalion until June 1918 when it returned to the Western Front as part of the 151st Brigade, 50th Division.

Badges: in August 1917 the Battalion CO informed the NWM that the 'battalion has never worn any distinctive badges on the sleeve or back of the Service Dress Jacket.' However, in Salonika the 27th Division ½" buff band should have been worn across the base of both straps. A green 2" × ¼" horizontal bar was worn on the left side of the pagri. To differentiate between the 3rd and 4th Battalions serving in the same brigade, other ranks did not wear the red cap badge backing and officers did not wear the scarlet boss, instead wearing the Maltese cross. In France, in 1918, a 1" square diamond in rifle green was worn on both arms, 2" below the shoulder straps; the shape showed the brigade and the colour the seniority of the battalion in the brigade. Collar badges were not worn by officers. A black silk lanyard was worn on the left shoulder.

In Salonika, dark khaki hose tops were worn. Buglers' lines were worn, 'hooked onto the left shoulder, across left breast looped over top button, from where they hung down'. Members of the band wore black patent leather waist belts-cross belts and pouches of black patent leather with silver bugle on pouch-lines as for buglers; a black sheepskin apron was worn for the big drum. Officers wore titles and badges of rank of black worsted on the shoulder strap. Black chin straps were used on the topee. In the summer of 1917 and 1918 shorts were Salonika pattern.

5th (Reserve) Battalion

The battalion served in the Sheerness area until the end of the war.

Badges: regulation cloth and metal.

6th (Reserve) Battalion

Like the 5th Battalion, the 6th was at Sheerness. It spent the last two years of the war at Queenborough where it was in the Thames and Medway Garrison.

Badges: regulation cloth and metal. Private A. Griffin who trained with the battalion in mid-1916 was certain that only regulation badges were worn.

Officers wore a red corded boss cap badge – known as the 'cherry' – rather than the standard blackened Maltese cross. This was a 'beehive'-shaped mounded coil of red cord surmounted by a strung bugle.

A representation of the 1st Battalion helmet badge painted by the son of Private Benjamin Harrop MM.

228   Badges of the Regular Infantry, 1914–1918

The 2nd Battalion did not wear a battalion badge but did use badges to identify specialists. The small diamond was worn on the back of the collar: green – rifleman; yellow – Lewis gunners; red – bombers; black – rifle grenadiers.

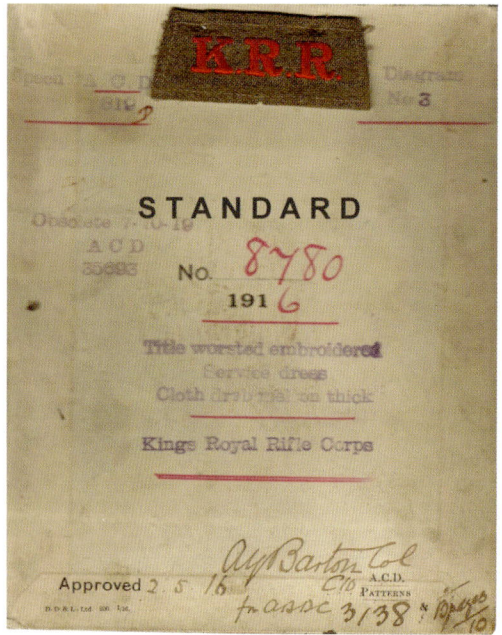

The KRRC was provided with a unique cloth title in red on khaki; authorised in May 1916 it was obsolete on 7/10/19.

A post-war studio portrait of a lieutenant in a regular battalion showing the boss cap badge, black buttons, lack of collar badges and metal regimental shoulder title.

In most of the battalions a red backing was worn behind the cap badge.

Both the 3rd and 4th Battalions served in Salonika where all divisions wore a coloured band on the shoulder strap base. The 27th Division wore a khaki/yellow band.

The King's Royal Rifle Corps 229

A lance corporal in the 1st Battalion which only wore regulation badges, like this bombers' badge in red over a khaki boss. Note the black rifle regiment buttons.

A stretcher bearer in either the 1st or 2nd Battalion. He has a two year good service chevron above his two wound stripes. The SB armband showed he was a trained soldier as well as a stretcher bearer. Below the shoulder strap he is wearing a red-on-khaki title and his cap badge has a red backing.

When the 4th Battalion returned to France in mid-1918 it joined the 50th Division and wore a rifle green diamond on both arms.

The 4th Battalion wore a horizontal green rectangle on the left side of the pagri to differentiate it from the 3rd Battalion.

In the 27th Division the 3rd and 4th Battalions wore the divisional sign on their shoulder straps. It was common in the KRRC for both officers and men to wear shoulder titles.

The Duke of Edinburgh's (Wiltshire Regiment)

Le Marchant Barracks, Devizes, was the Regimental Depot and home to the reserve battalion. During the war it processed over 5,000 recruits and 3,000 reservists. Neither regular battalion was at the depot: the 1st was at Tidworth, the 2nd in Gibraltar. All ranks wore a common cap badge, officers wore collar badges and other ranks wore a curved shoulder title – **WILTS**.

1st Battalion

On arrival in France on 14/8/14 it was part of the 7th Brigade, 3rd Division. In October 1915 the 7th Brigade was swapped with the 76th Brigade, 25th Division. In June 1918 it moved to the 110th Brigade, 21st Division.

Badges: on 17/8/17, Lieutenant Colonel Ogilvie, Battalion CO, told the NWM 'that beyond the official Cap Badge, this Battalion do not wear any special badges or mark of distinction. The Divisional sign, a red horseshoe, is worn on the back of the Service Dress Jacket and above the horseshoe is a red lozenge upon the collar of the jacket, this being a Brigade mark of distinction. This Battalion has never had a distinctive badge or mark since coming out to France in August 1914.' Although the Regimental Museum suggests that there are indications that after that date a maroon Maltese cross was worn on both sleeves and that coloured shoulder straps were used to identify companies. Private J. Wakeman, writing 1988, served with the battalion in early 1918 before becoming a PoW in the German Spring Offensive; he is certain that he did not wear any other sign apart from the horseshoe and bar. On transfer to the 21st Division, yellow squares were worn on both upper arms and on the back below the collar and were painted on the front, rear and both sides of the steel helmet.

The Duke of Edinburgh's (Wiltshire Regiment) 231

2nd Battalion

After nearly a month waiting to leave Gibraltar the battalion arrived at Southampton on 3/9/14. It joined the 21st Brigade, 7th Division, forming around Lyndhurst, landing at Zeebrugge on 7/10/14. On 19/12/15 the brigade was exchanged with the 91st Brigade, 30th Division. In May 1918 the battalion joined the 58th Brigade, 19th Division.

Badges: adopted in 1916, a light buff horizontal patch 2½″ × ½″ was worn 1″ below the seams on both arms with a smaller version, 2″ × ½″, painted on the left side of the helmet; no sign was worn on helmet cover.[30] Both badges were won by all ranks. Runners and signallers were identified by a 2½″ wide patch across the right strap under the shoulder title in red and blue respectively. In the 19th (Western) Division in 1918, the Regimental Museum suggests that the badge of the former 6th Battalion – a vertical green rectangle with a yellow edge – was worn on both upper arms, and a band of regimental colours – red/blue/buff – was worn round the crown of the steel helmet.

3rd (Reserve) Battalion

The battalion was stationed in Weymouth, Dorchester, Weymouth again and finally Sittingbourne. For the last year of the war it was part of the Thames and Medway Garrison.

Badges: Second Lieutenant D. Jeffries served with the battalion in 1917 and was clear in his correspondence in 1988 that only regulation cloth and metal badges were worn.

When the 1st Battalion was transferred to the 25th Division it adopted the divisional system of a red horseshoe for the division and a red bar for the brigade. The badges were worn on the back.

A yellow square was worn by the 1st Battalion when it fought with the 21st Division from June 1918.

---

30. IWM photo Q1145 shows a light coloured Maltese Cross sewn to the front of an officer's helmet cover at Bouzincourt in September 1916.

232 Badges of the Regular Infantry, 1914–1918

A family studio photograph taken on leave: the horizontal bar below the shoulder title shows he is in the 2nd Battalion. On the sleeve are two wound stripes and three good service chevrons indicating twelve years good conduct making him a pre-war regular.

The regimental museum suggests that when the 2nd battalion replaced the disbanded 6th Battalion in the 19th Division it adopted its badge: a vertical green rectangle with a yellow edge.

A group of soldiers serving with the 3rd Battalion all wearing regulation metal badges.

The Manchester Regiment

Although the regiment recruited from a very large metropolitan area it only consisted of two regular and two reserve battalions. The 1st was at Jullundur, the 2nd at The Curragh, and both the reserve and extra reserve were at the Regimental Depot, Ladysmith Barracks in Ashton-under-Lyme, on 4/8/14. All ranks wore a common cap badge, officers wore collar badges, and other ranks wore a curved shoulder title – **MANCHESTER**.

1st Battalion

Stationed in Jullundur, it was part of the Jullundur Brigade, 3rd (Lahore) Division. It fought on the Western Front from October 1914 to December 1915 when it was transferred to the Middle East. It fought there with the 8th Indian Brigade, 3rd Indian Division.

Badges: officers and men wore different pagri flashes: officers wore a fleur-de-Lis, vertically bisected green (front) and yellow, and men wore a square diamond bisected vertically green (front) and yellow; both were worn on the left side. However, in the letter from Lieutenant Colonel Hardcastle, the Battalion CO, he writes that he has sent a helmet badge worn by the battalion at that time – early October 1917 – and in about 1920 the IWM questionnaire confirmed that all ranks wore the same badge, a yellow and green diamond. Officer's cap and collar badge was the fleur-de-lys. No markings were worn on the steel helmet.

2nd Battalion

On 17/8/14 the battalion landed in France with the 14th Brigade, 5th Division. At the end of December 1915 the brigade was transferred to the 32nd Division and the 95th joined the 5th Division. The battalion was moved to the 96th Brigade of the same division in February 1918. It spent the entire war on the Western Front.

Badges: in the 32nd Division the divisional scheme was adopted with a red 90°, 1¼″ diamond showing the brigade with three red horizontal bars showing the seniority of the battalion. The colour of the bars was changed in 1917 to show the wearer's company: red – A Company; emerald green – B Company; yellow – C Company; mid blue – D Company; black – HQ Company. When the battalion was transferred to the 96th Brigade, the diamond became a triangle. RSM M. Lally, a pre-war regular who served throughout the war with the battalion, remembered the red badge denoting the battalion and also wearing a silver sphinx on his collars as a warrant officer.

3rd (Reserve) Battalion

It joined the Humber Defences at Cleethorpes and stayed there for the entire war.

Badges: regulation cloth and metal with the RSM wearing officer's collar badges.

4th (Extra Reserve) Battalion

Also part of the Humber defences for the war, the battalion was stationed at Riby, Tetney and Grimsby.

Badges: regulation cloth and metal.

Initially the 1st Battalion's pagri flash was a green and yellow fleur-de-lys for officers; men wore a vertically bisected square diamond in the same colours. Later all wore the same diamond flash.

A cloth title was made available from late 1916 to save metal.

The Manchester Regiment

In the 32nd Division, the 2nd Battalion conformed to the rigid system of colour – red – and shape – battalion. Being the third senior battalion it wore three bars in different colours to show the company affiliation: red – A Company; emerald green – B Company; yellow – C Company; mid-blue – D Company; black – HQ Company.

Soldiers of the 2nd Battalion displaying their signs at the end of the war.

The Prince of Wales's (North Staffordshire Regiment)

The home depot, Whittington Barracks, Lichfield, housed not only the 3rd (Reserve) and 4th (Extra Reserve) Battalions but also the 3rd and 4th Battalions of the South Staffordshire Regiment. Both regular battalions were out of the country: the 1st at Buttevant, the 2nd in Rawalpindi. All ranks wore a common cap badge, officers wore collar badges, and other ranks wore a curved shoulder title – **N.STAFFORD**.

1st Battalion

The battalion landed in France on 17/8/14 with the 17th Brigade, 6th Division. It was transferred into the 2nd Brigade, 24th Division, in October 1915 and remained with the brigade for the rest of the war on the Western Front.

Badges: in the 6th Division, the only badges worn were those permitted in the regulations. NWM correspondence from the Battalion CO, dated 3/8/17, states that the battalion adopted the 24th Divisional scheme when it was introduced on 25/7/16. All ranks wore a 3″ green cotton square on both arms below company indicators in the shape of a four-pointed star which was often worn as a diamond because it was easier to cut and sew on. The 3″ high star was worn on both arms: A Company – blue; B Company – green; C Company – red; D Company – yellow; HQ Company – no star. The square shape indicated the fourth battalion in the brigade, the colour indicated the brigade. When brigades were reduced to three battalions the square was changed for a green 2″ equilateral triangle; worn until January 1919. A 1½″ square, vertically divided in equal sections of red/black/white, was worn on the front centre of the helmet by all ranks. During 1918 a sergeant in charge of a platoon wore the letters PS in red cloth over their stripes.

Khaki regulation lanyards were worn for revolvers (right shoulder) and whistles (left shoulder). Bugler's cords were worn from the neck (front) to right shoulder and from the neck (rear) under left arm to the top button of the jacket. Bandsmen and drummers wore khaki wing epaulettes. Bandsmen wore a white music pouch slung from the right shoulder with a regimental crest in gilt on the flap. Officers wore bronze buttons.

2nd Battalion

The battalion remained in India for the duration.

Badges: as well as the regulation metal badges, all ranks wore a patch the width of the pagri on the left side: three ¾″ vertical stripes of red/black/white with red to the front.

3rd (Reserve) Battalion

In May 1915 the battalion left its war station in Plymouth and moved north-east. It served at Seaham, Forest Hall and Wallsend in the Tyne Garrison.

Badges: regulation cloth and metal.

4th (Extra Reserve) Battalion

After over three years as a home service battalion, it landed in France in October 1917. Initially attached to the 167th Brigade, 56th Division, it then joined the 35th Division, firstly with the 106th Brigade and then the 105th.

Badges: regulation cloth and metal; many units in the division did not wear signs but towards the end of the war some started to wear the divisional sign.

238 Badges of the Regular Infantry, 1914–1918

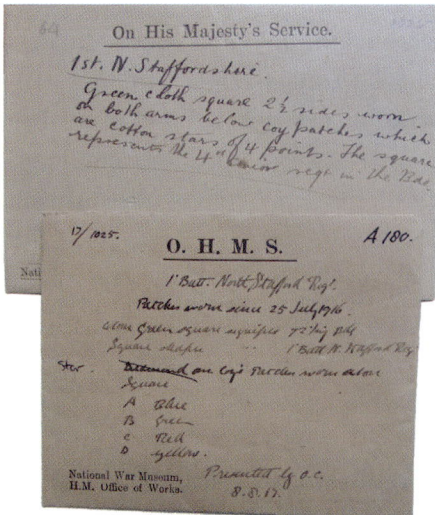

The envelopes containing the badges sent by the CO of the 1st Battalion on 8/8/17 detail the badges, their significance and when adopted.

In the 24th Division the 1st Battalion adopted the divisional system of a battalion badge and company sign. The battalion sign was a green 3" cotton square; the colour was the brigade, the shape, the battalion seniority, in this case fourth.

Company stars/diamonds were worn above the battalion badge on both arms: blue – A Company; green – B Company; red – C Company; yellow – D Company; no star – HQ Company.

The Prince of Wales's (North Staffordshire Regiment)

In February 1918 the brigade was reduced to three battalions and the 1st North Staffs became the third most senior battalion and adopted a green triangle. Both the officer and other rank are from the Company HQ and on the front of the helmet is a red/white/black painted square. The badge is recorded as being a 2" equilateral triangle but these are bigger and isosceles.

On the front centre of the helmet, all ranks of the 1st Battalion wore the same badge as the 2nd Battalion: a square of regimental colours.

Other ranks wore a metal shoulder title – NSTAFFORD. When the cloth title was introduced from mid-1916 it was shortened to NSTAFFS.

The 2nd Battalion remained part of the India Garrison and wore a red/black/white pagri patch on the left side. Men of the battalion out on campaign or exercises.

The York & Lancaster Regiment

The regiment shared its home depot with the KOYLI, so at the start of the war there were two 3rd Battalions stationed in Pontefract. Both regular battalions were out of the country with the 1st at Jubbulpore and the 2nd in Limerick. All ranks wore a common cap badge, officers wore collar badges and other ranks wore a shoulder title – **Y&L**.

1st Battalion

On arrival from Mumbai on 23/12/14 it joined the 83rd Brigade, 28th Division, landing in France on 17/1/15. After nine months service on the Western Front it moved to Egypt and then Salonika where it spent the rest of the war.

Badges: Lieutenant Colonel Wedgewood, CO of the battalion after the war, stated that the cap badge was worn on the front of the topee by all ranks and that a ¼″ piece of red braid was worn across the base of the straps. All other badges were regulation. Puttees were crossed twice in the front and centre of the leg. Shorts were of the Salonika pattern.

2nd Battalion

The battalion landed at St. Nazaire on 9/9/14 and fought on the Western Front for the entire war with the 16th Brigade, 6th Division.

Badges: only regulation badges were worn throughout the war. Lance Corporal J. Madeley served with the battalion during 1917 and is certain that the only badges he wore were metal.

3rd (Reserve) Battalion

For the entire war, the battalion was stationed in the north-east of England: Cleadon, Sunderland, Durham and Sunderland again from February 1916; part of the Tyne Garrison.

Badges: as a draft finding unit, only regulation cloth and metal badges were worn; puttees worn with two crosses in front. Lance Corporal J. Madeley who served with the battalion in mid-1916 remembered only wearing metal badges. Puttees were worn with two crosses in front. Helmets were only issued to men on draft and were factory finished.

A pre-war studio photograph taken in India of a private in the 1st Battalion showing the cap badge at the front and also a coloured line in the pagri folds.

The 2nd Battalion wore regulation badges throughout the war. This is Private Arthur Darwin number 8154 who was badly wounded at Armentières on 18 October 1914.

The York & Lancaster Regiment 243

In mid-1916 the battalion title was changed from metal to cloth. It was obsolete three years after issue.

The shoulder title was also produced in a shade of green and printed.

Other ranks wore a very simple metal shoulder title – Y&L.

The Durham Light Infantry

Fenham Barracks, Newcastle-on-Tyne, was shared with the Northumberland Fusiliers and was home to both regiments 3rd (Reserve) Battalions; the extra reserve battalion was at Barnard Castle where it had been originally raised in 1759. There were two regular battalions: the 1st at Nowshera and the 2nd in Lichfield. All ranks wore a common cap badge, officers wore collar badges, and other ranks wore a curved shoulder title – **DURHAM** below a bugle. A one piece version of the title was introduced during the war.

1st Battalion

The battalion remained in India throughout the war.

Badges: as well as the regulation metal badges a pagri patch was worn on the left side of the sun helmet: **D.L.I** in red on a horizontal green rectangle; the same badge was worn by the 18th Battalion in Egypt in 1915. The battalion lanyard was a green three-knot cord. Bandsmen wore a bugle with 68th in the centre on their pouch. Puttees were worn with one twist and hose tops were dark green. Bandsmen wore a badge on their pouch – 68 in a bugle.

2nd Battalion

On 10/9/14 the battalion landed at St. Nazaire and until the armistice fought with the 18th Brigade, 6th Division, on the Western Front.

The Durham Light Infantry 245

Badges: a steel helmet badge was adopted in August 1918 and worn by all ranks. Little is recorded apart from it being a 'shield in front with regimental colours': a green shield with two red vertical bars. The helmet was painted khaki. Question 8 of the 1920s questionnaire asked whether they had worn any recognition marks on their tunics. The reply was very clear: 'not used in 6th Division – being a regular Division.' Officers wore a light green whistle lanyard over the left shoulder. Puttees were worn in the regulation manner, except for transport men who wore them as for the mounted branches.

3rd (Reserve) Battalion

On the declaration of war, the battalion went to South Shields where it remained as part of the Tyne Garrison.

Badges: regulation cloth and metal.

4th (Extra Reserve) Battalion

Like the 3rd battalion, it was part of the Tyne Garrison based at Killingworth, Forest Hall and from October 1915 at Seaham Harbour.

Badges: regulation cloth and metal.

To conserve metal supplies shoulder titles were made from cloth after mid-1916. This reflects the metal title but the ACD STANDARD card does not show a matching pair.

In 1919, shortly before they were phased out, the ACD produced a matching pair of shoulder titles.

This is an interpretation of the IWM questionnaire information. The colours were those of the regiment, green and red, the positioning of the bars and their thickness was not given.

Acting Corporal Benjamin Whiteley, number 28613, served with the 1st Battalion during the war and after. He fought in the 3rd Afghan War in 1919. His pagri patch, red on green, was worn on the left side.

The Highland Light Infantry

One of the three Scottish regiments to form an extra reserve battalion; both reserve battalions were based at Garrioch Barracks, Hamilton, when the war broke out. The 1st Battalion was at Ambala and the 2nd in Maida Barracks, Aldershot. All ranks wore a common cap badge, officers wore collar badges, and other ranks wore a shoulder title – **HLI** sometimes with a bugle above.

1st Battalion

After a brief separation in Egypt, the Sirhind Brigade, in which the battalion served, arrived in France at the beginning of December 1914. A year later, the brigade, part of the 3rd (Lahore) Division, went to Mesopotamia. For a short while the battalion was detached and joined the Tigris Defences. In September 1917 it was part of the 51st Brigade, 17th Division; it fought with the division until the end of the war.

Badges: on the Western Front only regulation badges were worn but in December 1915, when the battalion moved to Mesopotamia, the pre-war pagri patch was reinstated. Cut from Mackenzie tartan with machined edges the badge was a 3″ high, a trapezium with red lines forming a cross on a green background: top edge 1¾″, base 2¼″.

2nd Battalion

The battalion landed at Boulogne on 14/8/14 and spent the war on the Western Front with the 5th Brigade, 2nd Division.

Badges: only regulation metal badges were worn but in early 1919 a light coloured 74 was worn on the left side of the steel helmet.

3rd (Reserve) Battalion

After ten months in Portsmouth the battalion returned to Scotland eventually becoming part of the Forth Garrison.

Badges: regulation cloth and metal.

4th (Extra Reserve) Battalion

Mirroring the 3rd Battalion after service in Portsmouth it returned to Scotland in September 1918 becoming part of the Tay Garrison.

Badges: regulation cloth and metal.

A non-standard version of the cloth title: painted but in matching pairs.

The Highland Light Infantry

An officer's collar badge was a two colour version of the cap badge.

A pre-war card showing the tartan, the cap badge and pre-war uniform.

Taken in India just before the war, the pagri flash and hackle can be seen on the left side of the helmet. He is wearing tartan shorts and coloured hose tops. The tunic is cut back in typical Scottish regiment style to show off the sporran. The badge is an original 1st Battalion flash sent by the battalion in 1917 to the NWM.

The Seaforth Highlanders
(Ross-shire Buffs, The Duke of Albany's)

Fort George, near Ardersier, was the depot of the regiment and home to the 3rd Battalion. The 1st was at Agra and the 2nd at Shorncliffe. All ranks wore a common cap badge, officers wore collar badges, and other ranks wore a curved shoulder title – **SEAFORTH**.

1st Battalion

In October 1914 the battalion arrived in France from India as part of the Dehra Dun Brigade, 7th 'Meerut' Indian Division. The brigade became the 19th Indian and went to Mesopotamia. After heavy casualties in February 1916 it was amalgamated with the 2nd Black Watch forming the Highland Battalion, 19th Indian Brigade. In July the battalion was reformed and continued to serve with the brigade and division in the Middle East.

Badges: writing on 14/11/17 from Mesopotamia and replying on behalf of the CO, Major J.H. Mackay Scobie informed the NWM that no badges were worn: 'since commencement of the war, I may state that beyond the official ones, none have been used. While in France the glengarry and afterwards the khaki round (or balmoral) bonnet was worn with the ordinary glengarry badge. Since being out here the khaki helmet has been in use but with no distinguishing badge or mark on it. Nor has the jacket (serge or drill kharki (sic)) had any marks of distinction at any time.' In 1991, Private S. Charters, who served with the battalion in France and Mesopotamia, could only recall regulation badges and the wearing of a Mackenzie tartan kilt.

The Seaforth Highlanders (Ross-shire Buffs, The Duke of Albany's)

2nd Battalion

The battalion landed in France about the 22/8/14 and spent the war on the Western Front with the 10th Brigade, 4th Division.

Badges: the battalion was allocated a vertical green rectangle 3″ × 1″, but just days before it was worn in action on the first day of the Somme, the battalion adopted a Mackenzie tartan segment, 2½″ wide (top) × 3½″ high, on 25/6/16. It was worn, apex down, until the end of the war by all ranks on both arms just below the seam. An additional badge was worn on 1/7/16, a large 6″ high light-coloured **C** was worn on the top of the left upper sleeve. In early 1917 the badge was placed below the mid-green divisional ram's head. A 3″ × 1″ mid-green strip of woven tape was worn vertically on both sides of the helmet cover, painted on when no cover was worn. The divisional sign was also worn on the helmet, position not stated in the NWM questionnaire.

3rd (Reserve) Battalion

It remained at its war station, Cromarty, for the entire war as part of the Cromarty Garrison.

Badges: regulation cloth and metal badges were worn, and Private S. Charters in 1991 remembered wearing a Mackenzie tartan kilt.

A private in the 1st Battalion during 1915. His kilt and cap badge are sufficient to identify him; he is not wearing shoulder titles.

A private in the 3rd Battalion towards the end of the war. He is wearing short puttees with coloured tabs in the hose tops, a Mackenzie tartan kilt with cut away jacket, and Balmoral with a tartan patch behind the cap badge. Although unclear in the photograph, he is wearing metal shoulder titles.

Although their kilts made them easily identifiable it was decided to add an additional badge on the left upper sleeve – a 6″ light coloured **C**.

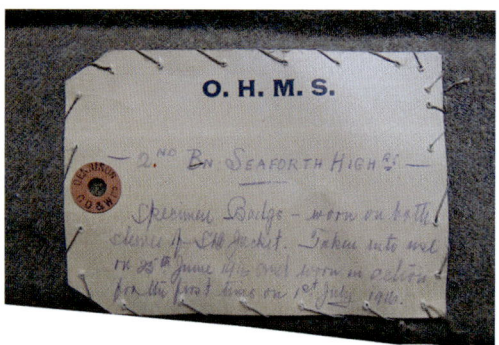

A tag stitched to the back of the tartan segment explaining the history of the badge.

In 1917 a green ram's head was placed above the tartan segment: the shape identified the 4th Division, the colour the brigade – 10th.

A tartan segment was adopted by the 2nd Battalion a few days before the first day of the Somme. It was worn on both arms.

A green vertical bar was worn on both sides of the helmet cover and painted on when no cover was worn. The divisional sign was also on the helmet, almost certainly on the front.

The Gordon Highlanders

Aberdeen was the regiment's depot and home to the reserve battalion in barracks at Castlehill; the 1st Battalion was at Plymouth, the 2nd in Cairo. The cap badge worn by officers and men was similar but the former was more stylised and smaller. Officers wore collar badges and other ranks wore a curved shoulder title – **GORDON**.

1st Battalion

The battalion landed at Boulogne on 14/8/14 with the 8th Brigade, 3rd Division. After heavy losses in the opening month of the war, the battalion left the division and became Army Troops to rest and re-form, re-joining the brigade at the end of September. In October 1915 the 76th Brigade was swapped with the 8th but the battalion remained in the division serving until the end of the war with the new brigade.

Badges: for the Battle of the Bluff, 2–3 March 1916, a special one-off badge was adopted for wear on the back of the tunic between the shoulders: a black 5″ cotton cross on a 6″ yellow cotton square. The usefulness of the badge was explained by Captain Pine on 23/9/17: 'this was the first occasion the Battalion went into action with any special distinguishing mark, and it proved the soundness of its adoption by the easiness with which the men knew each other when they occupied the captured German trench in the uncertain light of early morning.' On 1/7/16 a patch of yellow cotton cloth was worn on the flap of the haversack or the flap was painted yellow. Bright tin triangles were worn on the equipment between the shoulder blades. During the fighting at Delville Wood – 18/7/16 – and Guillemont – 18/8/16 – coloured shoulder straps were used to identify the wearer's company: A Company – blue; B Company – green (later changed to black); C Company – red; D Company – yellow; HQ Company

– mauve/violet. At Serre on 13/11/16 and Arras on 9/4/17 the same colours were used but only worn on the right strap. According to Captain Pine they were found to be a useful identification method when men became casualties during the fighting and adopted permanently as part of the 'fighting kit' of the battalion. In April 1917 the left side of the helmet, of all ranks, was stencilled in white with the regimental cap badge.

2nd Battalion

Arriving from Cairo on 1/10/14 it joined the 20th Brigade, 7th Division, forming at Lyndhurst. It landed at Zeebrugge on 7/10/14 and fought with the division on the Western Front until November 1917; the division was then transferred to Italy where it remained.

Badges: apart from regulation badges no special battalion marks were used. The steel helmet cover had a pagri with a bow on the left from 1917. The kilt was a distinctive emblem.

3rd (Reserve) Battalion

On 4/8/14 the battalion was in Aberdeen. It remained there throughout supplying drafts to the other battalions. It was part of the Aberdeen garrison.

Badges: regulation cloth and metal.

The officers' badge was very similar to that of the other ranks but not identical.

A special one-off badge was worn for the Battle of the Bluff on the night of 2/3rd March 1916. It provided easy identification in the dark during the fighting.

The Gordon Highlanders

A copy of the letter from the 1st Battalion, written in the field, on 23/9/17, describing the badges worn to that date and why.

```
From,
    The Officer Commanding,
        1st Battalion THE GORDON HIGHLANDERS.

To,
    The Secretary,
        National War Museum,
            L O N D O N.
            -----------
```

WAR MUSEUM
7 1119
2/10/17.

In answer to your letter I received some little time ago asking for any relic of this Battalion's actions during the present war. I am sending you the colours worn by the Battalion subsequent to the Battle of the Bluff.

These colours are being forwarded for inclusion in the collection of war material etc., for exhibition in the National Museum if you think them of sufficient interest for this purpose.

A short explanatory account is given hereunder to add a little information to the colours, and which I hope will prove of some small interest to the future generations who may be concerned in upholding the traditions of **THE GORDON HIGHLANDERS**.

PATCH. - <u>KHAKI CLOTH WITH BLACK ST ANDREW'S CROSS ON BLACK GROUND.</u>

During the Battle of the Bluff which was fought on the morning of 2/3rd March 1916. This patch was worn by the Battalion on the back of the Service Dress Jacket, between the shoulders.

This was the first occasion the Battalion went into action with any special distinguishing mark, and it proved the soundness of its adoption by the easiness with which the men knew each other when they occupied the captured German trench in the uncertain light of early morning.

SHOULDER COLOURS. - <u>WORN BY THE DIFFERENT COMPANIES AS FOLLOWS.</u>

"A" COY............ BLUE.
"B" " .... GREEN.
"C" " .... RED.
"D" " .... YELLOW.
"Headquarters COY..... MAUVE.

The above colours were worn on the two shoulder straps during the Battles of DELVILLE WOOD fought on 18/7/16 and GUILLEMONT fought on 18/8/16 on the SOMME, and on one shoulder strap (Right.) during the Battle of ARRAS fought on 9/4/17. AND Battle of SERRE fought on 13/11/16

The usefulness of these shoulder colours became apparent in helping to distinguish the men of the different companies when they became casualties during the fighting and were adopted permanently as part of the "Fighting Kit" of the 1st Battalion THE GORDON HIGHLANDERS.

In the Field.
23/9/17.   P T Vine Capt for   Major,
        Commanding 1st Battalion THE GORDON HIGHLANDERS.

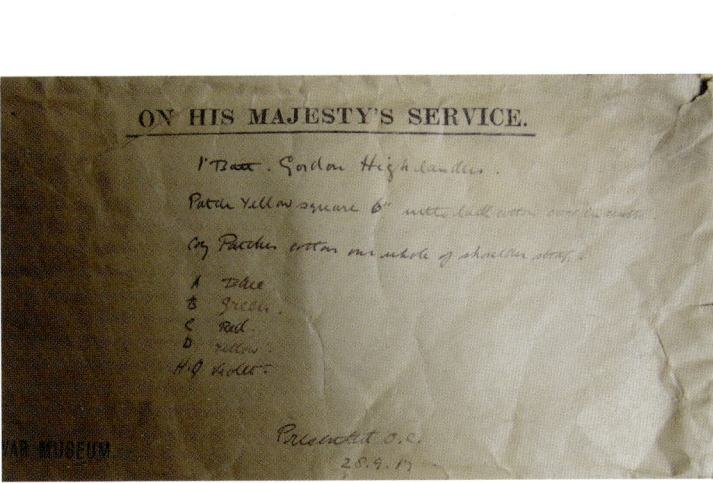

The envelope containing the 1st Battalion badges sent by the Battalion CO on 28/9/17.

Coloured straps were used to identify companies on the Somme; the same system was used at Arras but only the right strap was coloured: blue – A Company; green (later black) – B Company; red – C Company; yellow – D Company; mauve – HQ Company. They were found to be useful in identifying casualties and were retained until the end of the war.

The 2nd Battalion in Italy in the summer of 1918. Easily identifiable by their kilts and hats: the only identifying badge is the cap badge.

The Gordon Highlanders

A 2nd Battalion soldier; his kilt is enough of an identification. His left cuff badge suggests he is a runner, sniper or signaller.

A pre-war postcard showing the regimental tartan, and uniform worn in full dress.

A 7th Division sports meeting in May 1918 in Italy; the Gordon Highlanders are easily recognisable by their headwear.

The Queen's Own Cameron Highlanders

Cameron Barracks, Inverness, was the depot for the 3rd Battalion at the start of the war and also the processing centre for the volunteers of 1914. The 1st Battalion were in Edinburgh and the 2nd Battalion at Poona. All ranks wore a common cap badge, officers wore collar badges, and other ranks wore a curved shoulder title – **CAMERON**.

1st Battalion

The battalion joined the 1st Brigade, 1st Division, after a short period as Army Troops on landing in France on 14/8/14. In March 1916 the battalion absorbed the 1st/4th Battalion. It spent the war on the Western Front with the 1st Division.

Badges: a square of regimental colours, vertically divided blue/black/green, was worn on the upper arms. On the left side of the helmet, initially all ranks wore the bonnet badge, but it was quickly changed to just officers and warrant officers. In 1919, in Germany, a painted sign was adopted on the left side of all ranks' helmets: a white St. Andrew's cross on a blue disc. The battalion began the war with the regulation khaki drill apron but it was discarded at an early date and nothing worn after that. Sporrans were not worn. Steel helmets were first worn by bombers and then all ranks in March/April 1916 with a khaki cover from the summer until dulled helmets were issued.

2nd Battalion

On arrival from India on 16/11/14 it joined the 81st Brigade, 27th Division. It landed at Le Havre on 20/12/14 and fought on the Western Front until it sailed for Salonika on 29/11/15. It remained in Salonika for the rest of the war.

Badges: a ¼″ khaki band worn at the base of the shoulder strap was adopted in April 1916 and worn by all ranks. The Battalion CO also stated that all ranks wore two badges on the pagri. On the left was the pre-war regimental flash: a horizontal, 3½ × 1⅜″ patch of Cameron of Erracht tartan. The brigade sign, a vertical yellow tape 3″ × ⅜″ adopted in April 1917, was on the right side. A tartan patch was worn under the cap badge on the tam-o'-shanter.

3rd (Reserve) Battalion

After three years in Scotland the battalion moved to Ireland in November 1917.

Badges: regulation cloth and metal and a Cameron of Erracht tartan kilt. This was confirmed by Private Robert Burns who trained with the battalion in 1914/15.

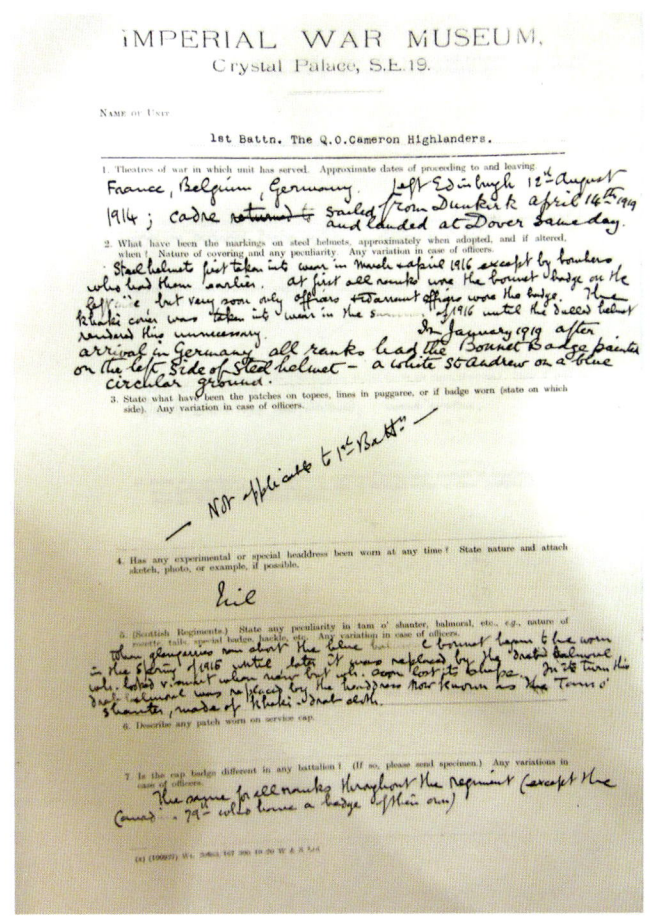

The answers provided by the 1st Battalion CO on the 1921 IWM questionnaire.

260 Badges of the Regular Infantry, 1914–1918

All units in the 27th Division wore a khaki/yellow band on the base of the shoulder strap.

A horizontal patch of Cameron of Erracht tartan was worn on the left side of the pagri; on the right side was the brigade sign, a vertical yellow tape.

An interesting photograph; the 1st Battalion soldier on the right has the battalion badge on the left of his pagri but the soldier on the left also has the brigade sign on the left.

A pre-war photograph showing the 1st Battalion sign in use.

The 1st Battalion wore a square of regimental colours on both upper arms.

The Queen's Own Cameron Highlanders   261

A pre-war postcard showing the regimental tartan and pre-war full dress uniform.

As part of the Army of Occupation, the 1st Battalion adopted a white cross of St. Andrew on a blue disc. It was worn on the left side of the helmet by all ranks.

In Salonika each division wore a different coloured sign on the shoulder straps. That of the 27th was khaki or yellow. Other ranks also wore a shoulder title.

The Royal Irish Rifles

Mainly recruiting around Belfast, the regiment was very large, consisting of two regular battalions, the 1st in Aden, the 2nd at Tidworth and three reserve battalions. The 3rd (Reserve) Battalion was based at Victoria Barracks, Belfast, the 4th was at Newtownards and the 5th at Downpatrick; the latter two were extra reserve battalions.

1st Battalion

Based in Aden, it embarked for England on 27/9/14. It landed at Le Havre on 6/11/14 and was part of the 25th Brigade, 8th Division, until February 1918 when it moved to the 107th Brigade, 36th (Ulster) Division.

Badges: the Battalion CO informed the NWM on the 22nd and again on the 29th August 1917 that in the 8th Division all ranks wore, on both sleeves, 1″ below the shoulder seam, a 2″ square, quartered in black – top left front and bottom right – and rifle green; black to the front. In the 36th (Ulster) Division, from February 1918, an inverted triangle, bisected vertically rifle green and black, was worn on both sleeves directly below the straps. The same cloth signs were worn on officer's helmets and painted on the men's in both divisions. A black cap badge was worn and puttees were worn spiral fashion. Buglers' lines were worn in green over the right shoulder.

2nd Battalion

The battalion landed in France on 14/8/14 as part of the 7th Brigade, 3rd Division, but on 18 October 1915 the brigade was exchanged with a brigade from the 25th Division;

days later the battalion was transferred to the 74th Brigade in the same division. In mid-November 1917 it moved again, this time to the 108th Brigade, 36th (Ulster) Division, where it absorbed the 7th Battalion. During the 1918 reorganisation it went to the 107th Brigade.

Badges: in the 25th Division, the first badge adopted, worn by all ranks, was a green shamrock, 1″, embroidered on a 2″ diameter khaki circle. In October 1916 the divisional sign – a red horseshoe – was worn on the back below a blue horizontal rectangle on the back of the collar. On joining the 108th Brigade, 36th (Ulster) Division in late 1917, a dark green minor arc was worn on the upper sleeve.[31] The battalion was exchanged with the 2nd Royal Irish Fusiliers on 8/2/18 and moved to the 107th Brigade where it wore a dark green inverted triangle on both arms. A silver cap badge was worn.

3rd (Reserve) Battalion

Moving from Belfast to Dublin and back, the battalion arrived in England during April 1918. It became part of the Irish Reserve Brigade.

Badges: regulation cloth and metal.

4th (Extra Reserve) Battalion

Like the 3rd Battalion, it remained in Ireland until joining the Irish Reserve Brigade at Larkhill in April 1918.

Badges: regulation cloth and metal.

5th (Extra Reserve) Battalion

Following the reserve and reserve battalions, the 5th moved to Larkhill after service in Ireland. The three battalions formed the Irish Reserve Brigade.

Badges: regulation cloth and metal.

---

31. IWM photo Q10678 Essigny, 7/2/18.

264   Badges of the Regular Infantry, 1914–1918

In the 8th Division all ranks wore a quartered square in black and rifle green on both arms.

On joining the 25th Division the 2nd Battalion adopted a shamrock worn on both arms.

Conforming to the 25th Division system the battalion wore the red horseshoe and a brigade bar on their back.

When the 2nd Battalion transferred to the 36th (Ulster Division) it adopted the sign of the 13th Battalion – a green minor arc.

When the battalion moved to the 107th Brigade it wore an inverted green isosceles triangle.

Private W. Graydon was killed in action on 9/5/28 serving with the 2nd Battalion.

When cloth shoulder titles were introduced they were supposed to be standardised. This is a printed version of the title; as a rifle regiment the original had the letters in green.

From February 1918 the 1st Battalion wore an inverted vertically bisected triangle in rifle green and black.

On joining the 108th Brigade, the 2nd Battalion wore a minor green arc on both shoulders.

A private in the 2nd Battalion photographed after February 1918; his inverted triangle is visible on the upper sleeve.

In black and white, the same sign was used by the 2nd, 7th, 8th and 9th Battalions.

The Princess Victoria's (Royal Irish Fusiliers)

Gough Barracks, Armagh, was the Regimental Depot and home for the reserve battalion. The extra reserve battalion was at Cavan, the 1st Battalion was at Shorncliffe, and the 2nd at Quetta. All ranks wore a common cap badge, officers wore collar badges and other ranks wore a range of shoulder titles – **RIF**, **RIF** below a grenade and **IgrenadeF**.

1st Battalion

Moving from Shorncliffe to York and then Harrow, the battalion landed in France on 18/8/14 with the 10th Brigade, 4th Division. On 3/8/17 it moved to the 36th (Ulster) Division, joining the 107th Brigade on 24/8/17. In February 1918 it was transferred to the 108th Brigade.

Badges: for the Somme offensive the battalion was allocated a 2″ green square to be worn on the helmet cover. This was later changed to being worn at the top of the arm, and from early 1917 it was below the divisional sign in green – a ram's head. In the 107th Brigade, 36th (Ulster) Division, all ranks wore, on both arms, an inverted mid-green isosceles triangle, base 1¾″, sides 2½″, and on transfer to the 108th Brigade it adopted a green minor arc, diameter 2½″ × depth 1¼″. All of these were clearly described to the writer in correspondence in 1988 by Private C. McLean who enlisted in 1911 and served throughout the war with the battalion. On 1 July 1916 attacking troops wore a tin triangle on their backs.

2nd Battalion

The battalion was stationed in India at the start of the war and arrived in England in mid-November. It joined the 82nd Brigade, 27th Division, and fought in France and Flanders from December 1914 to November 1915. In Salonika it replaced a battalion in the 31st Brigade, 10th (Irish) Division, and remained with the division for the rest of the war.

Badges: no battalion badges were worn on the tunic except the divisional bands of the 27th Division – khaki – and the 10th (Irish) Division – green – worn at the base of the straps. On the left side of the pagri, worn by all ranks, was a khaki drill patch with a green painted eagle. However, the regimental museum information gives the colours as a white cloth eagle on green. Steel helmets were not marked. Collar badges for other ranks were stopped during the war. Shorts were of the Indian pattern in Egypt and Palestine.

3rd (Reserve) Battalion

After nearly four years serving in Ireland, the battalion moved to England. First to Rugeley – April 1918 – and in July 1918 became part of the West Riding Reserve Brigade in Bawdsey, Suffolk.

Badges: Private J. Lovegrove served with the battalion before being commissioned into the Loyal North Lancashire Regiment in late 1917. He could recall the signs used by the Territorial Brigade he served with and was certain he only wore regulation cloth and metal badges with the 3rd Battalion.

4th (Extra Reserve) Battalion

Like the 3rd Battalion, it spent most of the war in Ireland and moved to England in April 1918 to Rugeley. There it was absorbed into the 3rd Battalion.

Badges: regulation cloth and metal.

268   Badges of the Regular Infantry, 1914–1918

A corporal in the 1st Battalion; although 1918 he is still wearing metal titles above his battalion badge. He is wearing regimental buttons and appears to have a 1 above the grenade.

A studio photograph of a youthful lieutenant wearing his full service uniform and sword. He is wearing badges on his collars and cap.

In the 107th Brigade all ranks of the 1st Battalion wore an inverted green triangle and when the 1st Battalion moved to the 108th Brigade it wore a minor green arc. These images show the 100-year-old colour and the real colour on the reverse.

The replacement cloth shoulder title unusually featured a raised grenade.

From early 1917 it was worn below the divisional sign – a ram's head; the colour indicated the brigade – 10th.

The first badge adopted by the 1st Battalion was a green square on both arms.

The Princess Victoria's (Royal Irish Fusiliers)

A khaki/yellow band was worn on the base of the straps by all ranks in the 2nd Battalion.

On transfer to the 10th Division the 2nd Battalion replaced the khaki/yellow band for one in green.

A soldier in the 3rd Battalion sometime in late 1918; the only badges are regulation.

The 2nd Battalion wore a green eagle on a khaki patch on the left side of the pagri.

In Salonika all divisions wore a coloured tab on their shoulders. Serving in the 10th (Irish) Division, the 2nd Battalion wore a thin green band with other ranks also wearing a shoulder title.

The Connaught Rangers

The regiment consisted of four battalions: the 1st at Ferozepore, 2nd at Barrosa Barracks, Aldershot, the reserve in Galway and the extra reserve at Boyle; the RHQ was in Mitchel Barracks, Castlebar. All ranks wore a common cap badge, officers wore collar badges and other ranks wore a curved shoulder title – CONN.RANGERS; the letter CR were sometimes worn on the greatcoat.

1st Battalion

Garrisoned in Ferozepore, it left India on 28/8/14 as part of the Ferozepore Brigade, 3rd (Lahore) Division. In early December 1914, in France, it merged with the 2nd Battalion. It left for Mesopotamia a year later. On arrival it was temporarily attached for a month to the 9th Indian Brigade, 3rd Indian Division. From February 1916 it served with the 7th Indian Brigade, 3rd Division, in Egypt and Palestine.

Badges: along with the regulation badges, all ranks wore a khaki drill patch on the left side of the pagri embroidered with **CONNAUGHT RANGERS** in green. According to correspondence with the CO of the 2nd Battalion just after the war, the 1st Battalion initially wore a green band on the pagri with the 3rd Lahore Division.

2nd Battalion

The battalion landed in France on 14/8/14, part of the 5th Brigade, 2nd Division. It joined the Ferozepore Brigade on 26/11/14 and was amalgamated with the 1st Battalion on 5/12/14.

Badges: during its short existence as an active battalion the only badges worn were regulation metal.

3rd (Reserve) Battalion

For nearly three years the battalion garrisoned Kinsale. In November 1917 it moved to Newcastle-upon-Tyne and in May 1918 became part of the Dover Garrison, based in Dover.

Badges: as well as the regulation metal and cloth badges, the cap badge was worn on the front of the steel helmet.

4th (Extra Reserve) Battalion

The battalion was absorbed into the 3rd Battalion in May 1918 after serving in Ireland and Scotland.

Badges: regulation cloth and metal.

All ranks wore a khaki drill patch on the left side of the pagri. The lettering is in green.

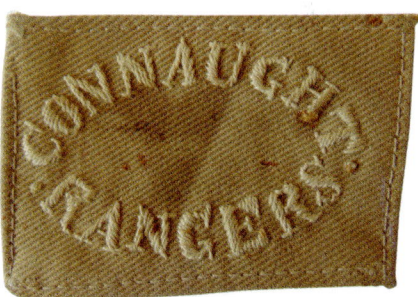

A close-up of the front and back of the patch showing fading to the front and the original colour behind.

By 1914 the CONNAUGHT title was supposed to have been replaced by CONN.RANGERS but both were worn.

The Princess Louise's (Argyll & Sutherland Highlanders)

A four-battalion regiment with its depot in Stirling Castle, the home of the reserve battalion. There were two regular battalions; the 1st was in Dinapore and the 2nd at Fort George. The extra reserve battalion was at Paisley. All ranks wore a common cap badge, officers wore collar badges and other ranks wore a shoulder title – **A&SH**.

1st Battalion

The battalion departed Bombay on 19/10/14 and landed at Plymouth on 19/11/14. It served throughout the war with the 81st Brigade, 27th Division, in France from 20/12/14 to 27/11/15, and for the remainder of the war in Salonika.

Badges: Lieutenant Colonel Elphinstone informed the NWM that in Salonika all ranks wore the divisional ½″ band in buff/khaki across the base of both straps from some time in 1915, and that a 2″ × 3″ horizontal patch of universal tartan was worn on the left side of the eight-fold pagri of the topee. There is also evidence of a brigade system of badges on the topee, so the battalion should also have worn a vertical red rectangle on the right side of the pagri. A back flap was worn on the steel helmet for protection against the sun. In 1915 when a soft felt hat with a four-fold khaki pagri was issued, the left side was pinned up. They quickly faded in the sun turning from grey-green to pink. 'The Battalion landed in France with glengarries. A few Balmorals were issued to Battalion shortly after landing in France and in July 1915 this was changed to a fawn colour, and issued to all. With both these bonnets the Regimental Cap Badge was worn on the left side and no rosette. Early in 1916 a Tam-o'-Shanter, known by the

Ordnance as "Caps Balmoral, large crown khaki cloth" was issued and is still in use. Officers wore the same pattern on all three occasions but a special tam-o'-shanter was eventually made by Barnard & Sons, London. This make all officers wore in the last year of the war. It had ribbons at the back, 12 inches in length.'

2nd Battalion

For its first week in France the battalion was LoC troops, joining the 19th Brigade at Valenciennes from 14/8 to 22/8/14. The brigade was attached to the 6th Division and at the end of May 1917 attached to the 27th Division. In mid-August 1915 the brigade replaced the 4th Guards Brigade in the 2nd Division, and in November it replaced a brigade in the 33rd Division. While the 19th Brigade stayed with the division it was split up and the 2nd battalion went to the 98th Brigade. It remained with the division until after the Armistice.

Badges: on 1/8/17 the Battalion CO informed the NWM that only regulation badges were worn. 'No such badges are worn by this battalion; the tartan is considered a sufficiently distinctive mark in the 33rd Division.' The wearing of only regulation badges was confirmed in July 1987 by Sergeant E. Turner who was certain that such things were only worn by brigade and divisional staff.

3rd (Reserve) Battalion

The battalion travelled the country during its service. From Stirling it went to Woolwich, Edinburgh, Dreghorn (near Kilmarnock), before arriving at Kinsale in Ireland. There it became part of the 25th Reserve Brigade.

Badges: Colonel Gordon, the Battalion CO, making reference to the distinctive badges worn by some of the other battalions sent the NWM a cap badge and a set of collar badges as worn by all battalions of the regiment. It is safe to assume from this that in this battalion only regulation cloth and metal badges were worn. This is confirmed by the replies to the IWM questionnaire in 1921.

4th (Extra Reserve) Battalion

Like the 3rd Battalion, it was well travelled: Paisley, Devonport, Sunderland, Plymouth, Edinburgh and finally Dunbar. There it was part of the Forth Garrison.

274 Badges of the Regular Infantry, 1914–1918

Badges: replying for the Battalion CO, Major Thomson informed the NWM on 2/8/17 that they wore no special badges: 'It is regretted that this Battalion has never served overseas as a unit since mobilization; consequently it has never worn this sleeve badge to which you refer. The only distinction in dress this Battalion has adopted since mobilization is that of wear (sic) a whole puttee instead of a half puttee and khaki hosetop, which I think is the practice in all other Battalions of the Regiment. This practice was adopted in this Battalion when the issue of diced hose and garters was discontinued early in 1915.'

All ranks of the 1st Battalion wore the divisional sign, a khaki band, on each shoulder strap.

In mid-1916 the ACD authorised a cloth title to replace the metal one.

Private W. Poole, number 27396, of the 4th Battalion, was based at Redford Barracks, Colinton, when this photo was taken in October 1916. He is wearing shoes, spats, and diced hose tops. He is wearing a Black Watch tartan kilt with a private soldier's sporran with the 'Swinging Six' tassels with silver coloured tops. The tunic is standard pattern with the hem pushed back rather than shaped. His glengarry bonnet has a cap badge with backing, a red toorie on top, two black tassels at the rear and red and white dicing. He is wearing cloth shoulder titles.

A horizontal rectangle of universal tartan was worn on the left side of the pagri.

A company of the 2nd Battalion shortly after their arrival in France. They claimed to be the first British troops to land in France on the outbreak of hostilities.

Three soldiers of the 3rd Battalion photographed in Cork. As second-line troops they have been issued with the American-made M14 Enfield. Two are wearing a glengarry, the other a tam-o'-shanter. The soldier on the right is wearing a cloth title, the one on the left a metal title and a cut away tunic.

Officer PoWs at an unknown camp. The officer standing on the left is wearing a kilt cover. Two officers have battalion badges on their upper arm; one is wearing an other-ranks tunic – often known as a funk jacket. Only the Argylls' officer is wearing collar badges.

An officers' collar badge; they came in matching pairs.

Serving in the 27th Division all ranks of the 1st Battalion wore a yellow/khaki divisional band on their straps; other ranks also had a shoulder title.

The Princess of Wales's Leinster Regiment (Royal Canadians)

Crinkill Barracks near Birr was the Regimental Depot and also the base for the reserve battalion. The extra reserve battalions were at Maryborough and Drogheda; the two regular battalions were at Fyzabad (1st) and Cork (2nd). All ranks wore a common cap badge, officers wore collar badges, and other ranks wore a curved shoulder title – **LEINSTER.R.C**.

1st Battalion

On arrival from India on 16/11/14 the battalion joined the 82nd Brigade, 27th Division, with which it fought, in France from 20/12/14 until November 1915 and Salonika until it was transferred to the 29th Brigade, 10th (Irish) Division, on 2/11/16. In September 1917 it left Salonika with the 10th (Irish) Division and fought in Palestine.

Badges: in the 10th (Irish) and 27th Division, all ranks wore the divisional band across the base of the shoulder straps – green and buff respectively. Correspondence from the Battalion CO, Lieutenant Colonel Wildblood, dated 6/10/17, gives exact details of two further badges worn by his men. The first replaced the cap badge worn on the pagri: a green cotton $2\frac{3}{4}''$ square with maple leaf shape cut out of the centre, backed with a patch of white cotton. This was made regimentally from material sourced locally and adopted on 12/8/17. It was worn on the left side. The second badge was taken into use the day before he wrote to the museum. On 5/10/17 a green vertical rectangle $2\frac{5}{8}'' \times 2\frac{1}{8}''$, with a white, loop embroidered maple leaf, $2\frac{3}{16}'' \times 1\frac{5}{8}''$, replaced the first badge. It was made in Cairo by Messrs J. Eskenayi & N. Babani of Khan Khalil.

2nd Battalion

On leaving Cork the battalion proceeded to France via Cambridge and Newmarket. On landing on 12/9/14 it was part of the 17th Brigade, 6th Division. On 26/11/15 the brigade was swapped with the 71st Brigade, 24th Division; the battalion was then transferred to the 73rd Brigade. In February 1918 during the reorganisation of British divisions it moved to the 47th Brigade, 16th (Irish) Division, absorbing men from the disbanded 7th Battalion. During April it also absorbed men from the disbanded 6th Connaught Rangers and by the end of the month it was fighting with the 88th Brigade, 29th Division.

Badges: in the 24th Division a yellow 2½″ felt square was worn below a four-pointed company star on both arms; it was also worn on the steel helmet. The stars were 2¾″ × 2¾″ and in different colours: blue – A Company; green – B Company; red – C Company; yellow – D Company; no star – HQ Company.[32] On transfer to the 16th (Irish) Division a green shamrock and a vertically bisected vertical diamond in white and blue were worn; position of wear is unclear, the divisional system was the shamrock on the arms and battalion badge on the back but Haswell-Millar records the battalion badge as being worn on the arm – white to the front. From April 1918 in the 29th Division the divisional red triangle was worn on both arms with a blue and green square diamond on the back, worn in different positions to show the wearer's company: blue over green – A Company; green left, blue right – B Company; green over blue – C Company; blue left, green right – D Company; divided middle top left to middle bottom right, blue to right and green to left – HQ Company. The divisional badge was worn on the front of the helmet with company signs on the sides.

Blue buglers lines were worn around the collar and fastened to the left shoulder. Pipers wore a saffron kilt, a khaki Irish bonnet with regimental badge, boots, puttees, green hose tops and white belts.

3rd (Reserve) Battalion

The battalion moved to Portsmouth in November 1917 after having served at Cork since August 1914. As part of the Portsmouth Garrison it absorbed the 4th and 5th Battalions in May 1918.

Badges: the IWM questionnaire confirms that the battalion only wore regulation cloth and metal badges.

---

32. IWM photo Q5850 Dickebusch 9/8/17.

278 Badges of the Regular Infantry, 1914–1918

4th (Extra Reserve) Battalion

Like the 3rd Battalion it moved to England in November 1917 becoming part of the Portsmouth Garrison before being absorbed by the 3rd Battalion. Before this it had served in Crosshaven, Devonport, the Curragh, Limerick and Tralee.

Badges: regulation cloth and metal.

5th (Extra Reserve) Battalion

This battalion served in three of the home countries: Ireland – Drogheda, Queenstown, Passage West, Mullingar, The Curragh, Laytown, Boyle and Birr; Scotland – Glencorse; England – Plymouth and Portsmouth. Like the 4th, it ceased to exist after May 1918.

Badges: regulation cloth and metal.

All ranks of the 1st Battalion wore a khaki/yellow band on their shoulder straps. When the battalion moved to the 10th Division it wore a green band.

Initially a cap badge was worn on the front of the pagri but this was replaced by a crudely made white maple leaf on a green square worn on the left side.

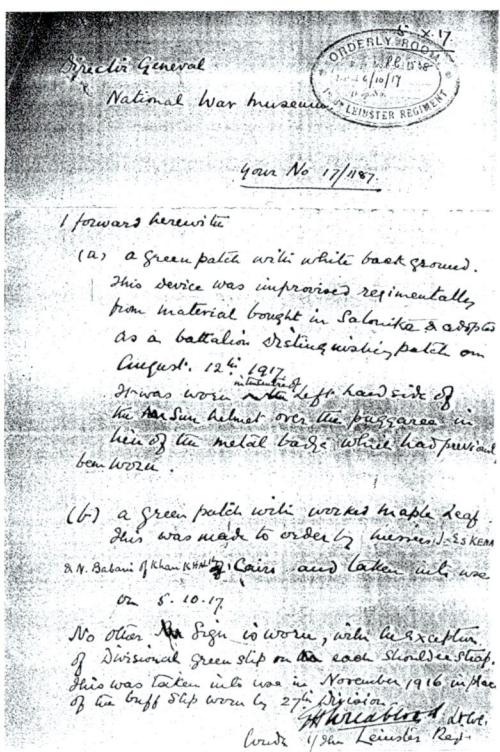

A copy of the letter written by the 1st Battalion CO on 6/10/17 describing the badges.

The Princess of Wales's Leinster Regiment (Royal Canadians)

In the 16th Division all ranks wore the Shamrock sign on both arms.

The second badge was professionally made in Cairo for the battalion; a white loop embroidered maple leaf.

In the 24th Division the 2nd Battalion wore a yellow square below a four-pointed star to identify the company: blue – A Company; green – B Company; red – C Company; yellow – D Company. The lack of a star indicated the HQ Company.

280 Badges of the Regular Infantry, 1914–1918

Three 2nd Battalion sergeants; their 29th Division badges are exactly in line with the top of the pocket.

In the 10th Division all ranks wore the divisional badge on their shoulder straps – a thin green band.

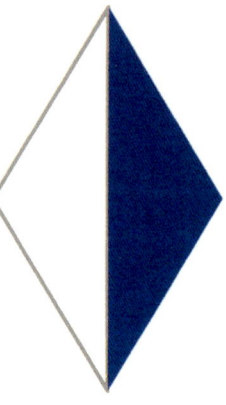

When the 2nd Battalion transferred to the 16th Division it adopted a vertical diamond in white and blue that was worn on the back.

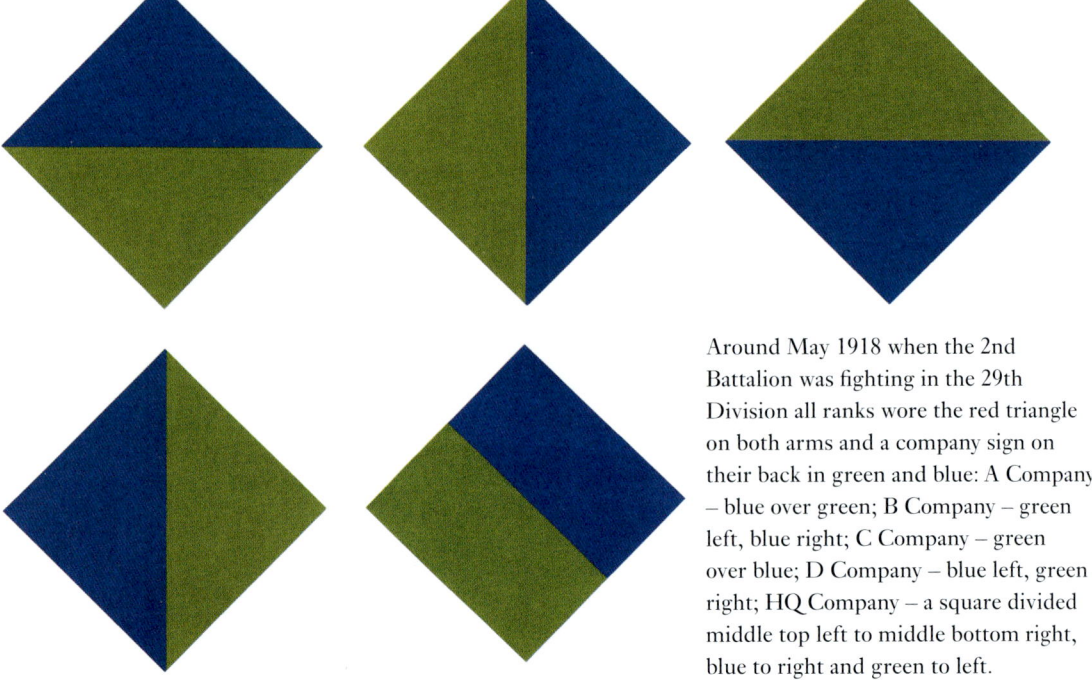

Around May 1918 when the 2nd Battalion was fighting in the 29th Division all ranks wore the red triangle on both arms and a company sign on their back in green and blue: A Company – blue over green; B Company – green left, blue right; C Company – green over blue; D Company – blue left, green right; HQ Company – a square divided middle top left to middle bottom right, blue to right and green to left.

The Princess of Wales's Leinster Regiment (Royal Canadians)

When the 2nd Battalion moved to the 29th Division in April 1918 it wore the divisional sign on both arms.

The 1st Battalion fought with two divisions in Salonika, each used a coloured band on their shoulder straps: yellow for the 27th, a regular division, and green in the 10th (Irish) Division, a Kitchener unit.

The Royal Munster Fusiliers

Recruiting across the south-west of Ireland, the regiment was formed of two regular, one reserve, and two extra reserve battalions. Ballymullen barracks in Tralee was the depot and housed the 3rd Battalion: two extra reserve battalions were at Kinsale and Limerick. The 1st Battalion was in Rangoon and the 2nd was at Malplaquet Barracks, Aldershot. All ranks wore a common cap badge, officers wore collar badges, and other ranks wore a shoulder title – **RMF** and later in the war **MgrenadeF**.

1st Battalion

The battalion sailed from Rangoon in December 1914. On arrival in England in early January 1915 it joined the 86th Brigade, 29th Division, with which it fought at Gallipoli. After sustaining heavy casualties the battalion was temporarily amalgamated with the 1st Royal Dublin Fusiliers to form what was known as the 'Dubsters'. In January 1916, having been re-formed in mid-May 1915, it moved via Egypt to France where it became LoC troops. At the end of May 1916 it was transferred to the 47th Brigade, 16th (Irish) Division, absorbing men from the newly disbanded 9th Battalion. In November it moved to the 47th Brigade and absorbed men from the disbanded 8th Battalion. When the 2nd Battalion was disbanded in April 1918 it absorbed its personnel before moving to the 172nd Brigade, 57th Division.

Badges: before sailing to Gallipoli, while in Coventry in February 1915, a green cloth shamrock was adopted. It was worn under the cap badge in two sizes: large for other ranks and a small padded one with beaded edge for officers. A green shamrock was worn on the left side of the pagri and a green and white hackle. On about 18/4/15, just before the Helles landings, 'battalions of the 29th Division were ordered to put up distinguishing badges'. A green cloth isosceles triangle, base 3″ × sides 2″, was chosen; they were worn on both sleeves. These remained in use until the divisional sign came into use when it was moved to the back of the tunic just below the collar in April 1916. Just days after joining the 16th (Irish) Division, all ranks put the new divisional sign on both sleeves with the green triangle on the back. The Battalion CO informed the NWM on 9/8/17 that when the battalion had absorbed the men from the disbanded 8th Battalion, by the special request of the Divisional Commander they adopted their shamrock sign and wore it on both arms; it was the same size as the shamrock behind the officers' cap badge. On the steel helmet a green shamrock with a white edge was painted on the front and sewn on when a cover was used.

2nd Battalion

Landing In France on 14/8/14 the battalion was part of the 1st (Guards) Brigade, 1st Division, and after serving briefly as Army Troops in September and October 1914 it was moved to the 3rd Brigade, 1st Division. In May 1916 it absorbed a number of men from the disbanded 9th Battalion. After brief service with the 47th Brigade, 16th (Irish) Division, it was reduced to training cadre and surplus personnel sent to the 1st Battalion. In June 1918 it was reformed with men from the disbanded 6th Battalion and became LoC troops until it joined the 150th Brigade, 50th Division.

Badges: the first sign worn was seen in August 1914 when the battalion landed in France. An unidentified major, still wearing his tropical helmet, had, on the left side, a green shamrock with **MgrenadeF** in bonze in the centre in front of white over green hackle. In the 1st Division ¾″ squares were used to identify specialist rolls: red – bombers; black – rifle grenadiers; yellow – Lewis gunners; green – riflemen. However, according to Lieutenant Colonel Neill, writing on 8/8/17, only a green shamrock was worn under the cap badge: 'No shoulder or back patches have ever been worn'. In the 16th (Irish) Division a green shamrock was worn on both sleeves with no battalion badge worn on the back. It is probable that the battalion wore a green square on both arms while in the 50th Division.

3rd (Reserve) Battalion

A well-travelled battalion: Tralee, Berehaven, Cork, Aghada, Ballincollig, Devonport, and Plymouth. It was part of the Plymouth Garrison from April 1918 until the end of the war, absorbing the 4th and 5th Battalions in May 1918.

Badges: regulation cloth and metal badges were worn with a sage shamrock behind the cap badge.

4th (Extra Reserve) Battalion

The 4th Battalion travelled in three of the home countries: Ireland – Kinsale, Queenstown, Aghada, Fermoy, Bere Island, The Curragh and Castlebar; Scotland – Dreghorn and Portobello; England – South Shields and Plymouth where as part of the garrison it was absorbed into the 3rd Battalion.

Badges: regulation cloth and metal.

5th (Extra Reserve) Battalion

Like the 4th, it served in Ireland, Scotland and England. Its final posting was Plymouth as part of the garrison; it was absorbed into the 3rd Battalion in May 1918.

Badges: regulation cloth and metal with a sage green shamrock behind the cap badge. These were confirmed by Major Roche, the Battalion CO, on 16/8/17.

A green shamrock was worn behind the cap badge when the 1st Battalion was in Coventry in February 1915.

The Royal Munster Fusiliers

Other ranks wore a large shamrock behind the cap badge; the officers' badge was smaller.

This shape of shamrock was more commonly worn behind the cap badge.

Just before landing at Helles the 29th Division ordered all battalions to adopt a distinguishing badge. The 1st Battalion chose a green isosceles triangle to be worn on both sleeves. When the divisional sign was introduced the green triangle was moved to the back.

A green shamrock with a white outline was worn on the front of the helmet

When the 1st Battalion absorbed the men from the disbanded 8th Battalion it adopted their shoulder badge: a shamrock very similar in size to the shamrock behind the officers' cap badge.

286   Badges of the Regular Infantry, 1914–1918

The 16th Division sign was worn by both the 1st and 2nd Battalions in the 47th Brigade.

In the 50th Division it is very probable that the 2nd Battalion wore a green square on both arms.

Specialist troops in the 2nd Battalion were identified by coloured squares on the back of the collar: yellow – Lewis gunners; red – bombers; black – rifle grenadiers; green – riflemen.

On landing at Gallipoli a green shamrock was worn on the left side of the pagri with a green and white hackle.

The IWM card with the 1st Battalion badges clearly shows the difference between the 1st Battalion officers and other ranks badge worn at Helles in April 1915.

The metal shoulder title worn by other ranks.

The Royal Dublin Fusiliers

Both of the extra reserve battalions were based in Dublin but the Regimental Depot was at Devoy Barracks, Naas, home of the 3rd Battalion. The 1st Battalion was serving in Madras and the 2nd was at Gravesend. All ranks wore a common cap badge, officers wore collar badges, and other ranks wore a curved shoulder title – a grenade above **RDF**.

1st Battalion

On arrival from India on 21/12/14 it joined the 86th Brigade, 29th Division, with which it served on Gallipoli. After heavy casualties it formed a composite battalion with the 1st Royal Munster Fusiliers – the 'Dubsters'. After further service with the division on the Western Front, it was moved to the 48th Brigade, 16th (Irish) Division, in October 1917 and absorbed the surplus personnel from the disbanded 8th/9th Battalion in February 1918. In April 1918 the 1st and 2nd Battalions amalgamated to form a new 1st Battalion; the 2nd was reduced to a cadre. The 1st Battalion then returned to the 86th Brigade.

Badges: between April 1915 and April 1916 a 2″ slate-blue square was worn on the left upper arm, point upward immediately below the shoulder strap. In France it moved to the back below the collar when the divisional sign was adopted for wear on the arm. The blue square was also worn on the left side of the pagri, and the top of the topee button was painted blue. The blue square was painted on both sides of the helmet. In the 16th (Irish) Division, only the divisional sign was worn on the tunic – a shamrock. On its return to the 29th Division it retained the shamrock as a battalion badge worn on the back.

2nd Battalion

The battalion landed at Boulogne as part of the 10th Brigade, 4th Division on 22/8/14. In November 1916 it was moved to the 48th Brigade, 16th (Irish) Division, absorbing the surplus personnel from the disbanded 8th/9th Battalion. After amalgamation with the 1st Battalion in April 1918 it was reduced to cadre, but was reconstituted and absorbed the surplus from the 7th Battalion. In June it joined the 94th Brigade, 31st Division, and after a few days was transferred to LoC and in mid-July to 149th Brigade, 50th Division.

Badges: Private Cahill, a pre-war regular, served with the battalion until late 1915. He told the writer he only wore metal badges in France. In the 4th Division the Battalion CO informed the NWM that a green diamond was worn on both sides of the steel helmet covers until 11/16. From that date a green minor arc 2″ across × 1½″ deep was worn 3″ below the collar in the centre of the back[33] with a small shamrock worn on both sleeves 1″ from the shoulder strap. However, there are two conflicting letters about the badges. Second Lieutenant Conway reported on 15/8/17 that the green half-moon was worn 'exactly below the shoulder strap on both shoulders'; a letter dated 22/9/17 by a major from the battalion states that during 1916–17 the patch was 'worn on the back close up to the collar of the S. D. Jacket. 2 small shamrock are worn on arm of S. D. Jacket 1″ from shoulder strap – on sleeve' – probably indicating when the divisional sign was worn by all units. On joining the 50th Division a blue half-oval was worn 2″ below the shoulder seams on both arms.

3rd (Reserve) Battalion

After over three years' service in Ireland, in November 1917 it moved to Pembroke and a month later to Gateshead. It absorbed the 4th, 5th and 11th Battalions and moved to the Grimsby area in the Humber Garrison.

Badges: regulation cloth and metal.

4th (Extra Reserve) Battalion

The war service of the 4th was similar to that of the 3rd, serving in Ireland and in England near Grimsby. It was absorbed into the 3rd Battalion in May 1918.

Badges: regulation cloth and metal.

---

33. IWM photo Q6152 27/10/17.

5th (Extra Reserve) Battalion

In May 1918 the battalion was absorbed into the 3rd Battalion at Grimsby. Before that it had served in Dublin, Queenstown, Sittingbourne, The Curragh, Longford and Glencorse.

Badges: regulation cloth and metal.

The two shoulder titles worn by other ranks during the war.

A lieutenant wearing his field uniform displaying cap badge and collar badges.

One of the many types of 16th Division sign used.

The 2nd Battalion wore a green diamond on both sides of the helmet.

A blue square was worn on the arm of all ranks of the 1st Battalion from April 1915 to April 1916 and was worn on the left side of the pagri. In France it moved to the centre of the back.

Badges of the Regular Infantry, 1914–1918

From November 1916 a green minor arc was worn in the centre of the back with the divisional sign on both shoulders. Three variations on the same badge.

An unknown Dublin Fusilier, identified only by his cap badge.

The red triangle was worn on both arms by all ranks of the 29th Division.

In the 50th Division, the 2nd Battalion wore a blue half-disc on both arms.

The Rifle Brigade

Like the King's Royal Rifle Corps, the regiment had no county affiliation. Its headquarters was at Winchester where the two reserve battalions were based in Peninsula Barracks. There were four regular battalions: 1st in Colchester, 2nd in Kuldana, 3rd in Cork, and the 4th at Dagshai. All ranks wore a common cap badge; officers wore collar badges and men wore the shoulder title RB in black.

1st Battalion

The battalion landed at Le Havre on 23/8/14 with the 11th Brigade, 4th Division. It fought on the Western Front with the division throughout the war.

Badges: according to the IWM questionnaire, a yellow cloth 2³⁄₁₆″ square Maltese cross was worn on both sides of the helmet during the winter of 1916/17 (adopted October 1916). Before that no badges were worn. This is contradicted by a 31st Division staff order that provided information about the battalion's badge for the Somme offensive: a 2″ yellow Maltese cross worn on the helmet cover. When covers were discarded in October 1916 the sign was painted on. During September 1916 a yellow ram's head was worn on both upper arms 1″ below the shoulder seams. It was worn until mid-1917 and was replaced by the yellow Maltese cross. In mid-1918 the yellow ram's head, was reintroduced and worn below a battalion sign: a horizontal rectangle 1½″ × 1″ in regimental colours: black (¼″)/dark green (¾″)/black (¼″). All of this was recalled by Private F. Stratford who joined the battalion in March 1918 who also remembered wearing the sign on the sides of his helmet. Evidence suggests that snipers wore a horizontal green bar below the right shoulder strap but this was denied in 1989 by Private Stratford who was a sniper; he said that they didn't wear them 'because if you were taken prisoner you didn't stand much chance with Jerry'.

2nd Battalion

After arriving from India on 22 October, the battalion joined the 5th Brigade, 8th Division. It landed at Le Havre on 6/11/14 and fought with the division on the Western Front for the duration.

Badges: a black 1½″ square with 1″ green bar across the centre was worn horizontally on both upper arms. It was originally 1″ square but enlarged in June 1917 and worn 1″ below the shoulder seams. In June 1916 cap badges were soldered to the front of the helmet and a year later a 2″ green square with black edges was painted on both sides; they replaced the cap badge which was thought to be too shiny. These were recalled in 1989 by Private Stratford who joined the battalion in late 1915. During 1917, 1½″ armbands, worn above the elbow, were adopted for specialists: signallers – Cambridge blue; scouts – green; runners – red; Battalion HQ runners – red with a small battalion sign sewn on. In the IWM collection is an A Company flag: green rectangle with black edges, white **A** superimposed.

3rd Battalion

The battalion landed in France on 12/9/14 with the 17th Brigade, 6th Division, and fought with the division until October 1915 when the brigade was transferred to the 24th Division with which it remained. Throughout the war it fought on the Western Front.

Badges: red 2¼″ cloth square, worn on both arms below four-pointed star. Company identifiers adopted before the action at Guillemont on 18th August 1916: blue – A Company; green – B Company; red – C Company; yellow – D Company; no star – HQ Company. The square indicated the 4th senior battalion in the brigade. 'Previous to this, no distinguishing mark of any description was worn.' In February 1918 the square changed to a red 2¼″ equilateral triangle when the battalion became third senior in the brigade. A blackened cap badge was soldered onto the helmet to be replaced in October 1916 by a coloured horizontal rectangle 1″ × 1¼″ on both sides: black (¼″)/ green (¾″)/black (¼).

4th Battalion

On arrival from India about 18/11/14 the battalion went to Winchester where the 27th Division was forming. As part of the 80th Brigade it went to France on 21/12/14 and in November 1915 moved to Salonika where it remained.

Badges: the only non-regulation badge worn was the buff ½″ strip worn across the base of the shoulder straps by all ranks. This was confirmed by Private W. Sims in 1989 who served with the battalion in Salonika before transferring to the Machine Gun Corps.

5th (Reserve) Battalion

From August 1914 to the end of the war, the battalion served in Minster as part of the Thames and Medway Garrison.

Badges: Rifleman Stratford, who trained with the battalion during 1915, told the writer in 1989 that while with the battalion he only wore regulation metal badges. This was confirmed by Rifleman Woolger who was there at the same time and Private S. Short.

6th (Reserve) Battalion

Like the 5th, the 6th Battalion was part of the Thames and Medway garrison throughout the war.

Badges: Private S. Short served with the battalion in 1918 and recalled only wearing regulation cloth and metal badges.

During the winter of 1916/17 a square Maltese cross was worn on both sides of the helmet by the 1st Battalion. It was painted on the helmet when no covers were worn.

From September 1916 until mid-1917 a yellow ram's head was worn on both shoulders by the 1st Battalion.

Badges of the Regular Infantry, 1914–1918

The yellow ram's head was replaced by a yellow Maltese cross from mid-1917 until mid-1918.

When the yellow ram's head was reintroduced by the 1st Battalion in mid-1918 it was worn below a new battalion sign in black and green.

The 2nd Battalion wore a black square with green band on both arms.

Specialists in the 2nd Battalion were identified by armbands: red – runners; green – scouts; signallers – blue.

The square was worn by the 4th most senior regiment in the brigade and when the brigade was reduced to three battalions the 3rd Battalion wore a red triangle.

The only badge worn by the 4th Battalion was the 28th Division sign – a khaki/yellow band on the base of the shoulder straps.

As a rifle regiment the cloth shoulder title was in green cotton. It was obsolete by October 1919.

The Rifle Brigade

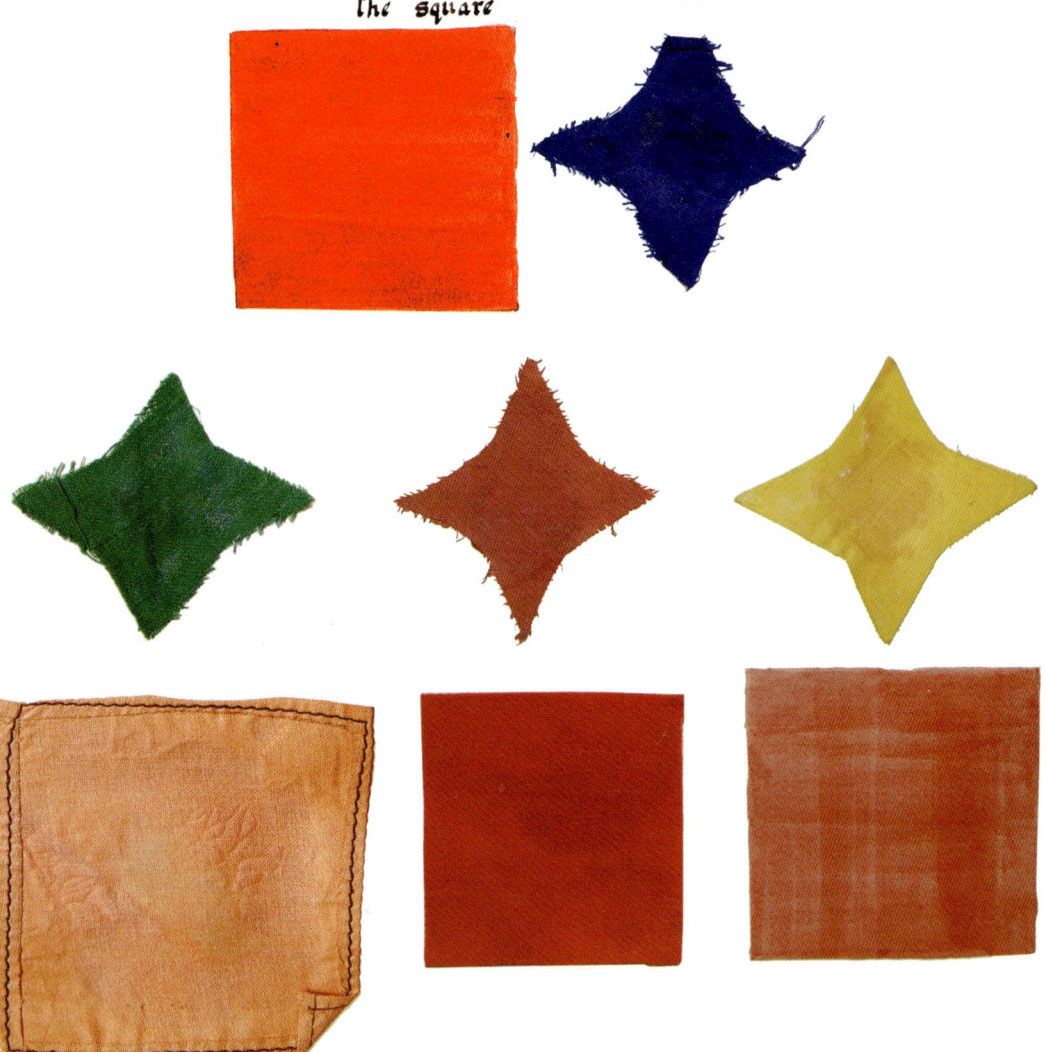

A red square was the sign of the 3rd Battalion in the 24th Division. Worn alone it represented HQ Company. The other companies were identified by a coloured star worn above the badge: blue – A Company; green – B Company; red – C Company; yellow – D Company. The red square was made from available cloth and was not always the same shade of red.

The letter that accompanied the badges sent by the 3rd Battalion explained what they meant and when they were introduced.

The 2nd Battalion sign is clearly visible on his arm and he is wearing a metal title and black buttons.

A Lewis gunner in the HQ Company of the 3rd Battalion with his parents. The battalion badge is at the top of his arm.

The only non-regulation badge worn by the 4th Battalion was the 27th Division band on each shoulder strap.

The RSM of the 3rd Battalion, photo taken sometime between August 1916 and February 1918. He is wearing the red square with a diamond above. On his chest is the MM ribbon.

Three very happy youthful privates in the 3rd Battalion. They are wearing a company diamond above the triangle, dating the photo as the summer of 1918.

A group photo of soldiers from the HQ Company after February 1918; they are wearing a red triangle at the top of the arm.

Bibliography/Further Reading/Sources

Museums

Argyll & Sutherland Highlanders; Black Watch; Border Regiment; Buffs; Cameronians (Scottish Rifles); Cheshire Regiment; Derby City; Devon & Dorset Regiment; Dorset Regiment; Duke of Cornwall's Light Infantry Regiment; Duke of Edinburgh's Royal Regiment (Berkshire & Wiltshire); Durham Light Infantry; East & West Surrey Regiment; East Lancashire Regiment; Essex Regiment; Gordon Highlanders; Imperial War Museum; King's Own Regiment; King's Own Scottish Borderers; King's Own Yorkshire Light Infantry; King's Shropshire Light Infantry ; Lancashire Fusiliers; Lincolnshire Regiment; Lincolnshire Life; Liverpool Museums; Manchester Regiment; Middlesex Regiment; National Army; Norfolk Regiment; Northamptonshire Regiment; Northumberland Fusiliers; Prince of Wales's Own Regiment of Yorkshire; Queen's Own Highlanders; Queen's Own Royal West Kent Regiment; Royal Hampshire Regiment; Royal Highland Fusiliers; Royal Irish Fusiliers; Royal Scots Regiment; Royal Sussex; South Lancashire Regiment; South Wales Borderers & Monmouthshire Regiment; Staffordshire Regiment; Suffolk Regiment; Welsh Regiment; Worcestershire Regiment; Yorkshire Regiment; Yorkshire & Lancaster Regiment.

Regimental, Unit and Campaign Associations

Argyll & Sutherland Highlanders; Bedfordshire & Hertfordshire Regiment; Black Watch; Devonshire Regiment; Dorset Regiment; Duke of Cornwall's Light Infantry; Duke of Wellington's Regiment; East & West Yorkshire Regiments; Essex Regiment; Gallipoli Association; Gordon Highlanders; Gloucestershire Regiment; King's (Liverpool & Manchester) Regiment; King's Own Scottish Borderers; King's Own Yorkshire Light Infantry; King's Shropshire Light Infantry; Lancashire Loyal North Lancashire Regiment; Middlesex Regiment; Northamptonshire Regiment; North Lancashire Regiment; Northumberland Fusiliers; Queen's Royal West Surrey Regiment; Royal Hampshire Regiment; Royal Inniskilling Fusiliers; Royal Irish Fusiliers; Royal Irish Rifles; Royal Regiment of Wales; Royal Sussex Regiment; Royal Ulster Rifles; Royal Welsh Fusiliers; Seaforth & Cameron Highlanders Regiment; Sherwood Foresters; Somerset light Infantry; South Lancashire Regiment; South Hales Borderers & Monmouthshire Regiments; North & South Staffordshire Regiment; Worcestershire Regiment; York & Lancaster Regiment; Yorkshire Regiment

Ex-service Homes

Royal British Legion – Maurice House, Halsey House, Galanos House and Lister House. The Royal Star and Barter Home, Richmond; Bournemouth Memorial Homes; Mr G. Church of Greenaways Home for the Elderly, Lancashire; Scottish Veterans Residences.

Royal British Legion Branches

Retford and Nottingham

B.L.E.S.M.A.

Crieff, Blackpool, Hull and York

Other Assistance

The editors of newspapers & regimental journals, too numerous to mention; Messrs Reed & Nixon of the Western Front Association; John Mollo; Major Astle of the Cheshire Regimental Association; Royal British Legion; Royal British Legion in Southern Ireland; The British Limbless Ex-Service Men's Association; The Forces Help Society; The Western Front Association; T. Tasker; Army Records Office in Hayes and Worcester; D. Clarke; Uppingham School Association; J.C. Nicholls; Officers' Pensions Society; Association of Jewish ex-Service men & women; H. Holland; Bundle School; Guildford Grammar School; H. Bayley; H. Staunton; Royal Grammar School Newcastle; Royal Grammar School Worcester; Exeter School; St. Peter's School, York; Giggleswick School; Highgate School; King's School, Chester; Felsted School; Aldenham School; King's School, Canterbury; Whitgift School; Hurstpierpoint School; Bristol Grammar School; Harwich School; Wellingborough School; Blundell's School; Eton College; Oakham School; Bolton School; Truro School; Sevenoaks School; Charterhouse School; Merchant Taylors' School, Crosby; Latymer upper School; Bradford Grammar; Wyecliffe College; Kingston Grammar; Cheltenham College; Barnard Castle School; Wellington College; Gresham School; Fettes College; Bloxham School; Merchant Taylors' School, Liverpool; Loretto School; King's School, Bruton; Colfe's School; Clifton School; Lancing College; Leys School; Rossall School; Epson College; John Lyon School; Sedbergh School; Wrekin College; Monkton Combe School; Denston College; Trent College; St. Edmunds School; St. Bees School; Tonbridge School; Coventry School; Merchant Taylors' School, Northwood; Culford School; Rydal School; Harrow School; Ashville College; Bromsgrove School; Tonbridge School; Radley College; Oratory School and Brighton College.

Veterans

L. Abel, 3rd Norfolk; A. Acland, 5th Grenadier Guards; Father J. Adamson, 2nd South Lancashire; T. Allen 3rd DCLI; Lord Ailwyn, TD, 2nd Norfolk; Anonymous, 29th Division; J. Armstrong, 1st Loyal North Lancashire; F. Ashman, 1st Worcestershire; D. Banks, 3rd Lincolnshire; Sir Charles Baring, JP, DL, Coldstream Guards; A. Barlow, 3rd and 5th Coldstream Guards; Major T. Barnard, 1st Gloucestershire; J. Benthall, 1st Life Guards; A. Birtwhistle 3rd East Lancashire; J. Blaber, 4th Worcestershire; W. Bowden, 3rd Worcestershire; Lieutenant Colonel J. Branscombe, 2nd Duke of Wellington's; G. Bray, 2nd Lincolnshire; T. Broach, 1st Hampshire; Brother David, 3rd Royal Welsh Fusiliers; R. Burns, 3rd Cameron Highlanders; E.M. Butler, 1st Rifle Brigade; J. Cahill, 2nd Royal Dublin Fusiliers; H. Calvert,

2nd and 5th Grenadier Guards; T. Charlton, 2nd and 5th Grenadier Guards; S. Charters, 1st Seaforth Highlanders; A.A.F. Chatfield, 7th and 29th RF; Lieutenant Colonel J. Codrington, 3rd Coldstream Guards; V. Cole, 1st Royal West Kents; Captain T. Clarke MC, 1st Scots Guards; J. Clarkson, 2nd East Lancashire; N. Clayton, 2nd Sherwood Foresters; J. Colville MM, 1st Royal Irish Rifles; F. Cornes, 2nd Royal Fusiliers; Lieutenant Colonel S. de Salis, 2nd KRRC; F. Dixon, 1st Leicestershire; F. Donnison, Grenadier Guards; Sir John Elliot, 3rd Hussars; H. Ellis, 1st Worcestershire; R. Emmett, 1st East Lancashire; A. Fairweather, 8th Hussars; B. Farrer, 2nd Yorkshire; Lord Ferrier, ED, DL, 4th Reserve Seaforth Highlanders; T. Fidler, 2nd Sherwood Foresters; R. Finch, 1st Worcestershire; H. Fosdyke, 1st Queens; P. Francis, 1st Somerset Light Infantry; A. Fripp, BM, FRCS, 1st Life Guards; Captain A. Fulton, 3rd Border; A. Funnell, 1st Royal Sussex; J. Galletly, 3rd Lincolnshire; H. Gibbons, 3rd Sherwood Foresters; G. Gibson OBE, 3rd Essex; Pte Gillies, 1st Royal Scots; H. Goodchild, 1st Dorsets; J. Goodwin, 2nd KOYLI; Major J. Gordon-Duff, 5th Rifle Brigade; H. Gray, 3rd Ox and Bucks L.I.; W. Grover MM, 2nd Royal Sussex; Sir James Harford KBE CMG, 2nd and 3rd Essex; B. Harrop, 1st KRRC; L. Hatch, 1st Life Guards and Life Guards Reserve Regiment; W. Hodges, 3rd Hampshire; V. Hogben, 3rd Dragoon Guards Reserve Regiment; W. Holland MM, 17th Lancers; E. Hoskins, 4th Worcestershire; G. Hudson, BEM, MID, Croix de Guerre, 1st King's Own; R. Hughes, 1st Sherwood Foresters; A. Illingworth, 4th South Staffordshire; E. Ingmire OBE, 1st King's Own; D. Jeffries, 3rd Wiltshire and 2nd Berkshire; Sir Raymond Jennings, 1st Royal Fusiliers; E. Johnson, 3rd Worcestershire; E. Jones, 3rd KSLI; W. King, 3rd DCLI; C. Kingswell, 4th Hussars; D. Knights, 3rd and 5th Grenadier Guards; RSM M. Lally, 2nd Manchester; Rev. S. Lamming, 2nd Lincolnshire; R. Langley, 4th Sherwood Foresters; Lieutenant Colonel J. Leach, 2nd Yorkshire; Lieutenant Colonel M. Lister, 2nd KRRC; H. Lloyd-Routh, 1st KRRC; Captain W. Lloyds, 4th South Staffordshire; J. Lovegrove, 3rd Royal Irish Fusiliers; E. Lowman, 1st SLI; H. Luxton, 1st Somerset L.I.; G. MacFarlane MSM MM (French), 1st Black Watch; C. McLean, 1st Royal Irish Fusiliers; . Madeley, 2nd and 3rd York and Lancaster; Major V. Matthews, 5th Dragoon Guards; A. Miller, 2nd Rifle Brigade; F. Molz, 1st Middlesex; Dr. R. Mortis, 3rd KSLI; Captain O. Meredith, R.N., 5th Grenadier Guards; A.W. Moren, 2nd Queens; S. Mansfield, 4th North Staffordshire; W. Nicholls, 2nd DCLI; F. Perry, 2nd and 3rd Lincolnshire; J. Plaskett, 1st KOSB; J. Pollitt, 1st and 3rd South Lancashire; Brigadier E. Ransford CBE, 2nd Norfolk; B. Sailles, 3rd Yorkshire; L. Seldon-Truss, 2nd Scots Guards; M. Sharp, 2nd Leinsters; T. Sharp, 3rd Cheshire; Lieutenant Colonel E. Simmons, 2nd Oxfordshire & Buckinghamshire Light Infantry; W. Sims, 4th Rifle Brigade; Major Skates, 1st, 2nd and 4th Bedfordshire; J. Smith, 1st and 2nd Worcestershire; Brigadier Hon. N.F. Somerset CBE DSO MC, 1st Gloucestershire; Lieutenant Colonel M. Solly MBE, 3rd Essex; The Earl of Southesk KCVO, 3rd Scots Guards; W. Spencer, 4th and 5th Grenadier Guards; Brigadier Sir Alex Stanier DSO MC DL JP, C.St. J., Welsh Guards; W. Stepney, Coldstream Guards; Major Sir H. Stewart, Bt., DL, 1st Royal Inniskilling Fusiliers; Rev. J. Stileman, 2nd Welch; D. Stirling, 5th Coldstream Guards; C. Stokes, 5th Rifle Brigade; Major G. Stone, 3rd Devonshire; F. Stratford, 1st, 2nd and 6th Rifle Brigade; J. Stringer, 1st Royal Dublin Fusiliers; J. Sutherland, 3rd Black Watch; J. Taylor, 3rd Sherwood Foresters; Rev. H. Tunnadine, 2nd and 3rd Loyals; G. Turberville, 3rd Queen's; E. Turner, 1st and 3rd Queen's; J. Wakeman, 1st Wiltshire; 3rd Dorsetshire; F. Walker, 2nd Cheshire; S. Walker, 2nd Devonshire; Captain A. Walsh, 3rd Manchester; P. Warwick, 2nd DCLI; I. Watkins, 2nd Welsh; W. Watson,

1st KOSB; Major Webster, 1st Suffolk; R. Weedon, 2nd Middlesex; C. Wells, 53rd and 4th Bedfordshire; B.W. Whayman, 1st Northants; Lieutenant Colonel G. Wheeler CIE CBE, 1st, 2nd and 3rd Queen's; A. White CMG OBE, 1st Wiltshire.

Other assistance

R. Franklin; Mr Harrop MM; F. Reading MC.

References

Anon. *Badges & Emblems of the British Forces*. Arms & Armour, 1968.
Audax, C.E. *Badge Backings & Special Embellishments of the British Army*. Ulster Defence Regiment Benevolent Fund, 1990.
Becke, Major A.F. *Order of Battle of Divisions, Part 1 - The Regular Divisions*. HMSO, 1934.
Bennett, R.W. *Badges of the Worcestershire Regiment*. Bennett, 1994.
Chappell, M. *British Battle Insignia (1): 1914–18*. Osprey, 1986.
Chappell, M. *British Infantry Equipments*. Osprey, 1980.
Chappell, M. *The British Soldier in the 20th Century Volume 1 Service Dress 1902–1940*. Wessex Military Publishing. 1987.
Chappell, M. *The British Soldier in the 20th Century Volume 2 Field Service Head Dress* 1902 to the present day. Wessex Military Publishing. 1987.
Chappell, M. *The British Soldier in the 20th Century Volume 4 Light Machine Guns*. Wessex Military Publishing. 1988.
Chappell, M. *The British Soldier in the 20th Century Volume 6 Tropical Uniforms*. Wessex Military Publishing. 1988.
Chappell, M. *The British Soldier in the 20th Century Volume 7 Personal Equipment 1903–1937*. Wessex Military Publishing. 1989.
Chappell, M. *The Gloucestershire Regiment*. Wessex Military Publishing, 1990.
Chappell, M. *Scottish Units in the World Wars*. Osprey, 1994.
Chappell, M. *The Welch Regiment*. Wessex Military Publishing, 1989.
Churchill, C. *History of the British Army Collar Badge*. The Naval & Military Press, 2002.
Churchill, C. & Westlake, R. *British Army Collar Badges 1881 to the Present*. Arms & Armour, 1986.
Cox, R. *Badges of the British Empire*. Benn, 1982.
Dux, R. & Hibberd, M. *British & Dominion Formation & Unit Vehicle Signage 1914–1918*. Privately published, Australia, 2018.
Endean-Ivall, D. & Thomas, C. *Military Insignia of Cornwall*. Penwith Books, 1974.
Fosten, D.S.V. & Marrion, R.J. *The British Army 1914–18*. Osprey, 1978.
Holohan, V.W. *Divisional and Other Signs*. Murray, 1920.
Imperial War Museum. Various contemporary documents.
James, Brigadier E.A., OBE TD, *British Regiments*. Samson Books, 1979.
Kipling, A.L. & King, H.L. *Head-dress Badges of the British Army Volume One*. Naval & Military Press, 2010.

Nash, D. 'The British Army 1914–1918'. *Airfix Magazine*, various issues. 1969.
Pegler, M. & Chappell, M. *The British Tommy 1914–1918*. Osprey, 1996.
Rosignoli, G. *The Illustrated Encyclopaedia of Military Insignia of the 20th Century*. Stanley Paul, 1987.
Rosignoli, G. & Whitehouse, C.J. *The Staffords 1887–1978. Badges and Uniforms*. Rosignoli, 1978.
Smyth, Major B., MVO, *The Lancashire Fusiliers' Annual 1917*. Sackville, 1918.
Steeple, W.J. 'Cloth Patches in the British Army'. *Journal of the Military Heraldry Society* Issue 62.
Steeple, W.J. Unpublished Identification Notes on the Cloth Badges of the East Yorkshire Regiment. ND.
Steeple, W.J. Unpublished Identification Notes on the Cloth Badges of the Hampshire Regiment. ND.
Steeple, W.J. Unpublished Identification Notes on the Cloth Badges of the King's Royal Rifle Corps. ND.
Steeple, W.J. Unpublished Identification Notes on the Cloth Badges of the Manchester Regiment. ND.
Steeple, W.J. Unpublished Identification Notes on the Cloth Badges of the Rifle Brigade. ND.
Steeple, W.J. Unpublished Identification Notes on the Cloth Badges of the South Lancashire Regiment. ND.
Steeple, W.J. Unpublished Identification Notes on the Cloth Badges of the Royal Sussex Regiment. ND.
Steeple, W.J. Unpublished Identification Notes on the Cloth Badges of the Yorkshire Regiment. ND.
Swinton, Major General Sir Ernest, KBE CB, *Twenty Years After* Volume 2. Newnes.
Various Officers. *Unpublished Record of the British Infantry and Cavalry Uniforms and Insignia 1914–18*, 6 volumes. Held at the IWM.
Waring, Major J. *Identification Pamphlet No.1, British Formation Signs & Shoulder Titles*. Military Heraldry Society, 1976.
Westlake, R. *Collecting Metal Shoulder Titles*. Frederick Warne, 1980.
Wheeler-Holohan, V. *Divisional and Other Signs*, John Murray, 1920.